Essay Index

A Matter of Dignity

A Matter of Dignity

Inquiries into the
Humanization of Work

EDITED BY

W. J. Heisler
John W. Houck

UNIVERSITY OF NOTRE DAME PRESS
NOTRE DAME ~ LONDON

Library of Congress Cataloging in Publication Data
Main entry under title:

A Matter of dignity.

  Includes index.
  1. Job satisfaction—Addresses, essays, lectures.
2. Labor and laboring classes—Addresses, essays,
lectures. I. Heisler, William J., 1942–
II. Houck, John W. III. Title: Humanization of
work.
HF5549.5.J63M27   301.5'5   76-51620
ISBN 0-268-01341-1

Publication of This Volume
Was Assisted by Grants from
The College of Business Administration Advisory Council Fund
The Herrick Foundation
and
The Vilter Foundation (Milwaukee)

Most of us have jobs
that are too small for
our spirit.

Studs Terkel, *Working*

Contents

Preface

THIS BOOK GREW OUT OF A CONCERN FOR THE WAY IN WHICH WORK AND work organizations are evolving in our society. While it would be inaccurate to say that all American workers are alienated or dissatisfied with their jobs, a growing number of segments of the American labor scene (younger workers, women, minority members, etc.) are becoming disenchanted with the work role as it is presently structured. And while discontent may be more apparent at some organizational levels than others and in some industries than others, no stratum of work society is exempt. There is evidence of the so-called "blue-collar blues" at all occupational levels. In fact, some management consultants point toward declining managerial productivity as a problem potentially far worse than diminished productivity among blue-collar workers. Even universities, the stanchions of "collegial" structure, appear haunted by these concerns as more consider and turn toward unionization.

Under a grant from the S&H Foundation, the editors were able to undertake sponsorship of a lecture series at Notre Dame on "The Design of Humanistic Work." It was the goal of the series to explore, from an interdisciplinary perspective, issues surrounding the design of more humanistic work. More specifically, it was the intent of the series to provide a forum to raise the issue of work-life quality in America and to examine the range of social alternatives available and necessary for the design and structuring of more humanistic forms of work and work organizations. This volume was prepared to make the content of the series available to a broader spectrum of the business, labor, academic, and policy-making communities.

We have enjoyed our participation in this activity immensely and feel we have learned a great deal ourselves from the interaction generated by the series. It is our hope that others, through this collection, can share with us in these discoveries.

We wish to thank the S&H Foundation for their underwriting of the lectureship series. Their generosity in supporting academic activities of this type in colleges and universities is worthy of special recognition because grants of this nature permit institutions to explore themes that otherwise may not be surfaced during regular courses of study.

We are also greatly indebted to Brother Leo V. Ryan, C.S.V., Dean of the College of Business Administration, University of Notre Dame, for his interest and faith in our vision. Without his support, the series could not have attained its expansive objectives, nor would this volume have been able to be published.

Special recognition must also be given to Dr. Yusaku Furuhashi, who as acting Dean encouraged and gave support to the series proposal, and to Vincent R. Raymond, Associate Dean, who provided necessary support services for completion of this manuscript.

Others who contributed to the completion of the lectureship series and to this volume through their ideas, support, and/or labor are the following (presented in alphabetical order): Mark Boyle, Janice Coffield, Edna Dolezal, Carole Froling, Jeanne Ray, and Peter Swain.

Our deepest appreciation.

W. J. HEISLER
JOHN W. HOUCK

Introduction

CAN THE READER ENVISION THE FOLLOWING "JOB WANTED" CLASSIFIED advertisement appearing in the local newspaper?

> Wanted: Steady eight-hour-a-day-job. Wages, conditions, and benefits must be competitive. No personal involvement desired.

There can be little doubt that this job seeker has stripped the World of Work down to its essentials—as that worker perceives it. Neither "Steady eight-hour" nor "competitive" salary and fringes would bother most of us. But why would a worker make the condition "no personal involvement" so clearly a requirement? The answer, of course, is obvious. This job seeker knows the territory he is attempting to enter. This job seeker is painfully aware that much of work is divided into the smallest operations that must be repeated again and again, thousands of times each working day. And all of this repetition is to be done to the harsh cadence of the machine, or possibly the assembly line. Moreover, the white-collar worker is not immune from this type of meaningless, repetitive activity. Our job seeker is fatalistically responding to the objective working conditions programmed for himself and many of his contemporaries—the Monotony Game.

Since every game must have a strategy in order to be played well, the Monotony Game pays off players who put in their time without getting involved. After all, involvement suggests a spectrum of human skills and possibilities from the conventional to the unexpected, from the submissive to the creative. Literature and poetry might celebrate this rich variety of human skills and possibilities, but not the industrial engineer who knows what is needed, down to the smallest micro-movement and micro-second, to make the system work. Involvement by the worker is like a benign-appearing barrel of

1

volatile chemical fluids; it is best to keep the lid on and to store it safely away from the operations.

However, there is a curious fact frequently overlooked in the industrial culture: it is the machine (the equivalent for white-collar workers is the bureaucratic system with its rigorously defined regulations and procedures), *not* the worker, that has the vital involvement. The machine dictates the extent of the division of labor into its smallest components and the speed of the line. The machine's needs and constraints determine how the operation is to be performed, what breaks in the tempo are needed, and even how machines can and ought to interact with other machines in a team effort. It is into this world that the worker goes as "an alien given admittance only in his capacity as an intermediary between machines and the things to be machined..." (Weil 1944, p. 370). We are so inured to this machine-human perversion that it doesn't even startle us. It has become for us a fact of life in too much of the World of Work that "things play the role of men, men the role of things" (Weil 1944, p. 373).

It is the contention of this volume that this perversion is questionable, dysfunctional, and too often unnecessary. There is no doubt that traditional arguments for the status quo in work design have a powerful hold on us. We believe, however, that the arguments are challenged convincingly in the essays from the various intellectual disciplines that are represented in this volume. A distinctive feature of the volume is that it draws from a wide variety of disciplines and methodologies: from philosophy and theology to human resource accounting; from intellectual history to the empirical; and from the academic theorist to the hardheaded, pragmatic union bargainer. But such an arsenal as this is necessary, as no one discipline or intellectual approach can adequately handle the complexity of the World of Work. In fact, much of the present difficulty stems from the monopoly that industrial economics and engineering have held for so long in our thinking about work and organizational design. By reducing human labor to simple paradigms of market mobility and economic motivation, ratios of input to output, and scientific management's "one best method," we have engineered what is "human" out of work. Historically, there has been a lack of effective counterveilance by other value systems and intellectual disciplines. But most contributors to this volume seem to expound the belief that work humanization is "an idea whose time has come."

"You're damn lucky to have a job!" captures the essence of one obstacle to work reform, especially when the labor market is weak and fears of unemployment grow. Discussions about the quality of work are "luxuries" that few can afford when the question of the quantity of work intrudes so powerfully. Professor Bowers points out in his essay (Part III) that employment fears and the business cycle can dampen both worker complaints and employer efforts to do anything about work.

Another variation on the same theme, the quantity of work, is found in this anecdote by the distinguished scholar, Eli Ginsburg:

> Many years ago I asked Jim Mitchell, the outstanding secretary of labor under Eisenhower... about his views concerning frustrated workers.... Mitchell replied, ''What are you talking about? In good periods when the labor market is tight and you have a job you cannot stand, you find yourself another job. When the labor market is weak and there is much unemployment you feel lucky if you have a job, even one that leaves something to be desired. I do not know any frustrated workers.'' (*Society*, p. 61)

Labor mobility as an approach to worker frustration requires sustained periods of economic growth and low unemployment, a requirement not met in our recent economic record of spurts and declines. In addition, we have to remember that labor mobility (the worker's ticket to more humanizing, rewarding work) becomes costly to all of us, employers and consumers, in the form of labor turnover. Finally, this approach is an issue-avoidance stance that never forces a probing, critical appraisal of work on its merit. It implies a ''freedom'' to run away from problems, a ''freedom'' endemic to the American experience of wide-open land and westward spaces: In pioneer times, if you feel crowded by the closeness of your neighbor's cabin, move on. If you feel pinched by the changing neighborhoods of the city, move on—to the suburbs and even farther out in the suburbs. In the context of the World of Work this attitude translates into: ''If you don't like this kind of work, move on.'' But today, the exhortation ''move on'' lacks an authentic and creditable ring: Where is the new frontier? The essays in this volume argue that it is time that we reject this traditional bromide and examine and confront the dysfunctional impact that work has on tens of millions of workers.

''There isn't any other way to design work without impairing efficiency.'' Another argument frequently made against improvement of work-design is that change will lessen efficiency. Not only is there solid evidence to the contrary regarding organizational redesign (see examples in Part III), but there are also valid reasons for claiming that technical efficiency is not the single objective of work. The worker is a resource with a wealth of talent, yet how little we draw from it. We extract little of his talents in thinking, planning, cooperating in teams, or in setting personal and group goals. We rely too often on muscle and manual manipulation as the unique contribution of our worker. By any standards this has to be an inefficient use of a resource. It can be compared to our petro-chemical industry drawing off only one product, automobile fuel, from oil and dumping the rest. Certainly no one would recommend this practice today. And no manager today would make a large investment in a piece of machinery or equipment which would continually be used at 10 to 15 percent of its total capacity. Yet this is precisely what we do with our workers.

Even if we grant, for the sake of argument, that efficiency is the prime indicator of an organization's success, many empirical investigations demonstrate that various, often inconsistent, techniques (e.g., specialization, formalization, decentralization, group) can be used to achieve this efficiency. The findings suggest that a particular technique may be largely irrelevant to an organization's success. In other words, an organization may be able to attain its goals effectively by any number of work-design possibilities, including many that are compatible with the humanization of work, thus opening the door to many low-risk opportunities for experimentation in work-design modes aimed at improving work life.

In addition, we have often overlooked the hidden and potentially serious costs of traditional work-design techniques. There is a growing recognition by social and medical scientists of the cost in mental and physical sickness, alcoholism, drug-use, and absenteeism. And while some of these costs can be allocated internally to the cost of goods and services produced, many would be classified as external costs that the society must bear through its hospitals, alcoholic wards, and divorce courts. These work-induced costs can be likened to the "free ride" given industrial air and water pollution in the past. Do we really believe that there are no significant effects from meaningless and monotonous work? Do we really believe that the worker can shake off the effects of this type of work as he walks out the plant gate or office door? The answers to both questions are the same: "Of course not." Management has recognized for a long time that worker performance is affected by marital and family troubles off the job. The reciprocal proposition rings just as true; the worker takes home considerable and costly baggage from the job. This "baggage" puts in jeopardy the instrumentalist view of work for the worker and the society: something to be patiently performed in order to be free and financed off the job. Present work-design techniques are not neutral as to these personal and social costs.

This efficiency argument against work humanization raises critical questions for the modern university, which has become a close collaborator with large organizations, bureaucracies, and industries. The university has become the ivy-covered site for research into new techniques of rationalization (e.g., efficiency, order, planning) of these large social units. A part of the university prides itself in designing sophisticated models that can "handle" human inputs as well as energies, machines, and materials. But to do this it must perforce keep the models relatively simple yet comprehensive, which can require the transformation of human polyvalence into a manageable, stripped-down factor. And while the university researcher (or the senior executive) might tingle with excitement about a new discovery in model-building, it can too quickly become a grind for the blue- and white-collar workers who must work within the confines of that discovery.

The university must be very careful *not* to ratify historic and potential techniques of work-design that are de-humanizing. To do otherwise would be a violation of its charter to speak the "whole" truth about what it discovers and espouses. It is the hope of the contributors, mostly members of the university from many of its diverse disciplines and traditions, that this collection of papers contributes to the whole truth about the World of Work.

REFERENCES

Ginzberg, E. Planning Full Employment. *Society,* 1976, 13 (4):57–64.
Weil, S. Factory Work. *Cross Currents,* 1976, 25:367–382. (First published in the journal *Politics,* Dec. 1946.)

PART 1

What Do Philosophy and Theology Tell Us about the Role of Work in Human Existence and Potential?

THROUGHOUT HISTORY, THE ACTIVITY COMMONLY REFERRED TO AS "WORK" has been viewed from a variety of perspectives. Many early civilizations regarded work as a curse; it was degrading to developed persons and took time away from contemplation and aesthetic experiences. Medieval Catholicism and the guild system glorified craft work. Under the craft system, work served to unite the worker, family, and religion. Typically performed in the home and involving family members in one fashion or another, work also was viewed as a way of serving God. Under these conditions, major life roles formed an organic wholeness.

With the advent of the Industrial Revolution, however, work moved outside the home, became segmented, and lost much of its intrinsic value. In the post-World War II era, work took on even more of an instrumental orientation. Today the question is even raised if work is a central life interest for a majority of the work force.

Regardless of the role work plays in life, to the philosopher or to the theologian the dignity of man must be of primary concern in its design. Human beings are deserving of dignity in and of themselves. To John Julian Ryan, the author of the first article in this section, a truly humane society is one in which the primal needs and rights of every man, as a full human being, are respected as sacred, not the least of these being that of leading a meaningful, consciously creative life as a worker serving others skillfully, personally, and honorably. Yet, Ryan cautions, while work cannot be looked upon merely as an opportunity to make money, neither can it be regarded primarily as a means of self-expression or self-satisfaction.

"Good work" is determined by a network of claims: social, domestic, professional, economic, and personal. But, according to Ryan, the claim of the client is primary; meeting the obligations of various claimants constitutes the worker's main source of satisfaction. Herein appears to lie a basic conflict: the ability to exercise one's particular talents freely and vigorously versus the very real demands of human community. The compromise suggested by Ryan asks much of the individual and of society. Its achievement would mean not only a restructuring of much of the economic processes of work, but also a change in one's attitude or philosophy toward work. Recognizing the magnitude of the changes proposed, Ryan nonetheless considers them necessary if work is to become truly humanistic, with workers performing as autonomous artists, producing suitable products of high quality and in adequate quantities to meet legitimate needs of society.

In the second article of this section, Francis Fiorenza explores the role which our theological heritage has played in developing our perceptions of work and its place in our total life situation. The two dominant contemporary views of work—"work is a means (usually unpleasant) to another end" and "work is a satisfying, noble, and fulfilling end in itself"—can be directly traced to earlier theological bases.

The legacy of ancient Greece is generally considered to be allied with the first view of work cited above. Manual labor and trading activity, for the most part, were considered corruptive of body and soul in that they rob persons of the leisure to participate in political, military, and contemplative activity. It should be noted, however, as Fiorenza points out, this view was not consistently held by all Greek philosophers.

While an examination of the seed-bed culture of Western civilization, Israel, reveals a similar diversity of attitudes toward work, the general orientation is more akin to the second contemporary view of work cited above: work is a fulfilling and rewarding activity in itself. The Jahwist view considers work to be basic to human existence and commanded by God. Rather than keeping people away from reflective activity and worship, work itself serves as a form of service to God.

Although New Testament writings do not offer any systematic teachings about work, it is readily apparent that it is not easy to work in contemporary society and be Christian in our thoughts and actions. In 1 Peter 2:18-19, for example, we are advised "Servants, be submissive to your masters with all respect, not only to the kind and gentle but also to the overbearing. For one is approved if, mindful of God, he endures pain while suffering unjustly" (RSV). But employees alone are not subject to such conditions and restraints. In Ephesians 6:9, employees are counseled "Masters, do the same to them [rendering service with a good will as to the Lord], and forbear threatening, knowing that He who is both their Master and yours is in heaven, and that there is no partiality with Him'' (RSV).

Fiorenza concludes that despite differences among various early theologies of Greece, Israel, and Christianity there is a consistent theme which runs throughout: Work is a basic and essential human activity. Through it, humankind can grow in freedom and share fraternally God's patrimony of material and spiritual resources.

Humanistic Work: Its Philosophical and Cultural Implications

by John Julian Ryan

> The control of the production of wealth is the control of human life itself.
>
> Hilaire Belloc

HAVING THOUGHT ABOUT THE SUBJECT OF WORK FOR MANY YEARS AND written a book that was largely concerned with it (Ryan 1972) and having conducted courses in which it is one of the central topics, I cannot help feeling the strain of having to deal with its most important aspects within the relatively small frame of one short paper. I feel somewhat like a person who has been asked to explain his theory of the universe in a few words. Maybe I can expedite matters by starting out with a story about three workers breaking up rocks. When the first was asked what he was doing, he replied, "Making little ones out of big ones"; the second said, "Making a living"; and the third, "Building a cathedral." While each of these answers was, of course, accurate, I hope to convince the reader that the third answer was "true"—that is, more faithful to our commonly shared potential of humanness.

Every Worker a Special Kind of Artist in Community

Let me begin my discourse by attempting to deal systematically with the basic philosophical concepts that are referred to by the term "humanistic" and by the term "work." Since, obviously, the first of these terms, "humanistic," means "that which is in accord with the nature of man as

11

man," we must start by taking note of certain essential characteristics of this strange creature.

One of the most basic of human characteristics is that, whatever else he may be, he is not a primarily passive creature. Rather, he is an active one. He does not need to be lured into action. Even the most seemingly slothful man hardly proves to be that *by nature*. If he takes a vacation (and when would he be likely to be more slothful?), he immediately appears astonishingly active: he swims, fishes, hikes, plays tennis, golf, and shuffleboard; he dances, and so on. Often enough, he returns from a vacation almost too well-exercised, sometimes muscle-sore. And even the typical desk-bound pencil-man is likely to enjoy, at the end of the day (and I would ask the reader to notice these words), a good "workout."

Second, our human is not a creature that can lazily rely on the guidance of instincts. True, he has certain in-built tendencies—and he is impelled to obey these more or less unthinkingly or subconsciously. But, instinctively? Never! Every one of us has to *learn* how to walk, *learn* how to talk, *learn* how to tie our shoelaces and to button our buttons. An animal, faced with a given situation, will respond to it in what is literally a given way. Usually untaught, it will with almost mechanical precision go through a complex sequence of actions designed to lead to a useful end. But we humans have no such built-in mechanisms; we have only general tendencies which we must *learn* how to translate into humanly effective actions. The frequently cited objection that the newborn infant instinctively grasps and instinctively sucks is hardly a very cogent one because these two instincts, if they are that, are hardly very complex. Neither are they very lasting. This is made clear by the fact that if the same grown-up who raises this argument were to have a lollipop thrown near him, he would not automatically seize it and start sucking it. Indeed, psychologists have gained so clear a recognition of this proposition that they refrain from using the word "instinctively" about man. Instead they employ terms such as "instinctual" or "instinctoid," which mean "*as* if instinctively."

Man, then, is essentially a creature who, in a sense, has to learn his own nature by working at living up to its norms. It would be hard to imagine a mother hen exhorting her young rooster, "Oh, snap out of it. Be a real rooster!" But it is not at all hard to imagine a human mother exhorting her son, "Oh, be a man! Act like a human being, will you!" Man earns his own nature by acquiring and using the kinds of skills called for in answering human needs. And although he is prompted by inborn instinctual tendencies, he still has to acquire his techniques deliberately and consciously (Eibesfeldt 1972). He does this until the exercise of them becomes habitual, subconscious, and seemingly "instinctive," if you will. By his very nature, therefore, man is called upon to be responsibly and creatively skillful in these techniques. In traditional language, every man is, quite literally, an artist.

Until recently, the first definition usually given of the word "art" was "skill." Even today in some dictionaries, this is still true. As Ananda K. Coomaraswamy, a great authority on the art of India, was fond of saying: "An artist is not a special kind of man, but every man is a special kind of artist." By nature, every man is truly a fine artist or is properly meant to be, not in the sense of being an excellent communicative artist such as a painter, a sculptor, a composer, or a dramatist (although I believe he has far greater potentialities for being one than our educational system allows him to suppose), but in the sense of naturally aiming at perfection. He is not content with *some* food, *some* clothing, or *some* shelter; he wants *good* food, *good* clothing, and *good* shelter. And he will struggle to improve, as animals will not.

The two tendencies we have been considering here, man's natural activism and his love of perfection, are both clearly manifested in how he deals with sports. Once man has devised a game, he does not make it easier to play, as he would were he naturally slothful. On the contrary, he makes it harder and more skillful:

> He refines the strokes and movements, improves the instruments used, whether racket, club, oar, bat, or ski, and even the court or playing field. The rules he makes stricter and more exacting, not only for the sake of fairness, but also for that of virtuosity. (Ryan 1971, p. 20)

He wants to enjoy its strenuousness and, beyond that, he wants to enjoy, either as a performer or as an interested spectator, the beauty of its rightness, the splendor of its perfection.

Like other creatures, moreover, man is gregarious or social. Hobbes to the contrary notwithstanding, man is not by nature simply a rugged individualist who strikes a contract with his fellowmen somewhat reluctantly. It is astonishing that the very same theorists who would like to reduce man merely to the status of a higher-order animal are unwilling to grant him a quality obvious in even the lowest animals, the insects—namely, the quality of an innate love of kind. Why should we be intrinsically less willing to cooperate, or if you will, less affectionate than, let us say, ants, bees, or termites, and at the other end, whales, elephants, or gorillas?

Therefore, it is natural for man to form communal organizations, such as the tribe, to answer his full range of physical, mental, and spiritual needs. Clearly it is necessary for humans to adopt specialization—to have each person do what he can to answer some need excellently by exercising his special skill responsibly. And as the tribe expands or joins with other tribes to form a city, it becomes necessary to have, not one or two men specializing in answering a given need, but whole associations of them doing so. All these conditions of human nature and societal life would result ideally in a humanistic social structure with its members working as the various kinds of artists they were meant to be. There would be artists in investigation (now called scientists, but once called philosophers) who would pursue knowledge. There would be artists in education who, relying on this knowledge, would foster the various kinds of skill called for by civilized living and occupational proficiency. Artists in production would fashion objects which, like our well-wrought antiques, would be true sources of use and delight. Artists in exchange would see that these objects found their way into the hands of those who needed them. Artists in governance would assure the mechanisms for peace and justice, as well as for communal services requisite for enabling men to live together safely, cooperatively, and harmoniously. There would be artists in athletics who would enable the citizens to gain the exercise which is needed for sound recreation, or to delight vicariously in it. Artists in communication would enchant men with insightful visions of reality and inspire them to live delightedly and nobly. And artists in priestly ministry would help citizens in their efforts to attain earthly and ultimate salvation. In short, a truly humane society would be one in which the primal needs and rights of every man, as a full human being, would be respected as sacred, *not the least of these being that of leading a meaningful, consciously creative life as a worker serving others skillfully, personally, and honorably . . . and being reciprocally served.*[1]

The Claims on the Artist-Worker in the Truly Human Society

Good work of every kind, no matter how humble or how important, is always determined far more deeply than is ordinarily supposed by a network of claims: social, professional, domestic, economic, and personal. And the more successfully and wisely a man evaluates and meets these claims, the more effective and happy he will be as a worker. The first and most obvious of these claims is the claim laid upon the worker by his *client* (and the word "client," let us remember, literally means "one in need"). Clearly, every maker or performer who approaches his work as a man of skill and responsibility—in other words, as a professional—must regard this claim as *primary.* He cannot look upon his work as a mere opportunity to make money. Nor can he regard his work as primarily a means of self-expression or self-satisfaction. Caslon, for instance, was a great type designer because we do *not* think of him when we scan his type. And when we observe a contemporary building, if we think first of its architect (Frank Lloyd Wright, let us say), then something may well be wrong. After all, it does not belong to the architect, it belongs to its owner-users. And while we must salute the worker and his special skills (and even his genius, as in the case of Frank Lloyd Wright), the test of its rightness nevertheless lies in its suitability to its owner-users.

Moreover, the claim of the client is a stringent one. It obligates the maker or performer to think about the client's true good, his true needs. The maker or performer has, in fact, to keep a hierarchy of values in mind. As striving himself to foster a humane civilization, he must keep particularly in mind the requirements of those who are also, at least potentially, striving to do likewise. He must try to afford them what they need for leading peaceful, profound, delightedly skillful, and generous lives. He must treat them as he would have them treat him. Ideally, therefore, his work should be so truly functional and appropriate as to be *humanly* effectual, enabling them to serve others as well as themselves, to live contemplatively without undue drudgery, and to enjoy products that are worthy of being meditated upon for their intrinsic rightness and excellence.

Moreover, since there is no such thing as an average person, there is no such thing, strictly speaking, as an average client. Consequently, the worker must make products that meet each client's unique set of needs. Usually, therefore, except in the making of servile mechanisms or very simple things or parts, he cannot permit himself the luxury of serving his client slothfully through mass-production or purely mechanistic methods. He must considerately hold himself to the solving of each technical problem afresh. This requirement does not mean that he must strive to be original, but it does require that he never fail his client by dodging the challenge of what is unique in every problem. He must be respectful of—indeed, imbued with—tradition; but he can never be lazily conventional or automatic. To be so is to sin against his client by treating him as a mere duplicate of another, rather than as a sacredly unique person.

Professionally, the normal maker or performer also feels obligated to meet the claims of his *fellow practitioners,* those of the past and of the future, as well as of the present. He must, therefore, maintain high standards of excellence for their sakes as well as for his own. And he must aid them to maintain a similarly high standard. More specifically, he must eschew all chicanery, all shoddy workmanship, all eye-catching glamor, and all huckstering. Further he should also support loyally all who are of like mind with him, cooperating with them to establish just standards, prices, and penalties, as well as responsible franchises. Moreover, through conferences, shop-talk, journals, and associations, he must educate them and himself for the common good of their art. Additionally, to insure the maintenance of this art for society, and also to serve younger men in affection and charity, he must accept the obligation of protecting, supporting, guiding, inspiring, and training apprentices. He should help them to establish themselves as independent masters, even at some risk to his own "trade."

The worker is also obligated, of course, to his *family*. In setting a fair price, he and his fellow practitioners must take into account the needs of their dependents—those encountered in the leading of a humane life. So too must he be fair to *himself,* striking a proper balance between the claims of his artistic conscience and those of his religious conscience. Naturally, he ought to exercise all of the virtues that good work inevitably requires: the fortitude necessary for resisting illegitimate dictation by clients, for accepting drudgery, for executing many revisions; the humility of avoiding exhibitionistic originality and of recognizing personal limitations; the justice of meeting his client's needs thoroughly and of never forcing materials or instruments or using them up needlessly; the temperance of refusing meaningless assignments and of keeping his designs classically and functionally austere. But he must also never lose himself so much in his art as to let it endanger his personal life, as Michelangelo had once complained of himself.

The Rewards of Humane Work

But if these considerations constitute the obligations of the worker, the meeting of them constitutes perhaps the main source of his satisfaction. Meeting them, he can be happy to feel himself becoming part of the past, the present, and the future in the building of society; being a member of a dedicated group; helping to overcome the challenges of his art; acquiring skill and exercising it effectively; seeing that his work is technically pleasing; realizing that his art is better than he found it; contemplating the sheer splendor of "work well done," his own included; sharing in that delightful fellowship, the fellowship of masters; educating and being educated generously. As far as possible, he has the deep contentment that comes from having served clients, coworkers, friends, family, his country, and yes, all mankind, unstintingly and creatively. With artistic and moral conscience clear, he can look upon his life as meaningful in the eyes of both man and God, as one truly dedicated, professional and, in the best sense of the term, vocational.

Through obsession with mere gain, man almost always cheats himself of certain rewards which are potentially available in work.[2] Tragically, he fails to enjoy these outcomes simply because he does not recognize their presence as clearly and appreciatively as he recognizes them in relation to a sport or a hobby. For example, when a person takes up golf or tennis, he enjoys a wide range of rewards simply because he expects to. He enjoys the reward of learning the nature of the game ever more thoroughly, of watching others play it well, of playing it well himself, and of being praised by others for so doing. Some even help to improve the game itself or its instrumentation. All of these rewards are meant for the worker, even the so-called ''menial'' worker, as much as they are for the player. Ditch-digging, for example, can be made quite as great an art as golf, and it can therefore assure much the same kinds and qualities of reward. Similarly, for most other jobs, much of the boredom apparent in the job results from a failure on the part of the worker to approach it with the right attitude and expectancy—namely, that of artistic achievement and *all* its attendant joys.

Too often, in fact, today's worker fails to enjoy not only the general rewards of which we have been speaking, but also the particular rewards of the aesthetic experience. Anything beautiful, whether product or action, has four qualities: unity, variety, vividness, and appropriateness. The worker should be able to find readily these qualities in his work as well as in his play. Indeed, his experience can be profoundly aesthetic. When work is carried out creatively and consciously, it possesses: (1) a clear unity of aim; (2) a variety of stages, subprocesses, materials, and instruments; (3) the vividness of hard challenges and conquests; and, (4) the appropriateness of happy solutions and techniques. Without these qualities, as Studs Terkel (1972) and Barbara Garson (1975) have reported, work can be devastatingly dehumanizing in its sheer boredom. With their presence, work can be profoundly recreative.

When work and play are approached as artistic performances, they are found to be remarkably alike, as the following hypothetical case demonstrates. Suppose that while on a vacation a professional tennis champion—a Connors or an Orantes—plays a casual match with a friend. Then, later in the year in a sports arena, he plays another match with this same friend (who has meanwhile become a professional) before a paying audience. The first match is obviously ''play''; the second is no less obviously ''work.'' How then do they differ? Clearly in the former instance, the players are under no pressure from without: they have no deadline to meet; they can choose their court, grass or clay, for themselves; they can stop whenever they wish; in short, they can concentrate fully on the game as an end in itself, without regard to satisfying an audience, to remuneration, or to professional standing. In the second, of course, they are somewhat constrained in all these matters. Yet, objectively, the two matches will differ very little from each other, even in quality of play. The first may even turn out to be the better match because of its very freedom from pressure. And if these men find their schedule, their opponents, and their living accommodations entirely suited to their tastes, they may hardly be able to tell whether they are working or playing. The chances are, in fact, that unless as players they feel something of that sense of wonderment which filled Babe Ruth who, when signing as a rookie, asked,

"You mean they *pay* you to play baseball?" they never will be the workers they should be. Every worker should have that same sense when he is in the right vocation; his joy in his work as an art should be such that there hardly could be a greater punishment for him than being forbidden from his workshop, his laboratory, his desk, his hospital, or his altar. For Thomas Edison to be banned from his workbench, even though he were to be recompensed in the millions of dollars, would cause him to feel trapped and frustrated. He would still yearn for the best form of play he knew, his work.

What the sound worker learns to do, then, is to accept the requirements of his work as so many ground rules and, having determined the limitations which these impose upon him, to pursue his art creatively within that framework. He pursues it, therefore, as if it were a game, if only because it is in such a spirit alone—the spirit of a liberal art—that he can work most fruitfully. Conversely, it is only when a game has the limitations of rules and requirements, which make it something to be worked at, that it becomes a game felt to be truly worthwhile. To work well, one must play at one's work; to play well, one must work at one's play.[3]

The truth is not, therefore, that one must normally go from unleisurely work to a leisurely play or contemplation. More properly, one goes from leisurely work to leisurely play and contemplation (all executed artistically) and back again, without regarding any one of them as simply *for* any other, since they are all indispensable to fully human living.

What is said of work and play here applies no less pertinently to that almost universally neglected set of human activities which are neither work nor play. These activities might be referred to as "behaviors," all that lies between formal work and play. Let me explain. Imagine a society in which

the members are normally skillful in all their non-economic and non-recreational activities. In this, they would be trained to move easily and gracefully, without apparent effort. They would speak resonantly and clearly. They would sing freely, melodiously, spontaneously. They would dance unselfconsciously—without any forced, wriggling, bacchaanalian gaiety. They would write a hand that was pleasantly calligraphic. The casual maps or diagrams they had to sketch, in giving directions or explaining something to a friend, would please both mind and eye. They would design and choose clothing which, while comfortably functional, would be expressively personal. They would build homes and shops that both in structure and appearance would foster a warmly human way of living. They would serve nutritious meals which would, without fattening, prove symphonies of tastes. They would converse, or compose letters, pointedly, wittily, or compassionately, as occasion demanded. In these, and the many other activities of daily living, therefore, they would continuously experience the delights both of performing things well themselves, and of enjoying the similarly skillful performances of them by others. (Ryan 1972, p. 6)

In an artistically determined society of this kind, a worker, because he could go from work to behavior to play and contemplation and back again almost insensibly, would be an incomparably better worker than one for whom life consists of boring, routine drudgery compensated for by pleasure-seeking dissipation, both interrupted by dully performed behavior. Why should a worker not enjoy an unbroken sequence of leisurely and pleasant artistic achievements in work, play, *and* behavior? What is the method that would aid the worker to meet the responsibilities and enjoy the rewards of his work, his play, and his general behavior?

"To Build a Cathedral"

In general, we can identify four factors which determine every act of skillful making or performing. We all realize, if only in the negative sense, that when we work with an inadequate purpose, inadequate material, inadequate instrument, or inappropriate form, we are likely to turn out something which is defective—something essentially inartistic. On the other hand, if we have the right purpose, choose the right material, and use the right instrument for casting it into the right form, we are likely to turn out something that is a work of art.

To make clear just what is properly meant by these terms would require a large book. However, a brief illustration of each of these factors may show how radically different their meaning is from that which is generally given them. Consider, for instance, "purpose." In general use, this term is understood to mean "the desire for money, fame, and/or self-expression, to be gained in the answering of wants." Artistically, however, it means the meeting of a particular set of needs felt by an individual in a way that is as satisfactory as possible to his body, mind, and soul, as he leads a creative life of self-realization in serving and being served communally. Let me illustrate the "answering of wants" by the example of a beer stein:

> Technically, for instance, the purpose of a beer stein is not to be thought of simply as the holding of beer. A stein is to be visualized as something that can readily be filled in such a way as to satisfy a drinker's need for a certain amount of beer, with a reasonable head of foam; that can be grasped by the whole fist easily and steadily; raised easily, but with enough weight to rhyme with the body of the beer and its slightly bitter taste; lifted gracefully aloft in a toast; tilted safely and emptied in the right volume for an easy swallow by an ordinarily large mouth; brought

down firmly, yet stably, in the expression of strong satisfaction. (Ryan 1971, p. 8)

Now consider the second factor, "material," which is generally understood to be the raw stuff on which is imposed a form that will make it a saleable article. Artistically, however, it means that dynamic stuff from which is educed, diplomatically, stage by stage, the set of products required by an artifact for filling a set of truly human needs. It is never strictly "raw" material, even when it is as pliant as putty. "Form" is ordinarily understood to be the shape or figure—above all, the mathematical pattern—that is given to the material, or more precisely, imposed upon it. Artistically, however, form is that whole set of specifications—color, texture, taste, smell, weight, etc., as well as shape—which are educed embryonically from the material. It is never simply "imposed." Generally, an "instrument" is thought of as that which imposes (the more precisely and repetitively the better) the shape on the so-called raw material. Artistically, however, it is thought of as that which educes persuasively, whether by tool, powered-tool, machine, or automated cluster, the particular qualities required for fostering the particular personhood of the client. Each instrument is to be used, therefore, primarily for *qualitative,* and only secondarily for *quantitative,* production.

Socially, the changes of attitude required for shedding the one set of beliefs in favor of the other are hardly less than revolutionary. The technological change-over alone would, for most people, be nothing less than startling. It would mean accepting a technology (and a workplace) that is *not* thought to be:

(1) a by-product of science developed by engineers, but *rather* an extension and refinement of technique and craftsmanship;

(2) workers who are employees of industrialists, but *rather* workers who are autonomous artists;

(3) turning out general, cheap products in great quantity, but *rather* turning out suitable products of high quality in adequate quantity;

(4) primarily for making a profit, but *rather* incidentally for earning a fee;

(5) to meet the largely created wants of "prospects," but *rather* to meet the legitimate needs of individual members of society.

What has been suggested throughout this paper is the transition from a mechanistic, economically oriented technology and way of life to another in which *all* work, play, and behavior will become, as far as possible, humanistic because it will be artistic, professional, and truly vocational. Can such a transition be easy? Hardly! With human nature and the economic system as they are, it may well be extremely difficult, if not impossible. However, without these changes in perspective, work can never become truly humanistic, nor can we hope to see work organizations evolve which are supportive of these ends.

NOTES

1. I do not need to recount for the reader that the society I have just described is *not* what the worker of today experiences. But let me share my critique: "Indeed, as worker, the ordinary man feels himself to be in a chill state of isolation. He feels alienated from God, his experience making it virtually impossible to appreciate Him as the Creator under whom one may work meaningfully, having been charged with filling out that part of the cosmos known as civilization. He feels no less alienated from his client, whom he is frequently trained to regard less as a fellow man to be served humanly than as a 'prospect' to be 'sold.' He feels alienated from his fellow workers, sharing with them, not a professional code of honor and solicitude, a love of perfection, mutual admiration for skilled work, basic technical sympathy, and understanding, so much as their common envy and their common hatreds and 'gripes.' Again, he feels alienated from his employer, under whom he has the status, not of fellow master, journeyman, or even apprentice, but of hireling. And he feels alienated from his very work, which technically is hardly his at all, since it is not the result of his own inventive choices or responsible decisions" (Ryan 1971, p. 2).

2. "Modern civilization takes it for granted that people are better off the more things they want and are able to get; its values are quantitative and material. Now, How much is he worth?, means, How much money has he got?... that an incessant 'progress,' never-ending in contentment, means the condemnation of all men to a state of irremediable poverty. But, as Plato already knew, 'poverty consists, not in the decrease of one's possessions, but in the increase of one's greed...'" (Coomaraswamy 1943, p. 2).

3. To be more specific, we might ask "what are the requirements of enthusiastic and enjoyable work?" "The worker should obviously understand the main objectives of his work. This work should never be so limited, through a mass production division of labor, as to prevent him from seeing its ultimate significance. It should be varied and complex enough to challenge, at one time or other, every one of his powers of mind and will, as well as of hand. It should be vivid in the sense of engaging these strenuously enough to afford them a good workout" (Ryan 1972, p. 42).

REFERENCES

Coomaraswamy, A. K. *The Bugbear of Literacy*. London: Dennis Dobson Ltd., 1943. (First published as *Am I My Brother's Keeper?* Freeport, N.Y.: Books for Libraries Press, 1947.)

Eibl-Eibesfeldt, I. *Love and Hate: The Natural History of Behavior Patterns*. Translated by Geoffrey Strachan. New York: Holt, Rinehart and Winston, 1972.

Garson, B. *All the Livelong Day: The Meaning and Demeaning of Routine Work*. New York: Doubleday, 1975.

Ryan, J. J. The Hope For Humanization. *Cross Currents*, 1971, 22 (1):1–24.

————. *The Humanization of Man*. New York: Newman Press, 1972.

Terkel, S. *Working*. New York: Pantheon Books, 1972.

Work and Critical Theology

by Francis Schüssler Fiorenza

ONLY HESITATINGLY DOES A THEOLOGIAN APPROACH THE SUBJECT OF WORK. He or she must run the gauntlet set up by August Bebel's often quoted statement that "strictly speaking the worker who drains sewers to protect humanity from unhealthy miasmas is a very useful member of society, whereas the theologian who seeks to befog the brain with supernatural, transcendental doctrines is an extremely harmful individual" (1913, I:409f.).

Bebel's censure offends, but it raises a crucial question: what can a theologian say about work? Can it be anything else but a befogging of the brain with supernatural transcendental doctrines? Does a theologian have only questions to raise about work (Rahner 1966)? Or can a theologian contribute to a better understanding of work? Since these questions concern the role of theology today, I should like to contrast three ideal types of theology before reflecting on work.

Three Theological Approaches

A *literalist* or *scripturalist* type of theology maintains not only that God has revealed certain truths necessary for humanity's self-understanding and salvation, but also that these truths are primarily (and for some, exclusively) in the Bible. The theologian concerned with work would search the Bible for the divine revelation or the inspired teachings on the meaning of work. This biblical teaching would be the measure and standard for evaluating the modern situation of work.

This approach presupposes that God's revelation in the Bible can be applied to all times and covers every situation. Overlooking historical and societal differences, all ages are seen as standing *directly* and *immediately* under the revealed Word of God (Barth 1918, p. 1f.). Technological, social, economic, and political differences between biblical times and the present are often not sufficiently brought into focus. The approach is literalistic whenever it interprets the biblical writings as isolated texts independent of their socio-cultural contexts. Although the historical-critical method has highlighted the theological, cultural, and historical differences within the biblical writings and has underscored the distance between these writings and our present situation, several have sought to elaborate a biblical doctrine of work and to make it directly relevant for today's industrial world (Bienert 1954; Haes 1958; Richardson 1958; Rondet 1955).

The second type, the *transcendental* or *anthropological* approach, acutely perceives not only the theological diversity within the scriptures, but also the differences between the biblical past and the contemporary situation. It consequently seeks for a certain standard underlying the diversity of biblical teachings and the flux of history. This standard is seen in the fundamental a priori transcendental structure of humanity or in the fundamental religious dimension of experience which then provides the basis for the constructive task of theology.

This transcendental approach assumes that a basic fundamental human structure or religious experience underlies all religious statements. Biblical and doctrinal teachings are seen as expressions of this structure of experience. The approach does not elaborate a theology of work as a biblical theology, but rather as an anthropological theology. Work is analyzed in its relation to human nature and to the religious dimension of human experience. Since religious experience is seen as the culmination of this dimension, it is taken to be the highest activity of humanity. And work is evaluated from the perspective of such human religious activity. Such a transcendental approach has been exemplified by Friedrich Schleiermacher (Germany) and Horace Bushnell (USA) in the nineteenth century and by Karl Rahner in our day.

The transcendental approach often takes as its starting-point human nature or human experience in isolation from societal factors and cultural processes. Its analysis of religious experience and of even the work experience abstracts from the economic, political, and symbolic structures of human reality. Its origin in the Romantic movement and its relation to the industrial revolution can indicate the difficulties of its position on work and of its fundamental method.

The third type of theology, *critical theology*, reflects upon the historical context and societal function of religious truth. Since religious truths are formulated within a specific historical context and often have definite societal functions, religious truth cannot be reduced to some pure revealed word of God or to a banal religious experience. Instead theology as a critical theory of religious truth examines the fundamental interests and basic orientations that underlie religious worldviews and are expressed in religious truths (Fiorenza 1975).

The approach *does not neglect either the significant role of the Bible or the importance of human experience for theology; but it suggests these can be understood, interpreted, and evaluated only in the larger context of a historical, societal, and practical analysis.* Despite its recency this approach seeks to establish the continuity of its conception of the theological task with the Christian tradition by underscoring the significance of Christianity's belief in transcendence as historically mediated and as an eschatological, redemptive hope. Hence, it searches for the meaning of religious symbols not in abstraction from societal praxis nor in terms of a legitimation of that societal praxis. Rather, it searches for meaning in terms of a critical analysis of present and past societal praxis for the sake of uncovering emancipatory symbols and tendencies. In this approach, theology does not interpret the present solely in terms of some normative past tradition nor does it interpret the past in terms of some present normative value. Instead, it seeks to evaluate the interrelation between theory and praxis in the past as well as in the present to arrive at its interpretative categories and normative values.

This essay approaches work from the perspective of a critical model of theology. First, it explores the heritage of Greece and Israel as the two seed-bed cultures of the Western world. Second, it analyzes one major historical understanding of work within the history of Christianity. Finally, it discusses the meaning of work in contemporary society.

The Legacy of Antiquity

The legacy of Greece

"To the Greeks work was a curse and nothing else." This verdict, pronounced by Adriano Tilgher (1958, p. 3), is often the favorite prejudice of theologians seeking to contrast a Greek attitude toward work with the biblical (Rondet 1955; Schoonenberg 1964; Chenu 1971). Whereas the former is negative, the latter is positive. This prejudice is widespread because Aristotle and Plato are mistakenly taken as representative of all Greek literature. Greek and biblical (Hebraic) notions of work should not be simply contrasted. Instead, the respective writings of each should be analyzed in their historical and societal contexts so as to perceive the function and evaluation of work within each context.

Not only does Greek literature not see work only as a curse, but *three* attitudes toward work become evident: first, as basic to humanity and divinity; second, as religious; and finally, as negative.

Work as basic to humanity.   The epics of Homer, dealing with the landed aristocracy, take work as a matter of course. Even gods and goddesses perform manual labor. Odysseus's agricultural and pastoral labor is praised for being unexcelled (Odyssey 10. 366–75). Like Paris, he builds with his own hands his house and furniture (Odyssey 7. 103). Nevertheless, his slaves do the real work. Although Odysseus excels in work, his genuine achievements are the outstanding feats of courage and warfare during his journeys.

Work as religious.   Written at the end of the Homeric age, Hesiod's poem *Works and Days,* praises work as religious during a period of tragic transition for the small farmer. They are losing their farms and are becoming slaves or hired persons. Having lived among these farmers and shepherds of Ascra in Boetia, Hesiod is sympathetic to their plight (Solmsen 1949, pp. 76–100). He contrasts the difficulty of work in the present situation with the past Golden Age of Cronos, an age without the evils of pain, worries, and hard work.

Nevertheless, the poem praises agricultural work. As a way of life it is a form of religious experience. In farming, everything must be done at the right time and in the right form. Only then can the farmer trust divine justice and expect that the divine earth will yield its fruits. Justice, the favorite daughter of Zeus, blesses and rewards those working in accord with the laws of nature and justice. Hesiod's praise of the work of the farming life therefore is at the same time a praise of the divine order of justice (Solmsen 1949, pp. 86–94; Vernant 1968, pp. 16–36).

Small household farms decrease in Greece. Yet, the praise of farming continues. Xenophon (434–355 B.C.) attributes a religious dimension to the farming life. Farmers, just as the warriors, depend upon the gods for success. Not only do they sacrifice to the gods for the growth of the crops, but their work itself in the fields is a cult. The land, which is a god, teaches justice. Whoever best cultivates the land, will receive the most from the gods. In cultivating the land, the farmer participates in an order that is natural and divine and is taught humility and justice (Vernant 1968: 16–36).

But while Xenophon praises the work of farming, he disdains the work of artisans. The craftperson's sedentary work weakens the body, robs it of strength, and makes the person physically and morally unfit for warfare (*Oeconomicus* 4. 3; LCL 390). Hence, only farmers and not craftpersons are virtuous and reliable (4. 2–5, LCL 391 and 6. 7, LCL 409). Xenophon's and Hesiod's praise of work is obvious. For both, work is religious and teaches justice, but for Xenophon it also prepares one for the military.

Work as negative. The negative attitude toward manual labor as well as toward various trades is found in the classical philosophical writings of Plato and Aristotle. This emergence of a negative attitude toward work has been attributed to the transformation of Greek society into two classes, slaves and free persons. The praise of work in Hesiod (or, for Roman history, in Virgil) took place before the rise of slavery (Mosse 1969, p. 29). After the inception of slavery, the manual labor of the slaves came to be looked upon as unfit for citizens.

Hannah Arendt has suggested that "[the] opinion that labor and work were despised in antiquity because only slaves were engaged in them is a prejudice of modern historians. The ancients reasoned the other way around and felt it necessary to possess slaves because of the slavish nature of all occupations that served the needs for the maintenance of life" (1959 p. 74). Instead she claims that the work of craftsmanship, trade, and farming was first disdained and only consequently was slavery instituted. It was not because work came to be performed by slaves that it came to be despised; rather the reverse was true.

Although Arendt's thesis challenges any reductionistic interpretation of cultural history, it can be questioned: Why was manual labor disdained for only a very limited period of time and why by only a minority of thinkers? What caused the change between the time of Hesiod and the time of Plato and Aristotle? More significantly, Arendt's thesis overlooks the attitude toward manual labor among the working class itself. If nonphilosophical or nonliterary texts are examined, a view of manual labor can be obtained from various inscriptions that differs from that of the Athenian aristocracy. The ancient laborer looked at his or her work as under the protection of a deity. Sepulchral bas-reliefs present a smith as a heroic figure with the implements of the trade. Similar evidence from drawings on pottery, epitaphs on graves, and inscriptions in temples caution against any attempt to claim that the despisal of manual labor in Plato and Aristotle was general or that it led to slavery (Conze 1893, p. 119 plate 2; Wilhelm 1909).

More helpful than speculation about the causes and origin of this despisal of manual labor would be an analysis of the values expressed in this despisal and to observe its societal context. Plato and Aristotle regard free peasants and slaves as almost equally ignoble, as Arendt notes, because the exigencies of life compel them to perform labor. This labor (understood in a narrower and more pejorative sense than work) consists of that work required for the obtaining of the necessities of life. It does not leave time for the truly active life of politics and war.

Here lies the crucial argument: Labor robs persons of the leisure to participate in political and military activity. These activities are proper to the upper class and are appropriate only to free citizens. This argument that labor and the trades do not allow persons free time for moral and intellectual pursuits loses its feasibility, however, when one considers that political debates or military warfare were not seen as impeding the development of intellectual or moral virtues. Moreover, the concern for the contemplative life and the virtues of the intellectual is not solely operative in this despisal of manual labor. Early Christian monasticism could reconcile manual labor and the contemplative life, but not military or political activity with the spiritual life. The Athenian despisal of work is not so much based upon the esteem for the intellectual and contemplative as it expresses the sensibility of an aristocratic class (Levi 1974, pp. 39–99). Plato betrays this sensibility when he has Socrates ask Callicles whether he or his son would marry the daughter of an engineer (*Gorgias* 512). Plato's argument against material and business success becoming standards of virtue is well made. However, its application only to manual labor or the trades, and not to military warfare or to political activity, expresses the prejudices of the Athenian aristocratic class (Jaccard 1960, pp. 66–74).

This disdain of manual labor was not shared by all, nor was it even consistently held among Athenian philosophers. Antisthenes, the founder of the Cynic School, urged his followers to imitate the toil of Hercules. Even Plato admits that laborers have their part in knowledge and virtue (*Philebus* 56c), and Aristotle argues against communism that it removes people's desire to work (*Politics* 1261b. 33–38). Nevertheless, the legacy of Ancient Greece for Western civilization lies in the opinion that manual labor and trading activity is corruptive of body and soul. Even though this prejudice was not universal in antiquity, it remains the dominant influence of Greek thought upon the Western cultural tradition.

The legacy of Israel

The other seed-bed culture of Western civilization, Israel, also has diverse attitudes toward work. The Israelites saw work as basic to humanity, as a difficulty, and as a positive force. But much more stands behind these simple evaluations.

Work as basic to humanity.   Although it is commonly assumed that the Bible negatively evaluates work by viewing it as a curse, the opposite is expressed by a large portion of the Hebrew scriptures. Genesis 2:15, for example, indicates how the Jahwist author (known for his use of Jahweh as a name for God) understands work. In the Jahwist description of the creation of humanity, God commands Adam to till and to keep, to cultivate and to protect the fields. Adam's task is twofold: he should work the field and he should watch over it. Work is demanded of him even in the garden.

This aspect of Adam's existence in the garden is often overlooked by many who think that work is only the result of sin. It has been suggested that this phrase "to till and to keep" must be an insertion by some secondary editor. After all, humans are not in paradise to work (Budde 1883, p. 83). Here the interpreter's imagination of paradise and his own views on work are expressed and not those of the Genesis text itself. The basic meaning of the word "paradise" (used in the Hebrew text) is "fenced orchard." As a Persian loan word, it evokes images more in accord with the Koran's description of paradise as a primordial place of peace and abundance. The Genesis text does not conceive of the gods in some past golden age. Instead it teaches that work is an essential component of human existence even in paradise (Westermann 1974, p. 300). The words "till and keep" represent two basic complementary aspects of not only farming, but of all human work.

This positive evaluation of work contrasts sharply with neighboring Sumerian and Babylonian myths of creation. In these latter works, humans are created specifically to do the difficult work for the gods. One Sumerian myth relates how the higher gods supervise the burdensome work of the lower gods: Nammu, the mother of the gods, requests that the god Enki create substitutes who can unburden the gods of their work. In this ancient Oriental myth, humans were created to take away drudgery from the gods. Humans build their temples and till their fields and were created for this purpose as Enuma Elish and the Atrahmhasis myth document (Westerman 1974, pp. 299–308).

In contrast to these myths, Genesis does not have God create humans to take over drudgery. Adam is not placed in a field of a god so as to work for God. Instead, he is given his own field in which to work. *Work belongs to human existence and is commanded by God.* In comparison to these myths, the Genesis account demythologizes work. The culture arising from the tilling and keeping of the land has meaning for human existence. The ensuing chapters of Genesis describe the development of various trades and crafts and so depict culture and civilization as resulting from the creator's basic command to work (Westermann 1974, pp. 305ff.).

Work as a curse.   Despite the essential nature of work, the Jahwist account notes the difficulties and hardships of work, but these are interpreted as the result of sin. In Genesis 3:17–19, God curses the ground and humans must now earn their bread by the sweat of their brows. What does this cursing of human work mean? The classic commentary on Genesis sees this text as an "extremely pessimistic view of human life and agriculture" (Gunkel 1922).

The verses themselves do not justify this view. Originally two different versions can be detected.

The first version in verses 17c, 19a, and 19b is: "Cursed is the ground because of you//in toil you shall eat of it all the days of your life//in the sweat of your face you shall eat bread//till you return to the ground for out of it you were taken." This version obviously describes the life of the peasant (fellah) and the difficulties of obtaining a harvest from the clods of the earth. Nevertheless, verses 18, 19c represent a second version: "Thorns and thistles it shall bring forth to you//and you shall eat the plants of the field//you are dust and to dust you shall return." This view envisions the life of the Bedouin in the steppe, where existence is not plagued by the difficulties of tilling the grounds, but afflicted with the poverty and skimpiness of the Bedouin life (von Rad 1963, pp. 91-94).

By combining both versions, Genesis 3:17-19 traces the misery of the primary forms of life in Palestine back to the mythic past. Yet even in this passage, *work in itself is not seen as a punishment or a curse.* Instead, the hardship and difficulty that accompanies work is the result of sin. The lack of proportion between human effort and success does not come from creation, nor was it originally intended by God. Rather, it comes from human sin (von Rad 1963, p. 92).

The praise of work.   The wisdom-teaching of Israel in the Book of Proverbs praises work (Wolff 1973, pp. 192-195). Proverbs teaches that a regularity governs life: work and industry bring success, whereas laziness and sluggardness brings poverty. "A slack hand causes poverty, but the hand of the diligent makes rich" (Proverbs 10:4). The social opposition of the rich and poor result from either industry or idleness. Even the difference between free persons and slaves is seen as dependent upon industrious work. "The hand of the diligent will rule, while the slothful will be put to forced labor" (Proverbs 12:24). These didactic poems minutely describe the consequences of laziness, for they seek to convince the youth that idleness causes poverty and subjection, whereas hard work is the pillar of success. These proverbs are pedagogical sayings by which the educated upper-class, living in an urban cultural milieu (von Rad, 1972, pp. 74-77), seeks to explain distinctions of wealth and class in terms of a work ethic and endeavors to impart this work ethic to its youth.

These texts demand a nuanced evaluation. On the one hand, they should not be labeled as ideological, for they do stress that both the rich and poor stand under Jahweh's judgment. Riches do not suffice for the day of wrath, but only righteousness. Proverbs does not make the will of Jahweh the basis of social inequality as do the Laws of Manu, composed by Hindu priests around 200 B.C. They describe the creation of four classes as divinely ordained by

God and see it as the Lord's will that the Sudra serve the other three castes (Muller 1886, 25:13–14, 24). In contrast, Proverbs explains social stratification as the result of industry or laziness, but not divine will.

On the other hand, the praise of work often rings false. Sayings such as Proverbs 20:4 "the sluggard does not plow in the seedtime, he will seek at harvest and have nothing," strike one as ludicrous. What farmer does not plow in seedtime and still expect a harvest. Moreover, although Proverbs praises work, it is nonetheless often performed by others. For example, Proverbs 31:10–31 describes women as the primary workers (managers of the household and business), whereas men sit at the gates and engage in political discourse.

By so justifying the existing social structure, Proverbs' attitude toward social inequality differs from the prophetic writings. The cause of social distinction for the Book of Micah is not idleness or industry, but the exploitation and greed of the rich. The rulers of the land "abhor justice and pervert all equity" (3:9). "They covet fields, and seize them; and houses, and take them away" (2:2). Amos sees the rich as "oppressing the poor and crushing the needy" (4:1). Although the social historical interpretation of this prophetic critique is complex (Fendler 1973: 32–35), the contrast to the Book of Proverbs is obvious.

Summary

On an informational level, this survey clears away the misconception that the Greeks viewed work as demeaning and the Hebrews saw it as a curse. Instead, as I have argued, both societies have traditions affirming work as basic to humanity and as a religious command. Likewise, both societies are aware of the difficulties and tribulations of work. The Bible traces these difficulties back to some fault or misdeed on the part of humans; Greek literature places the fault with the gods. In both, a golden age of the past is depicted with work, but without hardships.

An analysis must move to another level beyond the mere unraveling of ideas, convictions, and tenets about work. Theology as a critical theory of society and its symbolic traditions must observe how the various beliefs about work function in their respective societal contexts. Our survey also points to a salient paradox: Both the despisal and praise of work have served to explain social inequality. The Athenian distinction between freepersons and slaves was related to the despisal of the work of slaves. The Book of Proverbs by praising work attempts to encourage its youth to diligence. Both attitudes have had similar functions throughout Western history, even today. The ethic of work has been invoked by politicians to hold down increases in welfare benefits for the poor. And the praise of leisure has served to impede an equal emphasis upon reforming the work situation and making it meaningful. If a lesson is to be learned from the legacy of antiquity, it is that *theology must attend not only to convictions and beliefs about the meaning of work, but must also become sensitive to the praxis that flows from those beliefs and convictions.* Such a theology would be critical. It would have the therapeutic function of analyzing the distortions that might flow from various religious evaluations of work. This task demands a further look at the evaluation of work in the history of Christianity and in modern theology.

Work in the History of Christianity

New Testament writings offer few systematic teachings about work. To construct a New Testament "theology of work" is neither feasible nor possible. Not only does the theological diversity of New Testament writings weigh against it, but work is not a central concern. Nevertheless, since several occasional and incidental references to "work" in the New Testament have become significant for Christianity's understanding of work, they should be examined.

The earliest historical references to work are found in the Gospel of Mark and in Q (the source material common to Matthew and Luke). Mark 6:3 refers to Jesus as a worker. "Is this not the carpenter, the Son of Mary?" Matthew's gospel, written approximately twenty years later, sought to present Jesus as a rabbi or teacher. It slightly modifies this text into "Is not this the carpenter's son" (Mt. 13:55) so that Jesus appears as the son of a carpenter. The apocryphal gospels about the infancy of Jesus are legendary and stem from the second century. They relate stories of Jesus helping his father at work.

Much more significant are the sayings attributed to Jesus in Q: "Do not worry about your life, what you will eat, or what you will drink, nor about your body, what you will wear. Is not life more than food and the body more than clothes? See the birds in the sky: They do not sow nor reap nor gather into barns and yet your heavenly father feeds them" (Mt. 6:25–26//Luke 12:22–24). It further adds: "Take no gold, nor silver, nor copper in your belts, no bag for your journey, nor two tunics, nor sandals, nor a staff; for the laborer deserves his food (wages)" (Mt. 10:9–10//Luke 10:4 and 7c). These sayings of Jesus' call to discipleship refer to the situation of the early Christian missionaries who are following the itinerant life-style of the Lord (Did 11. 8). The sayings bring to the fore the harshness of the homeless existence of these early Christian missionaries. They probably came from small rural areas and left behind the security of a livelihood to go about the country without possessions to preach the gospel (Theissen 1973, pp. 245–271). In this context, the proverb "the laborer deserves his/her food or wages" means that the itinerant missionaries should trust in God and rely upon living from the results of their preaching. Its attribution to the historical Jesus gives the saying its authority (Hoffmann 1972, pp. 264–267).

In his first letter to the Corinthians (9:1–27), Paul refers to this saying in defending his apostleship. It is one of only two times in which Paul quotes Jesus. By writing "in the same way the Lord commanded that those who proclaim the gospel should get their living by the gospel," Paul indicates that the early Christians missionaries as a rule live totally from their preaching as was the Jewish custom. Nevertheless, he and Barrabas did not use this right, but have preached the gospel in freedom.

Paul argues that his praxis contrasts with the Lord's command but for the same reason. Whereas according to the sayings of Jesus, the disciples should live from their preaching and have the trust and freedom to do so, Paul states that for the sake of freedom and autonomy, he has, as a rule, not used this right, but has supported himself by work. The proverbial statement that the laborer deserves his wages was thus first invoked to insure the total dedication and freedom of Christian missionaries to preach and live from that preaching. But Paul exempted himself because in his situation the opposite praxis would guarantee his freedom and right to preach.

The second letter to Thessalonians (3:7–12) deals with their idleness. Because of their eschatological beliefs and conceptions, they thought that they could lead a life free from the burden of work. They are scolded for their idleness in comparison to Paul's own example: "We did not eat anyone's breakfast without paying, but with toil and labor we worked night and day that we might not burden any of you. It was not because we have not the right, but to give you in our conduct an example to imitate. For even when we were with you, we gave this command, if anyone will not work, let that person not eat." Paul's example went against the Pharisaic teaching of the Torah and was contrary to the Lord's command. Yet it is invoked against the Thessalonians.

Although these two texts touch upon work only tangentially and occasionally they show how the New Testament writings have influenced Christianity. Often texts are taken out of context and are applied to quite different situations. Even though these texts deal only with missionary activity and its remuneration, they have been applied within Christianity and even outside of it to all work situations. Paul's defense of his example with the proverb "if anyone will not work, let him not eat" has become the so-called "golden rule of work." Its application has been quite diverse. The clergy of England, especially Townsend and Malthus, used it to argue for the repeal of the Speenhamland Law. This law, passed in England in 1795 to provide financial relief for the unemployed poor (with the hope of avoiding a revolution), was the first example of social welfare. Since it seemed to undercut the market economy, one appealed to Paul's statement quite out of context for the law's successful repeal. The verse is also quoted in Article 12 of the 1936 Constitution of the Union of Soviet Socialist Republics as a basic principle. With no reference to its origin! (Bell 1962, pp. 252–255). Similarly, the saying that the laborer deserves his wage became a principle underscoring the demands for a just and living wage for workers.

Work and Theology in Contemporary Society

Despite enormous diversity, three basic approaches to work can be delineated. Each should be analyzed and evaluated as to how it meets the challenges described above. These approaches are: the enconomium of leisure, the praise of work, and the demand for social reform.

The enconomium of leisure

One major theological evaluation of work in the modern industrial society comes from the liberal transcendental approach to theology. It associates technology and industrial society, and views technology as making possible humanity's mastery over nature and freeing it from the struggle for survival over nature. Since technology increases free time and leisure, it enables individuals to give more time to intellectual, cultural, and religious pursuits. This approach is represented by Schleiermacher (1824/1884) and by Bushnell (1848/1881), Karl Rahner (1959/66) and his brother Hugo (1965), as well as such philosophers as Pieper (1952) and Huizinga (1949).

Schleiermacher (1824/1884) assumes that Christian morality involves the domination and shaping of nature. He hopes that technological mechanization will humanize both technology and nature so that the human spirit can express its religious and artistic nature and can more fully penetrate both nature and society. Aware that industrial development, with its division of labor often impedes the formation of human personality and personal talents, he therefore suggests that labor be divided according to the talents of each and that dehumanizing work (work that reduces persons to machines) be rejected. Christianity's task, as he sees it, is to encourage a lessening of mechanical work and an elevation of industrialized work to the realm of art. These reflections betray his attachment to the Romantic movement. The criterion for his evaluation of industrialized work is the aesthetic and religious dimension of human nature. Writing in 1820, Schleiermacher expects that spirit and nature, human freedom and machines, will in the future become reconciled. Later in the century Ritschl will shift the emphasis to the liberation of the human spirit from nature, rather than its penetration through a humanized technology.

In an 1848 lecture, Bushnell, the father of American liberal theology, analyzes work and play as the two basic forms of human activity. Whereas work is done with conscious effort, play is spontaneous. Consequently, work is temporary, transitory, and finds its realization and fulfillment only in the state of play (see also Simon 1971). The desire for play underlies all culture. *One works to have the opportunity for play.* This centrality of play is underscored by religious evolution insofar as religion has developed from one of legal obedience to one of spontaneity. Bushnell optimistically hopes for a time when society, under the influence of Christianity, will become a life of play.

A century later, Karl Rahner (1959/66) observes the large decrease in working hours from 1850 to 1950. Finding no economic, medical, or physical reason for the increase in leisure, he suggests an anthropological foundation: humans are spirits in the world. The increase in free time due to the human spirit's domination of nature enables it to dedicate itself more fully to the pursuit of the intellectual and spiritual. More nuanced than Bushnell, Rahner suggests that this spiritual activity of humans involves a type of both work and play, but a work different from the securing of the necessities of life. It is an activity that is its own end.

This anthropological approach presupposed that by increasing humanity's domination over nature, modern technology will increase humanity's leisure and cultural pursuits. The early nineteenth century hoped that technology would bring this about. In the mid-twentieth century the rise of automation led to the same belief. This evaluation however overlooks significant data. First of all, despite a considerable reduction in time at work between 1850 and 1950, recent studies (e.g., Carter 1970, pp. 52–67) indicate that this trend has been reversed, primarily through overtime and partially through dual jobholding. Moreover, contemporary economists expect work activities to increase, rather than decrease (Galbraith 1967). Secondly, this theology overlooks how the length and effort of work impede a person's ability to engage in meaningful pursuits in leisure time. According to recent studies, leisure does not compensate for meaninglessness in work and is not capable of providing the basis for an individual's life-satisfaction in the same manner that meaningful work can (Wilensky 1966; Meyershon 1972). Insofar as a society's occupational system becomes increasingly unsatisfactory, leisure also becomes dissatisfying (Seligman 1965). The objectification of the work situation in a rationalized society has had its effects on leisure. Leisure offers some rest, restoration, and respite, provides some entertainment, but does not necessarily lead to self-realization.

The theological praise of leisure is inadequate to the problem of work. It rightly questions "to what purpose work?" but it too easily answers by making leisure meaningful in itself and the culmination of human activity. Instead, it should ask how can work be structured so that a meaningful interrelation between work and leisure can evolve and so that both human activities can be made meaningful. The degraduation of work to mere functional preparation for leisure bifurcates the human person; unless this separation is overcome, neither work nor leisure can be meaningful.

The glorification of work

In contrast to viewing work only as a preparation for leisure, this second approach glorifies, sacramentalizes, and absolutizes work. Whereas the first approach becomes prevalent at the beginning of industrial development or at times of technological innovation, this positive theology of work dominates the period that immediately followed World War II. The writings of Auer (1966), Chenu (1963), Rondet (1955), Todd (1960), Truhlar (1961) are just a few samples of the literature that arose in Europe during a ten-year period. At this time, the feast of St. Joseph the Worker was instituted on May 1st in Europe or on Labor Day in the USA (Filas 1957). The World Council of Churches issued studies on work (Oldham 1950/61; Richardson 1952/58) and so did the *Opus Dei* (Illanes 1967). Several causes can be given for this sudden praise of work. A biblical renewal underscored the Bible's positive attitude toward work against the false view of work as a curse. Moreover, both the growth of Communism and the task of reconstruction that took place in Europe after World War II created both the disposition and the need for a positive attitude toward work. Consequently most of these theological studies are optimistic toward work and the world.

How is this praise of work formulated? Monsignor Cardijn writes, "The workbench becomes an altar on which the lay priesthood prolongs the sacrifice of the Mass" (Todd 1960: 220), and Herbert McCabe asserts that "in itself the business of human work is to externalize and effect the rule of Christ the King, the rule of man over the whole Universe" (Todd 1960, p. 219). A theology of work must exist, according to McCabe, because of the difference between the secular and the Christian attitude toward work. Whereas for the former work means wealth, honor, and comfort, for the Christian it is a "sacramental."

This theological approach is also inadequate in analyzing the present societal imprint upon work because it merely selects biblical and theological motifs positive toward work and elaborates them into a constructive synthesis. It declares work to be meaningful in the face of the increasing fragmentation of work and the growing instrumentalistic attitude toward it. What significance can be gained by applying to work the following theological categories: partnership in creation, stewardship over the world, sacramental activity, continuation of the sacrifice of Christ, redemptive or eschatological activity? Does it lead to a neglect of work's hardships and frustrations and does it cover up its rationalization and fragmentation? Or does it serve to appropriate this positive vision as a cultural force for reforming the praxis of work, as has often been done? Does this approach sufficiently perceive how much job satisfaction often comes from the job situation rather than from the work itself and urge not only the enrichment of the job, but also of its situation. Does its purely theoretical approach overlook the cognitive dissonance that exists between religious worldviews and the public sphere (Berger 1964, pp. 211–241; 1973, pp. 119–178)? In the face of the complexities of work in modern industrial society, the theological attempt to sacramentalize work reminds one of Adorno's complaint that Marx wanted to "turn the world into a giant workhouse" or Horkheimer's judgment that the making of labor into "a transcendent category of human activity is an ascetic ideology" (Jay 1973, p. 57).

The demand for social reform

If the two previous theological approaches exalt either leisure or work, the third approach seeks to reform the work situation itself: amount and conditions of work, security of work, salary for work, etc. This approach is represented by diverse movements: The Social Gospel in America, Religious Socialism in Switzerland, the Christian Social Movement in England, and the Papal Catholic Social Teachings. These movements cut across denominational and national lines in confronting work as a human and social problem. Faced with the inequalities, brutalities, and exploitations of the modern work situation, prophets of social reform seek to change it.

Emerging at the end of the nineteenth century and the beginning of the twentieth, these movements combine realism and idealism in their appraisal of work and the work situation. They strongly criticize the effects of capitalistic competition; they point out the negative effects of industrialization; and they censure the exploitation of the workers. The inhuman conditions of work, the poverty and squalor of the working person's situation are all censured. But they also had positive recommendations. Some suggested moderate changes that would enable workers to earn a fair wage, to work under decent conditions, and to live decently within the capitalistic system. Others suggested a radical transformation of capitalism into socialism.

Yet, these religious social movements were also idealistic. They exhibited a strong preference for preindustrial forms of life. A return to the rural agricultural life was often seen as desirable. Leo XIII argues in *Rerum Novarum* that it would be advantageous if workers could also own their own farms (66). And Pius XII still considered tilling the soil the noblest form of work. The moral integrity of the nation depends in his opinion on the farmers and on contact with nature (1950, pp. 442).

Religious socialism primarily recommended placing private ownership with public ownership. It had "no idea of reverting to the simple methods of the old handicrafts, but heartily accepts the power machinery, the great factory, the division of labor, the organization . . . as the most efficient method of producing wealth. But it proposes to give to the whole body of workers the ownership of these vast instruments of production and to distribute among them all the entire proceeds of their common labor" (Rauschenbush 1907/1964, p. 407). This conviction—that the transfer of power from private ownership to state ownership will solve the main social defects of industrialized work—overlooks the extent that technocratization, rationalization, and efficiency are just as much a part of advanced socialist societies as they are of capitalist societies. Lenin's demand that the efficiency of Taylorism be introduced into socialism readily shows that socialism alone does not solve the problem of work. Some work will remain more desirable than others; the division of labor remains necessary; planning is often mistaken; and increased efficiency and higher productivity will be as forcefully felt in socialism as in capitalism. Both systems must balance equity and growth. Although socialism might be more effective for the developing countries and more equitable than capitalism, as an economic system it must also face the problem of work.

These Christian social movements seriously attempt to come to terms with work. On the one hand, they draw upon the Christian vision and its utopian content of eschatological fulfillment and personal redemption as a source to criticize the inadequacies and brutalities of certain societal practices. On the other hand, they have often coupled this critique with the appeal to return to some preindustrial ideal of society or to some socialistic form. Because of this inadequacy, it becomes necessary to develop a critical theology of work that draws from the same utopian content and semantic potential of the Christian tradition as a source of criticism. And at the same time, it refuses to become a simplistic theology that too readily recommends concrete programs as solutions.

Critical Theology and Work

Reappropriating the semantic potential of the Christian tradition places theology before a theoretical and practical task. Theoretically, theology interprets its religious tradition and retrieves its cultural heritage to illumine not only the past but also the present (Fiorenza 1972). Likewise it undertakes the practical task of considering how its religious heritage can be best communicated and realized in praxis.

My interpretation of this religious tradition points to a dialectical view of work: work is positive but not absolute. The positivity of work was affirmed throughout the whole religious tradition. Nevertheless, neither work nor its hardships were divinized. The hardships of work are the result of human sin and not God's eternal will. In praising work and a work-ethic, the book of Proverbs still does not absolutize it as the Laws of Manu did. An analysis of this biblical tradition displays a correspondence between the biblical belief in creation and the positive evaluation of work. The world and work are good because created. Yet because created, they are not absolute, but relative. Paul's appropriation of Jesus' saying manifests a similar dialectic. His own praxis documents the positivity of work, yet his recommendations point to its relativity. It can be chosen for the sake of the freedom to preach Jesus, just as it can be renounced for the same reason. This vision has two poles: positivity and relativity. They must be kept in constant balance. To lose the balance is to lose the vision.

The dialectic of this vision can illumine the anthropological data that I brought to bear in my criticisms of the theologies of leisure and work. Against the theologies of leisure, I have pointed out that the self-concept and self-value of persons often depends upon their occupational and vocational task. Leisure and free time can provide opportunities for fulfilling activities only if a work situation exists that is meaningful and not destructive. Against the theologies of work, I have pointed to the rationalization of work and to the increasing instrumental attitude toward work. Vocational satisfaction often comes from the job situation or the environment of work rather than from the work itself. In the perspective of the vision that I have suggested, this data indicates the importance of making work meaningful and positive without over-emphasizing its importance. In my opinion, a comprehensive anthropological analysis of work would corroborate the Christian vision of work as positive but relative.

Although the religious heritage and its vision provides a perspective for viewing the anthropological data, the question remains: what relation does the religious vision of work that I have suggested have to our present societal praxis. On the one hand, the rationalization of society manifests trends of de-democratization with its neglect of interests, bifurcation of roles, and erosion of privatism. All militate against the meaningfulness of work. On the other hand, this same society includes reform movements seeking to counter de-democratization by "participatory democracy," to lessen work fragmentation by "job enrichment" and to combat the erosion of privatism by cultural and communal renewal. The culture of our society is, therefore, ambiguous.

On the one side, there is an excessive emphasis on a work-ethic and on a competitive vocational spirit. On the other hand, this same competitive spirit readily accepts the fragmentation of work as natural and productive so much so that it resists any reform of the work situation that would lessen its efficiency and productivity. After all, it is argued, work is work.

Insofar as theology seeks to recapture for our culture the binary dialectic of the religious heritage's vision, it moves against two interlocking fronts. Its retrieval goes contrary to any societal demeaning of work that would impede reform of the work situation just as it equally counters an absolutization of the work ethic that hinders social or welfare legislation. Its reappropriation of the positive value of work critically functions to marshall its society's cultural heritage against any functional collapse of work as humanely and socially efficient into work as solely productively efficient. Such a positive appropriation of the meaning of work is often neglected by a theology glorifying leisure. Its retrieval of the relativity of work enables it to perceive—what a theology of work might not—that the growing instrumentalistic attitude toward work needs to be criticized only insofar as it hinders reform of the work situation, but not insofar as it aids persons to face occupational changes, disappointments, and losses, and not insofar as it encourages reform of the private sphere and job environment.

Theology as a critical social theory, consequently, does not so much reject the theologies of work and of leisure as it strives to sensitize to their correct appropriation and right application by surveying how the praise or disdain of work functioned in different societal contexts. I should like to suggest that the twofold dialectic of the religious heritage can be best preserved by not constructing an abstract theology either of work or of leisure but rather by appropriately drawing on the relevant affirmations of this religious heritage to influence attitudes, to shape culture, and to inform prudential judgements toward work and leisure as well as toward their reform. By tracing the history of the relation between symbolic affirmations and their societal praxis, critical theology's method is reconstructive. It seeks to give contour and content to the criteria of comprehensiveness and appropriateness by which the historical and constructive task of systematic theology proper can be evaluated and better enabled to interpret and appropriate the tradition for the present.

In my opinion, the theologies of leisure and work have not been sufficiently comprehensive. They have selected those stories, myths or metaphors either glorifying leisure or work, but have neglected the contrasting traditions. Their anthropological analysis was likewise selective. It viewed persons mainly as free spirits or as workers. As a consequence these theologies often failed to appropriately retrieve their tradition and bring it to bear on their societal culture and praxis. Did they analyze whether their culture's praise of work fostered an excessive competitive spirit, disregarded those caught in the dysfunctioning of the market system, and hindered welfare legislation for the unemployed? Or did they analyze whether the praise of leisure often hindered the reform of the work situation? How the religious tradition is appropriated makes all the difference. Does the appropriation support a praxis consonant or in contrast with the total vision of the religious tradition? Although religious symbols do not have an internal logic that guarantees their correct appropriation, a comprehensive analysis of these symbols of the religious tradition can provide insights and skills enabling us to determine whether the appropriation of a particular cultural attitude to support a particular praxis accords with the total vision of that tradition or does not. By seeking to maintain the double accent of the Christian vision, I have sought not only to avoid the weakness of these theologies, but also to sensitize to the problem of their correct application. My endeavor differs from those reform movements that have too readily recommended preindustrial or utopian schemes insofar as it places more emphasis upon the problem of society's cultural heritage (Fiorenza 1972). Theology has a theoretical task as well as practical. By underscoring the duality of the vision and the need for its correct appropriation, I have sought to underscore the need for a cultural retrieval that could inspire societal reforms and encourage social legislation with absolutizing any particular movement or legislation.

The rationalization of society, however, subjectivizes religious beliefs and also weakens the social power of religious symbols. Critical theology therefore has a practical task. It must also initiate a praxis incorporating and expressing its retrieval of the religious vision. As a part of ecclesial institutions, theology must incite these institutions to become *mediating communities* that link theory and practice. As concrete communities, the churches should provide not only opportunities for communal worship, but also for ethical discourse. This discourse would be the democratic and communal endeavor to interpret the religious heritage and its relation to present societal custom. As living communities, the churches could provide occasions of social interaction among persons of diverse interests and vocations. This interaction would help individuals transcend the limitations of their professional and private self-understandings and become a formative and supportive force. As experiential communities, the church could provide society with alternative life-styles and practical paradigms expressing the meaningfulness of work and leisure as contained in its religious heritage. But to exercise this critical function countering the trends of de-democratization, bifurcation of roles, and erosion of privatism, the churches must become much more self-critical and express more the truth of their religious vision than the rationalized bureaucratic structures of their society. Only then can they become the catalytic paradigms of vision and application, initiating and inspiring some socio-cultural patterns and resisting others. Only then can they be a light to the world.

In conclusion, I have proposed a religious vision. It exhibits a meaning of work that is not exhausted either by society's glorification of a competitive work ethic or by its fragmentation and functionalization of work. By confronting our society's praxis with this vision, theology does not fall under August Bebel's verdict.

REFERENCES

Arendt, H. *The Human Condition*. New York: Doubleday, 1959.

Auer, A. *Christsein in Beruf*. Düsseldorf: Patmos, 1966.

Barth, K. Preface to the First Edition (1918). In *The Epistle to the Romans*, E. C. Haskyns, trans., Oxford: Oxford University Press, 1933.

Bebel, A. *Die Frau und der Sozialismus*. Stuttgart: J. H. W. Dietz, 1913.

Bell, D. Work and Its Discontents. In his *The End of Ideology*. New York: The Free Press, 1962, pp. 227–272.

Berger, P. L., ed. *The Human Shape of Work*. Chicago: Henry Regnery Co., 1964.

Berger, et al. *The Homeless Mind*. New York: Random House, 1973.

Bienert, W. *Die Arbeit nach der Lehre der Bibel*. Stuttgart: Evangelisches Verlagswerk, 1954.

Budde, K. *Die Biblische Urgeschichte*. Giessen: Richter, 1883.

Bushnell, H. *Work and Play*. New York: Charles Scribner, 1881.

Carter, R. The Myth of Increasing Non-Work vs. Work Activities. *Social Problems*, 1970; pp. 52–67.

Chenu, M. D. *The Theology of Work*. Translated by L. Soiron. Chicago: Henry Regnery, 1963.

———. Arbeit. In *Historisches Wörterbuch der Philosophie*, J. Ritter, ed. Darmstadt: Wissenschaftliche Buchgesellschaft, 1971.

Conze, A. *Die Attische Grabreliefs*. Berlin: W. Spemann, 1893.

Fendler, M. Zur Sozialkritik des Amos. Versuch Einer Wirstschafts- und Sozialgeschiccht-lichen Interpretation Altestamentlicher Texte. *Evangelische Theologic*, 1973, pp. 32–53.

Filas, J. The Mass and Office of St. Joseph the Worker. *American Ecclesiastical Review*, 1957, pp. 289–303.

Fiorenza, F. S. Progress and Eschatology within the Context of Ernst Bloch's Notion of Cultural Heritage. In *Philosophy of Religion and Theology*, D. Griffin ed. Chambersburg: AAR, 1972, pp. 104–114.

———. Critical Social Theory and Christology. *Proceedings of the Thirtieth Annual Convention of the Catholic Theological Society of America*, 1975, pp. 63–110.

Galbraith, J. K. *The New Industrial State*. New York: Houghton Mifflin, 1967.

Gunkel, H. *Genesis Übersetzt und Erklärt*. Göttingen: Vandenhoeck & Ruprecht, 1922.

Haes, P. de. Doctrina de Labore in Novo Testamento. *Collectaenea Mechliniensia*, 1958, pp. 597–601.

Hoffman, P. *Studien zur Theologie der Logienquelle*. Munster: Aschendorff, 1972.

Huizinga, J. *Homo Ludens*. London: Routledge & Kegan Paul Ltd., 1949.

Illanes, J. J. *On the Theology of Work*. Translated by N. Adams, Chicago: Scepter Books, 1967.

Jaccard, P. *Histoire Sociale du Travail de L'antiquité à nos jours*. Paris: Payot, 1960.

Jay, M. *The Dialectical Imagination*. Boston: Little, Brown, 1973.

Levi, A. W. *Philosophy as Social Expression*. Chicago: University of Chicago Press, 1974.

Meyersohn, R. Leisure. In *The Human Meaning of Social Change*, A. Campbell and P. E. Converse, eds. New York: Russell Sage Foundation, 1972.

Mosse, C. *The Ancient World at Work*. Translated by J. Lloyd. New York: W. W. Norton, 1969.

Müller, M., ed. *The Laws of Manu*. Translated by G. Bühler, Oxford: Clarendon Press, 1886.

Oldham, J. H. *Work in Modern Society*. Richmond, Va.: John Knox, 1950/1961.

Pieper, J. *Leisure: The Basis of Culture*. New York: Pantheon, 1952.

Pius XII. Address to the Italian Farmers' National Federation. *Catholic Mind*, 1950 (Talk given on Nov. 15, 1946).

Rahner, H. *Man at Play, or Did You Ever Practise Eutrapelia?* London: Burns & Oates, 1965.

Rahner, K. Theological Remarks on the Problem of Leisure. In his *Theological Investigations*, IV. Translated by K. Smyth. New York: Seabury Press, 1966.

Rauschenbush, W. *Christianity and the Social Crisis*. New York: Harper & Row, 1964.

Richardson, A. *The Biblical Doctrine of Work*. London: SCM Press, 1952/1958.

Rondet, H. Eléments pour une Théologie du Travail. *Nouvelle Revue Theologique*, 1955, pp. 27–48 and 123–143.

Schleiermacher, F. *Die Christliche Sitte*. Edited by L. Jonas, 2nd edition. Berlin: G. Rimer, 1884.

Schoonenberg, P. *God's World in the Making*. Pittsburgh: Duquesne University Press, 1964.

Seligman, B. On Work, Alienation, and Leisure. *American Journal of Economics and Sociology*, 1965, pp. 337–360.

Simon, Y. R. *Work, Society, and Culture*. Edited by V. Kvic. New York: Fordham University Press, 1971.

Solmsen, F. *Hesiod and Aeschylus*. Ithaca, N. Y.: Cornell University Press, 1949.

Theissen, G. Wanderradikalismus. Literatursoziologische Aspekte der Ueberlieferung von Worten Jesus im Urchristentum. *Zeitschrift fur Theologie und Kirche*, 1973, pp. 245–271.

Tilgher, A. *Homo Faber: Work Through the Ages*. Translated by D. C. Fisher. Chicago: Henry Regnery Co., 1958.

Todd, J. M. *Work: Christian Thought and Practice*. Baltimore: Helicon, 1960.

Truhlar, C. V. *Labor Christianus*. Rome: Gregorian University Press, 1961.

Vernant, J. P. *Mythe et Pensée chez les Grecs, II*. Paris: Francois Maspers, 1968.

von Rad, G. *Genesis*. Translated by J. H. Marks. London: SCM Press, 1963.

————. *Wisdom in Israel*. Translated by J. D. Martin. Nashville, Tenn.: Abingdon Press, 1972.

Westermann, C. *Genesis, I*. Neukirchen-Vluyn: Neukirchener Verlag, 1974.

Wilensky, H. Work as a Social Problem. In *Social Problems: A Modern Approach*, H. S. Becker, ed. New York: Wiley, 1966.

Wilhelm, A. *Beiträge zur Grieschischen Inscriftenkunde*. Vienna: A. Holder Verlag, 1909.

Wolff, H. W. *Anthropologie des Alten Testaments*. Munich: Chr. Kaiser Verlag, 1973.

PART 2

What Does Socio-Psychological History Tell Us about Work and Its Effects upon the Worker?

PROGRESS, AS OUR SOCIETY HAS COME TO VIEW AND DEFINE IT, IS COMMENSU-rate with the increasing satisfaction of material wants. Our efforts in seeking "progress," however, have not only taxed our physical resources, but have strained much of our social fabric as well.

Since the advent of the Industrial Revolution, the invisible hand guiding the design and structuring of work has been technical efficiency. Apparently, man would find satisfaction in the fruits of his work (i.e., a higher level of material affluence), even if he did not find fulfillment in the toil which bore that fruit. For a young and poor nation with masses operating at a subsistence level, this criterion was acceptable, and perhaps appropriate.

But this rationale is not without its critics. As early as the mid-1800s, Karl Marx was outlining the dysfunctional consequences of such lines of thought. And if these consequences were true for early industrial man, modern industrial man feels the effects much more forcibly.

The three articles in this section trace the development of the psychological and social effects of industrialization, and more specifically, bureaucratization characterized by extensive division of labor, formalization, and impersonalization.

In the first article, John Houck examines the first expressions of the concept of alienation by Karl Marx, the German philosopher, and Emile Durkheim, the French sociologist. Writing in the nineteenth century, both recognized the dynamic, organic nature of modern capitalism which drew together and rationalized the means of production, creating at once a power that individual man could neither contest nor do without. Not only was the individual no longer in control of the means of production, he was subordinate to them. Where once as a craftsman he owned not only the means of production but the output as well, with the growth of industrial processes man himself became a product to be bought and sold.

While Marx and Durkheim present a vivid and suggestive picture of the dysfunctional human consequences of industrialized work, their recommendations for dealing with alienating conditions at work are unacceptable. Neither the rebellion called for by Marx nor the near acquiescence called for by Durkheim are viable alternatives for modern society. We cannot tolerate the disruption of revolution whose outcome is uncertain. But neither can we accept the perpetuation of a state of affairs which threatens the psychosocial well-being of the individual and the community.

The second article in this section, by William Heisler, considers the phases through which concern for alienation in the work place has passed in this century. Early concern for worker reaction to dehumanizing conditions of work, Heisler points out, was generated so that the effects of the individual's dissatisfaction would not counterbalance or diminish the effects of the precisely designed and engineered technical system. If there was an advantage to producing like goods on like machines, there was thought to be an equally great advantage in training the individual to perform as a machine.

A genuine concern for the psychological well-being of the worker appears just about the time that white-collar workers and managers themselves began to feel for themselves the alienating consequences of work. If the blue-collar worker is alienated by his sterile relationship to the production process, the white-collar employee has become alienated by the equally sterile nature of bureaucracy.

While work processes have remained relatively static over the past century, the educational level of all ranks of employees has continued to rise phenomenally, generating expectations no longer compatible with many contemporary organizational design strategies. As a result, malaise, dissatisfaction, and restlessness grow. Sometimes it is expressed in the form of rebellion, as through the 1972 automobile strike at Lordstown. More frequently it is expressed in the form of half-hearted involvement or simply "putting in one's time."

While considerable steps have been taken to protect the worker physically and reward him materially, it is in the area of psychological fulfillment that the schism between the needs of the worker and the seemingly immutable demands of the organization becomes most apparent. In the third and last article of this section, Stanislav Kasl examines this link between mental health and work environment.

To fully understand the relationship between mental health and work environment, Kasl points out, one must first define and conceptualize mental health itself. Part of the difficulty with contemporary approaches to the study of work and work organizations lies within what one defines as "mental health.'' If one assumes that the satisfactory execution of one's role or job is a priori an indication of mental well-being, then perhaps there is little wrong in the world of work. But can we truly equate desensitized, robot-like performance with mental health?

There are those, Kasl adds, who contend that anything less than growth, development, use of valued skills, etc., contributes to poor mental health. But can business afford to function as a personal growth center? To resolve this dilemma Kasl advocates that we stop searching for the *one* index of mental illness–mental health because any single measure will always be too narrow and too broad. Rather, he proposes we use a multiplicity of criteria as a good ''working definition'' of mental health.

After reviewing contemporary research associated with job dissatisfaction and mental health at work, Kasl concludes that poor mental health has been shown to be related to (1) conditions at work, (2) the nature of the work itself, (3) shift work, (4) the type and competency of supervision, (5) one's location within the organization, and (6) wages and promotion. Each of these relationships, however, are mediated by individual differences (age, aspiration level, work background, etc.).

While no immediate conclusions are drawn from Kasl's review, he does propose that a ''person-environment (P-E) fit'' model be used as a framework for designing work and work organizations. Such a model recognizes that job satisfaction and mental health are the results of interaction and are not determined by either dimensions of the person or the environment alone. In addition, the P-E fit model forces organizations to adopt a dynamic perspective since either facet of the model is capable of autonomous change. Such a perspective should contribute functionally to diminishing some of the disparities apparent in contemporary work organizations.

Early Historical Traces of the Contemporary Debate about Work Alienation

by John W. Houck

IT IS IN WHAT APPROXIMATES THE NINETEENTH CENTURY IN WESTERN Europe that we find the most discernible details of the great social and technological phenomenon, Industrialization, and its concommitant philosophy, Industrialism. Life will never be the same again for anyone, anywhere on this planet, given the boldness and sweep of what occurred in the nineteenth century. It is true that this revolution started earlier and its blessings or curses were debated earlier than 1800; still, it is in that most pivotal of centuries that the "world of work" was permanently, irrevocably changed. What had been isolated and modest in scope became pervasive (at least in Western Europe and starting in the U.S. by the 1840s) and nearly totalitarian in its grip on people's imagination, ways of working and living, and patterns of value formation. With a slight modification, substituting industrialist for bourgeoise, we find one of the best descriptions of all this in Marx and Engels' *Communist Manifesto* of 1848:

> The bourgeoisie [industrialists], during its rule of scarcely one hundred years, has created more massive and more colossal productive forces than have all preceding generations together. The subjection of nature's forces to man and machinery; the application of chemistry to industry and agriculture; [the development of] steam navigation, railways and electric telegraphs; the clearing of whole continents for cultivation; the canalization of rivers and the conjuring of whole populations out of the ground [off the land?]—what earlier century had even a presentiment that such productive forces slumbered . . . ? (*Essential Works of Marxism*, p. 17)

We can almost see the great armies of people leaving the countryside and becoming workers in factories; or members of craft guilds leaving the smaller shops and joining the ranks of machinists using the new energies of steam, and later, electricity. This was undoubtedly one of the greatest migrations of all time.

What happened to these workers who were drawn to the new factories, after cutting their ties with the old ways of work and traditional patterns of village and guild life? We will find out by examining the assessments of three major thinkers of the period: Adam Smith, Karl Marx, and Emile Durkheim.

The man whose whole life is spent performing a few simple operations generally becomes as stupid and ignorant as it is possible for a human creature to become

Adam Smith set the tone and, more importantly, the standards of one of our greatest intellectual achievements, the discipline of economic science. The role of detailed observation, the analytical approach to knowing "what is going on," and finally the drafting of theory are all illustrated in his volume *The Wealth of Nations*. Smith set out to uncover the key cause of the noticeable increase of wealth in countries such as England, France, and Poland, during his part of the eighteenth century. It was, he concluded, "a consequence of the division of labour." The effect of the division of labor is demonstrated by his use of the example of the making of pins. He writes: "One man draws out the wire, another straights it, a third cuts it, a fourth paints it, a fifth grinds it at the top . . ." (Smith, p. 4). The advantages of this approach to organizing work and workers are several:

(1) It reduces "every man's business to some one simple operation," which increases the output of each workman by repeating thousands of times the simple operation.

(2) A saving of time is commonly made because the worker no longer has to move from one operation to another.

(3) It leads "to the invention of a great number of machines which facilitate and abridge labour," enabling one man to do the work of many.

All of this is simple enough as a work design concept with the workman repeating his assigned operation thousands of times each day. This is especially true if we measure only the benefits of increased output. But we must uncover the costs to this new worker.

In his nearly one-thousand-page volume, Smith expounded on the role of markets and money, pricing, profits, rents, joint-stock companies, interest, and much more, for over seven hundred pages before saying anything about the impact of the division of labor on the personality of the workman. This is quietly tucked away in his chapter on the education of youth:

> In the progress of the division of labour, the employment of the far greater part of those who live by labour, that is, of the great body of the people, comes to be confined to a few very simple operations, frequently to one or two. But the understandings of the greater part of men are necessarily formed by their ordinary employments. The man whose whole life is spent in performing a few simple operations has no occasion to exert his understanding. . . . He naturally loses, therefore, the habit of such exertion, and *generally becomes as stupid and ignorant as it is possible for a human creature to become.* The torpor of his mind renders him, not only incapable of relishing or bearing a part in any rational conversation, but of conceiving any generous, noble, or tender sentiment, and consequently of forming any just judgment concerning many even of the ordinary duties of private life. . . . It corrupts even the activity of his body, and renders him incapable of exerting his strength with vigour and perseverance, in any other employment than that to which he has been bred. (Smith, p. 734, italics mine)

And if this determination were not bad enough, he contrasted the worker in industrial society with his counterpart in nonindustrial societies, or, to use his quaint term, barbarous societies:

> It is otherwise in the barbarous societies, as they are commonly called, of hunters, of shepherds, and even of husbandmen in that rude state of husbandry which precedes the improvement of manufactures, and the extension of foreign commerce. In such societies the varied occupations of every man oblige every man to exert his capacity, and to invent expedients for removing difficulties which are continually occurring. Invention is kept alive, and the mind is not suffered to fall into that drowsy stupidity, which, in a civilized [industrialized] society, seems to benumb the understanding of almost all the inferior ranks of people. (Smith, p. 735)

We can properly score Adam Smith for failing to juxtapose adequately the costs of the division of labor with its benefits. Certainly Smith saw these costs as anything but modest. For if he was right that the new worker was being condemned to becoming "as stupid and ignorant as it is possible," then we can wonder about his moral reticence. He was capable of being very severe: witness his sharp comments about businessmen who "seldom meet together, even for merriment and diversion, but the conversation ends in a conspiracy against the public, or in some contrivance to raise prices" (Smith,

p. 128). One possible explanation was Adam Smith's judgment that the effects of the division of labor on man, the worker, was an acceptable cost to pay for a greater wealth of goods and services for man, the consumer.

This is the trade-off that haunts us two hundred years after Smith published his volume. We can only speculate what might have been the history of industrialization if Smith had dramatized more effectively the heavy cost to the minds, personalities and health of the workers. He was, after all, a person of immense influence. In any case, today, as in the past, there are many who debate the legitimacy of the trade-off: the costs have always been and still are too great; or, the costs are no longer justifiable, given our greater surplus of wealth. It is this last argument, the greater surplus, that probably is operational in our times for more and more social critics and workers. It is understandable that perceptions about the trade-off shift as genuine necessities are satisfied, i.e., food and shelter. Then the question becomes: "How much can we ask the worker to put up with in order to obtain less-than-genuine necessities?" It is a pity that Adam Smith did not force the debate.

Division of labor perfects the worker, and degrades the man

We turn now to a later period of industrialization in Western Europe, to Karl Marx's *Economic and Philosophic Manuscripts of 1844*, sometimes called the "Paris Manuscripts" because Marx wrote them during his exile in Paris from his native Prussia. These are described by the Institute of Marxism-Leninism of the Soviet Union as "a rough draft of Karl Marx's first economic investigation," and as an "unfinished work, which has come down to us incomplete" (Marx, p. 7). They have also been described as the most "commented upon" pieces of philosophical literature of the twentieth century (Mészáros, p. 11). The *Manuscripts*, about fifty thousand words in length, were not printed and made available until the 1920s and 1930s in European intellectual circles and were not translated into English until the 1950s. Since publication, the *Manuscripts* have been the subject of fierce controversy, very much like the early reactions to the discovery of the *Dead Sea Scrolls*. (This analogy is particularly apt given the fragmentary nature of the writings in Marx's notebooks, which are the sources of the *Manuscripts*. They also, like the Scrolls, could have been irretrievably lost, to use Marx's phrase, "to the mice that would chew the pages.") Why are these unpublished, incomplete notes so controversial? The search for the answer to this question has to be made in the context of the hefty corpus of Marx's writings that would, or so we would think, adequately explain his point of view, his system of thought. Certainly political and economic history will never be the same because of his already well-known and readily available works. Before the publication of the *Manuscripts,* Marx was that rarity, a giant of thought and a mover of history. But to answer the question about their controversial nature, one must explore how "unsettling" these writings are to Marx's constituents, both friendly and unfriendly. I will briefly sketch some reactions, and because of the brevity, inevitably do some injustice to the fullness of their respective positions.

First, the Central Committee of the Communist party of the Soviet Union was wary of the *Manuscripts* because the Central Committee, under Stalin, had used other parts of Marx's thinking to justify a rigidly materialistic determinism, emphasizing especially the villainous role of the capitalist class. Once the capitalists were overthrown, and the Communist party was in power (vigilantly uncovering latent capitalist tendencies within the state and imperialist drives outside the state), then it followed that automatically a better social system would result. To use a medical analogy: "Remove the tumor and health will follow." But, as we will see, the *Manuscripts* put man, the active worker, at the root or center, a philosophical and ethical point-of-view that forces an assessment of any economic or political system, even a Communist one. To use our medical analogy again: "To remove the tumor may result in an improvement, but not necessarily in good and complete health." This question of "good and complete health" is important in its own right, and demands a full exploration and judgment. Marx can be used to assess the handiwork of a Marxist regime, or to put it another way, Marx can be cited against Marx's chief disciples—by any standard, an embarrassment.

Second, anticommunists will similarly want to play down the importance of the *Manuscripts.* They are either "immature" (Marx was twenty-six when he wrote them), or inconsistent with his later writings, and therefore unimportant.[1] But they do appear to "modify" Marxism, to put it in new perspective. Thus they can serve as the catalyst for the rehabilitation of Marx in Western thought. After all, during the Cold War, most of us learned to handle Marx, the materialist and class determinist, but not Marx, the humanist. And the *Manuscripts* have caused a revival of Marxist thought as evidenced by the recent outpouring of books and articles.

Third, those Marxists badly burned by Stalin can use Marx against Stalin's heirs who have constructed an immense technostructure of their own, as alienating as anything the capitalists could do. More importantly, these neo-Marxists can now examine the technostructures of both the West and East with effective results. Finally, all social thinkers and critics, no matter what their persuasion, can use the richness and complexity of these fragments to criticize contemporary society with considerable success (witness, for example, Erich Fromm's *The Sane Society,* with its central contention that advanced capitalism's impact on the personality of all—worker, manager, and consumer—is active alienation).

What exactly do *The Economic and Philosophic Manuscripts of 1844* say? For one thing, they state that existence, life, reality, both personal and social, is not static, but dynamic. Or, at the risk of the lyrical, reality is a whirl, always changing, always moving. Marx, with his collaborator Engels, gives a concrete example of this dynamic in the century under discussion, the nineteenth, when he writes in *The Communist Manifesto of 1848:*

> The bourgeoisie [we can read capitalist, industrialist, technologist, or innovator] cannot exist without constantly revolutionizing the instruments of production... Constant revolutionizing of production, uninterrupted disturbance of all social conditions, everlasting uncertainty and agitation.... All fixed, fast frozen relations... are swept away, all newly formed ones become antiquated before they can ossify. (*Essential Works of Marxism*, p. 16)

Does this mean that we can say nothing meaningful, or pragmatic, about this dynamic, except maybe the essentially passive, "Isn't it all amazing, or incredible!" No, we can sort out from all these forces, circles within circles, some tendencies and potentials which are important. One issue that appears central is the relationship between these forces and changes and the human (to Marx, the human as worker). Again and again, Marx explores this central relationship by describing what is happening to the worker as he is being affected, pulled, and snared by the new industrial forces.

But what then is Marx's concept of human nature? He doesn't give his definition. He cannot do so and still remain faithful to his philosophic perspective, for to define humanness is to adopt the "worldview" of the static, and reject the dynamic. However, the dynamic can be viewed from this critical dimension—as either alienating or nonalienating. And what is "alienating" depends on the potential that social circumstances open up for the nonalienating. To use an example, slavery isn't alienating until there is some realistic potential of abolishing slavery. Then we can move to a time of nonalienating. But of course, and this so infuriates many including the Stalinists, the cycle does not end. A new perception of alienating is developed as a new *potential* for nonalienation is uncovered. (It goes without saying that we are reaching into the immensely difficult tangle of "knowing" anything about humankind.)

This is why Marx had such ambivalent feelings about the role of the capitalist. The feudal order became alienating when the capitalists created the potential for escape from that order. After all, *The Communist Manifesto of 1848* contains many things, but one thing we are sure of, it is a glowing description of capitalists as a class

> [which] has been the first to show what man's activity can bring about. [Which] has accomplished wonders far surpassing Egyptian pyramids,

Roman aqueducts, and Gothic cathedrals. [Which] has conducted expeditions that put in the shade all former Exoduses of nations and crusades. (*Essential Works of Marxism,* p. 16)

But what then can be said of such an extraordinary achievement, the capitalist revolution? Very simply, it had become alienating because of the potential which capitalism had made possible for moving to the nonalienating. Some might wish to exclaim "such ingratitude!" But we must remember that by the 1840s when Marx wrote, the capitalist revolution had held sway for nearly one hundred years. This for Marx was long enough to express gratitude, and in addition the dynamics of the potential beckoned.

It is necessary to probe the new alienating conditions created, keeping in mind the goal: a further and higher plateau of the nonalienating, an evolutionary ideal. Marx analytically breaks down what has happened to the worker into four alienating relations:

(1) The worker's relations (interacting and being acted upon) to his productive activity;

(2) the worker's relations to his output or product;

(3) the worker's relations to his species;

(4) the worker's relations with other workers.

Concerning the first of these, Marx writes[2] that "labour is *external* to the worker, i.e., it does not belong to his essential being. . . ." Why? Because the worker does not "affirm himself but denies himself, does not feel content but unhappy, does not develop freely his physical and mental energy [Marx plunges deeper into describing the alienating conditions of this new industrial order] but mortifies his body and ruins his mind." Shades of Adam Smith. To be an alienated worker means that the worker "only feels himself outside his work, and in his work feels outside himself," (Marx 1959, p. 72).

Marx goes on to say that "the worker is at home [with all that the term connotes in way of psychological and biological rewards and supports] when he is not working, and when he is working he is not at home" (p. 72). The productive order has become so affected by the division of labor and repetitive tasks that human powers are stunted, causing a "cretinism." Activities in which a worker would normally take pride are turned against the worker: his work becomes "suffering"; his strength becomes weakness; and even "begetting" becomes its frightening opposite for the worker, "emasculating" (p. 73).

The second course of alienating relations is that the output, the product, is not the worker's, "but someone else's that it does not belong to him" (p. 73). In the industrial and capitalist order, the worker has given up his birthright, so to speak, to another class and to the world of things. As worker, he is not at the center, as he should be, but at the edge, both in being an appendage to a machine and as a functionary in the division of labor. Marx writes in his volume *Capital* (p. 310), "It is no longer the laborer that employs the means of production, but the means of production that employs the laborer." The final ignominy is the classical exploitational theme of Marxist literature: The worker's output goes to another, the capitalist class.

The third alienating relation is that the worker as worker is separated from the true uniqueness of his species. Here Marx demarcates all other species from humankind, which is marked by the capability of being active, of working freely, consciously, and "in accordance with the laws of beauty" (p. 76). Unlike animals, work (obviously not degrading or alienating work) is to Marx here like creativity, or artistry. "Why," Marx asks, "does man produce even when he is free from physical need?" Marx answers:

> But an animal only produces what it immediately needs for itself or its young. It produces onesidedly, whilst man produces universall. It produces only under the dominion of immediate physical need, *whilst man produces even when he is free from physical need and only truly produces in freedom therefrom.* An animal produces only itself, whilst man produces the whole of nature. (Marx 1959, p. 75, italics mine)

Finally, the worker, internalizing the three alienating relations, must then confront other workers, similarly alienated. This makes for twisted relationships and strange perceptions of humans by humans. The worker becomes alienated even from his brother workers. To use contemporary parlance, "The workers do not see others in their humanness, as persons, but as capitalist and worker, farmer and landlord, cog and cog, functionary and functionary, used and user." This state of affairs can not make for relationships that are either wholesome or invigorating.

To sum up Marx "on the world of work," let me use an analogy. He wants work to be a potluck dinner, and not a catered affair. First, a catered affair is prepared by specialists, salad-makers, vegetable-preparers, cooks, bakers, etc.—uniformity, simplification and the division of labor prevail.—Even the consumer, here the eaters of this bland fare, are treated as ciphers, dutifully, almost by the numbers, finishing one plate so another can be served. Little involvement is exercised, or even possible, by the preparers or the eaters, except the money paid or received. The potluck is different, assuming "good will" by the participants, which is a difficult assumption—given the "catered affair" mentality and conditioning that is operational. Some planning is needed, allocating who will bring salads, vegetables, wines, desserts, etc., but kept to the minimum. The preparer is also the eater. The preparer wants to make and share a favorite dish which is an important form of self-expression. When the different dishes are laid out on the table, very likely the preparers will sample almost every dish as an eater. Comparisons can be made, recipes exchanged, new possibilities explored, as the preparers (the workers) eat and talk. To paraphrase Marx: "The more the preparer expends himself the greater becomes the potluck he creates for others and himself, the richer he becomes in his inner satisfaction, and the more belongs to himself and others."[3]

Workers are privates in an industrial army on an important mission

Our next important observer is the French sociologist Emile Durkheim, called by some the "father of modern sociology." His series of lectures on the theme, and entitled *The Division of Labor in Society,* was first published in 1893. So Durkheim had a fifty-year advantage on Marx, who in turn had nearly seventy years on Adam Smith, all three of them trying to understand the dynamics, and meaning, of the Industrial Revolution. It goes without saying that each subsequent thinker stands on the shoulders of his predecessor, seeing better because others saw. This is, of course, true of all learning. Another aspect worth considering is the interdisciplinary (to use the modern term) capacities that these thinkers needed to have in dealing with the immense complexity of the phenomenon under study. Disciplinary barriers had to be breeched, but in truth in some cases intellectual disciplines had to be invented. Adam Smith, a social moralist, had to "father" classical economics. Marx, a philosopher, had to become an economist and historian, and had, in fact, to change history. Durkheim was a sociologist who had to move to social and legal philosophy and back again.

But let us begin the examination of Durkheim's contribution. We might recall that the pervasive division of labor was to Adam Smith the cause of *The Wealth of Nations,* to Marx a source of alienation, but to Durkheim it was a perfectly normal dimension of society which is capable of producing social solidarity and higher forms of achievements:

> Society becomes more capable of collective movement, at the same time that each of its elements [through the division of labor of different crafts, occupations, functions and professions] has more freedom of movement. This solidarity resembles that which we observe among the higher animals. Each organ, in effect, has its special physiognomy, its autonomy. And, moreover, the unity of the organism is as great as the individuation of the parts is more marked. (Durkheim, p. 131)

This solidarity stemming from the division of labor is called by Durkheim, "organic," which implies "life" and "integrated" and "on-going." He contrasts his concept of the organic with "mechanical" solidarity, which does not have the division of labor. It is, as the term mechanical implies, dead, lifeless, hemmed in by a minimal collective conscience, and by necessity, repressive law. He is suggesting that mechanical solidarity integrates the members of the society through a set of similar, basic judgments: patriotism, respect for authority, some bodily security. Not much can be expected in this solidarity. But he judges "the greater the diversity of relations [division of labor] . . . the more it creates links which attach the individual [worker] to the group" (Durkheim, p. 109). The group, whether neighborhood, family, profession, craft, or industry, is human-scale and manageable. It teaches the individual restraints and values and generates loyalties; it is a mediating form for social cohesion that draws the isolated rootless person into its web of meaning and purpose.[4] Without these intermediate groups made possible by the division of labor, our choices would be dismal: harsh, repressive laws because of the mechanical solidarity, or no solidarity at all, that is, an "aimless," "rootless" existence.

Let us step back a moment, and contrast Marx's implied conception of human nature when he describes the worker in alienation, and Durkheim's. It is apparent that Marx sees the worker as an artist, or no less than a craftsman, in control of his talents and doing his work, not out of fear or requirement, but because it is inherently human. Man is a worker, whose "species" requires self-realization (as a worker-artist or craftsman) existing as an inner necessity, a need. We can recall the similar point made by John Julian Ryan, a contemporary humanist, elsewhere in this volume:

> by nature, every man is truly a fine artist, or properly meant to be . . . he is a fine artist in the sense of naturally aiming at perfection. . . .

In contrast, Durkheim sees human nature in constant need of restraint and the ordering function of groups. In the great debate about human nature, human freedom and "what makes for a decent social existence," Durkheim adopts something akin to Thomas Hobbes' view in the *Leviathan* (Chap. XIII) that humans are so equal that they struggle with each other to obtain an incremental advantage over each other, to rise above one another, through greed and the need to dominate. This is a species whose life, to quote Hobbes, is "solitary, nasty, brutish, and short. . . ." What is needed, then, for this unfortunate species is, to Hobbes, "a common Power to keep them all in awe. . . ." To Durkheim, what is needed is life in a determinate, limited environment with rules telling each of the workers his rights and duties, not vaguely in general terms but in precise detail. Humans' unruly passions are moderated, not so much by the "awe" of authority of the essentially Hobbesian "mechanical solidarity" that Durkheim talked about, but by membership in the division-of-labor groups. These groups are the mediating agencies through which "the individual becomes cognizant of his dependence upon society; from (them) come the forces which keep him in check and restraint" (Durkheim, p. 401). Finally, Durkheim rejects Marx's view of worker-artist, and the companion school of humanistic work, when he writes:

> our duty is not to spread our activity over a large surface, but to concentrate and specialize it. We must contract our horizon, choose a definite task and immerse ourselves in it completely, *instead of trying to make ourselves a sort of creative masterpiece, quite complete which contains its worth in itself and not in the services that it renders.* (Durkheim, p. 401, italics mine)

Or, to put it bluntly, a worker is a private in the industrial army on an important mission, and that ought to be enough for him to know and to be satisfying for him. For, Durkheim writes, "in more advanced societies, his nature is, in large part, to be an organ of society, and his proper duty, consequently, is to play his role as an organ" (Durkheim, p. 403).

If the division of labor produces social solidarity, does it sometimes happen that there are contrary results? The answer is yes, and Durkheim characteristically examines the pathological anomie, or rootlessness that can result. The first type is caused by industrial or commercial crises (recessions and depressions) which are so many breaks in organic solidarity. Apparently, occupational groups are not adequately adjusted to one another, do not cooperate sufficiently and the resultant "warfare has become even more violent" (Durkheim, p. 335). The lack of cohesion unleashes forces of greed and passion which are difficult to check. Competition and an unregulated economy are the villains here, where each individual finds himself in a state of war with every other. New conditions of industrial life naturally need a new organization (to protect social solidarity), "but as these changes have been accomplished with extreme rapidity, the interests in conflict have not yet had the time to be equilibrated" (Durkheim, p. 370).

The forced division of labor is Durkheim's second abnormal type. Humans must not be forced into occupations but by a form of natural selection, "the free unfolding of the social [talents] each carries in himself." There can be no obstacles that would prevent a person from occupying the place in the social framework which is compatible with his faculties or talents. Social cohesion is, in short, a meritocracy in which "labor is divided spontaneously only if society is constituted in such a way that social inequalities exactly express natural inequalities" (Durkheim, p. 377). Durkheim believes that members of the society will spontaneously reach the level of their competence, and will readily appreciate the inherent justice of the status, privilege, and income that results. Of course, this requires "a subtle organization in which each social value, being neither overestimated nor underestimated by anything foreign to it, would be judged at its true worth'' (Durkheim, p. 377). Under his schema those who find themselves in a disadvantageous position are to be helped unless they are the cause of their own disability.

Finally, the last state of social pathology described by Durkheim is inefficiency, caused by employees not sufficiently occupied, movement of work from factory bench to factory bench badly organized, and a lack of an effective overall plan. He wants a managerial class to take charge. He writes that ''the first care of an intelligent, scientific [manager] will be to suppress useless tasks, to distribute work in such a way that each one will be sufficiently occupied, and, consequently, to increase the functional activity of each worker ... that work is more economically managed'' (Durkheim, p. 389).

When we put together the pieces, we have a coherent picture of Durkheim's Good Society. It accepts enthusiastically the division of labor: life ''becomes richer and more intense as it becomes more specialized'' (Durkheim, p. 404). Secondly, to use contemporary language, there is need for a managed macro-economic policy for full employment and regulation of competition. Next, it is a society in which merit freely floats to its appropriate level. Finally, there must be a large cadre of scientifically-oriented managers (officers) to lead the industrial army of workers. It is a society where the rationalization of all aspects of existence have fairly well been completed. It is also a society which has fully integrated the worker and his world, but we can ask: ''At what price and to whose advantage?''

A Possible Reconciliation

It is appropriate at this point to attempt to reconcile the views of Marx and Durkheim about the worker and his world. (We can disregard Adam Smith, since he saw at best the worker as consumer, with little hope for improving the state of work or the role of the worker.) We must ask ourselves this question: How can the spontaneous, inner-directed worker-artist of Marx collaborate with Durkheim's well-adjusted worker who knows his place in the social schema? After all, Marx's alienation is a different psychological state and sociological setting than Durkheim's anomie, indicating the absence of organic solidarity. It would seem that a convergence of these contraries is impossible, especially if we put the two side by side at the same point in time. But what if we took a longitudinal approach, that is, as causal, sequential steps in the dialectic; a possible scenario would read as follows:

> As alienation in the society increases, then under the pressure, social structures start collapsing. There is consequently an increasing anomie, the loss of organic solidarity. But, as we described above, alienation is

possible (and most vividly felt) when the nonalienation opens up, pointing the way toward a new social order which can capture the loyalties of the rootless. This would lessen anomie, fulfilling Durkheim's belief about the social need for organic solidarity.

But, like the marriage of two strong-willed individuals, the critical question is "which partner, Marx or Durkheim, will be willing to give up more, to offer compromises, to save the bond?" My suspicions are that Durkheim might play that role initially. First, Durkheim was aware of the dangers of alienating work (too great a division of labor):

> [If the worker] repeats the same movements with monotonous regularity . . . [has no] interest in them . . . without understanding them . . . [then] he is no longer a living cell . . . but an inert piece of machinery . . . [and] one cannot remain indifferent to such debasement of human nature. (Durkheim, p. 371).

Secondly, Durkheim will have to accept a modified version of Marx's model of the worker-artist, a less optimistic version of what Marx implied to be sure, but still an approximation. Otherwise he cannot realistically expect a worker to be (to use Durkheim's biological analogy) "a living cell of a living organism which unceasingly vibrates with neighboring cells, which acts upon them, and to whose action it responds and with whose needs and circumstances it changes" (Durkheim, p. 371). It goes without saying that worker-robots can do none of this!

Marx, on the other hand, will have to accept some forms of the divisions of labor that both Adam Smith and Durkheim judged to be the basis for the immense material progress of the last two hundred years. To reject an adequate material base is to reject what makes alienation so possible and what makes the movement toward nonalienation so plausible. In addition, Marx must confront the mediating role of groups of workers, craftsmen, professionals and neighborhoods that provide Durkheim's organic solidarity. Otherwise his beloved worker-artist will sink into the masses of isolated individuals, the state of so many even in political regimes claiming Marx's patrimony. To revert to the catered affair/potluck analogy, if we are correct in assuming that Marx would prefer the potluck, he must recognize that there will have to be considerable group, or communal, loyalty to make the potluck work. Without this loyalty, and what it demands in solidarity, it is very easy to slip into the catered-affair mentality.

In any case this has been a partial tracing of the question of work and the worker in the nineteenth century. Other papers will bring us up to the contemporary. We can only ask: Have the issues *really* changed much since the times of Adam Smith, Marx, and Durkheim?

NOTES

1. Daniel Bell is a sensitive representative of this school of criticism of neo-Marxist thought. He argues that in the *Manuscripts* Marx saw the new industrial worker losing both control over the conditions of work because of the division of labor (dehumanization) and losing the results of his work (exploitation by the capitalists). But Bell further argues that Marx in his later and comprehensive writings, *Capital,* glossed over dehumanization and put his major emphasis on the exploitation theme of private property and the class struggle. By doing this, Bell argues that the Marxist solution became one-sided: "abolish private property, and the system of exploitation would disappear" (p. 367). But what of dehumanization of the worker, Bell asks, whether in a socialist state or in a capitalist country, both practicing evermore sophisticated techniques of the division of labor? See Bell's essay "Two Roads from Marx" in *The End of Ideology,* and Mészáros' spirited rejoinder, p. 227 of his *Marx's Theory of Alienation.*

2. The references, unless otherwise noted, will be from the seventeen pages of his fragment, entitled "Estranged Labour," *Economic and Philosophic Manuscripts of 1844.*

3. Marx was actually describing alienating labor, not the nonalienating suggested by the potluck analogy. Marx writes: ". . . that the worker is related to the *product of his labour* as to an *alien* object. For on this premise it is clear that the more the worker spends himself, the more powerful the alien objective world becomes which he creates over against himself, the poorer he himself—his inner world—becomes, the less belongs to him as his own" (Marx 1959, p. 70).

4. "Conceivably, a plant or factory could fill the soul through a powerful awareness of collective—one might say, unanimous—life, all noises have their meaning, they are all rhythmic, they fuse into a kind of giant respiration of the working collectivity in which it is exhilirating to play one's part" (Weil, p. 368). While this is a description of what Durkheim has in mind, it should be noted that Simone Weil is using irony here. In fact, she rejects this description as sham: "If factory life were really this, it would be only too beautiful but such is, naturally, not the case" (Weil, p. 369).

REFERENCES

Bell, D. *The End of Ideology.* New York: The Free Press, 1965.

Durkheim, E. *The Division of Labor in Society.* Translated by George Simpson. New York: The Free Press, 1964.

Fromm, E. *The Sane Society.* New York: Holt, Rinehart and Winston, 1955.

Hobbes, T. *The Leviathan.* London: Cambridge University Press, 1904.

Marx, K. *Capital,* Volume I. Translated by Samuel Moore and Edward Aveling. Moscow, 1958.

Marx, K. *Economic and Philosophic Manuscripts of 1844.* Translated by Martin Milligan. Moscow, 1959.

Mendel, A, ed. *Essential Works of Marxism*. New York: Bantam Books, 1961.
Mészáros, I. *Marx's Theory of Alienation*. New York: Harper & Row, 1972.
Smith, A. *The Wealth of Nations*. New York: The Modern Library, 1937.
Weil, S. Factory Work. *Cross Currents*, 1976, 25: 367–382. (First published in the journal *Politics*, 1946.)

Worker Alienation: 1900–1975

by W. J. Heisler

MORE THAN 100 YEARS AGO, KARL MARX (1844) SAW THE ALIENATION OF man from his work as a central problem of industrial society. According to Marx, alienation assumes a variety of forms. First of all, the worker is alienated from the product of his labor: he has no ownership rights or control over the disposition of the products he produces. Second, the worker is alienated from the means of production: with the advent of the factory system, he no longer owns the means (tools, machinery, etc.) by which products are produced. Third, the worker is alienated from himself. Under the factory system, the worker becomes a product to be bought and sold in the labor market. And work becomes a means, rather than an end in itself. It takes on instrumental value only. Thus, the worker finds himself engaged in a job which provides little or no opportunity for identification, growth, or creative self-expression. Marx described this form of work as follows:

> Work is external to the worker... it is not part of his nature; and consequently, he does not fulfill himself in his work but denies himself, has a feeling of misery rather than well-being, does not develop freely his mental and physical energies but is physically exhausted and mentally debased. The worker feels himself at home only during his leisure hours, whereas at work he feels homeless. His work is not voluntary but imposed forced labor. It is not the satisfaction of a need, but only a means of satisfying other needs. (Marx, 1844)

Since Marx's time, concern for alienation in the workplace has experienced a number of cyclical fluctuations. It is the purpose of this paper to present a somewhat skeletal outline of these cyclical trends, pointing out the unique focus and concern of each era. Considering the immense volume of material related to investigations of alienation, some injustice is likely to be done by any attempt to review these developments in a single paper of modest length.[1] Nevertheless, it is hoped that the sampling of writings and research presented herein will capture the essence of the perspectives, concerns, and trends.

The Rise of Scientific Management

The turn of the twentieth century saw the continuation and burgeoning of the Industrial Revolution. Organizations continued to grow in size and complexity with such innovations as steel, electricity, and railroads. Increasingly, mass production techniques replaced individual craftsmen and home industries. In these circumstances, new organizational problems developed. A higher form of rationalization or systemization appeared needed. Further, in a growing product market characterized essentially by free competition, a premium was placed on productivity and efficiency. In the vacuum of formalized management and organizational theory, the stage was set for the emergence of scientific management.

Introduced around 1910, "scientific management," or "task management" as it was sometimes called, caught on and soon even acquired an evangelical tone. Perhaps the scope and flavor of what Fredrick Winslow Taylor, its founder, was advocating can best be summed up by a passage from his own book, *Principles of Scientific Management* (1911):

> Perhaps the most prominent single element in modern scientific management is the task idea. The work of every workman is fully planned out by the management at least one day in advance, and each man receives in most cases complete written instructions, describing in detail the task which he is to accomplish, as well as the means to be used in doing the work.... This task specifies not only what is to be done but how it is to be done, and the exact time allowed for doing it.

The essence of Taylor's philosophy was that there was a "one best method" of doing each piece of work, and that through observation and "scientific" investigation, this method could be discovered. All similar positions could then be reconstructed to conform to this procedure. Once this "one best way" was established, focus could then shift to determining the exact amount of time that it should take a worker to perform his function. According to Taylor (1911), the essential principle of this facet of scientific management was the following:

> *the substitution of science for the individual judgment of the workman....* In most trades, the science is developed through a comparatively simple analysis and time study of the movements required by the workman to do some small part of his work, and this study is usually made by a man equipped merely with a stop-watch and a properly ruled

notebook. . . . The general steps to be taken in developing a simple law of this class are as follows:

First. Find, say 10 or 15 different men . . . who are especially skillful in doing the particular job to be analyzed.

Second. Study the exact series of elementary operations or motions which each of these men uses to do the work which is being investigated, as well as the implements each man uses.

Third. Study with a stop-watch the time required to make each of the elementary movements and then select the quickest way of doing each element of work.

Fourth. Eliminate all false movements, slow movements, and useless movements.

Fifth. After doing away with all unnecessary movements, collect into one series the quickest and best movements as well as the best implements.

Another aspect of the scientific management program called for the "scientific" selection and training of workers, rather than permitting them (the workmen) to select their own work as they had done in the past. Additionally, management was to share more intimately the responsibilities of the workers, doing that part of the work for which they are best fitted. In other words, they were to "relieve" the worker of the responsibility for "methods, implements, speed, and harmonious cooperation."

Although controversial when introduced (as will be explained in the paragraph which follows), "soon no self-respecting manufacturing firm was without the paraphernalia of Scientific Management: time-study men, methods engineers, work standards, piece rates, job classification schemes, and more" (Leavitt, 1965). If inventors and engineers were king in the design of factories and machines, their success, Taylor believed, could be duplicated in designing a worker and his work.

As Davis (1975) points out, several key assumptions are implicit within this management philosophy. One is that ownership carries with it absolute authority. Accordingly, organizational managers can dictate and impose upon the workers whatever is felt to be in the best interest of the organization (i.e., the owners), almost without concern for its impact upon the worker. But more importantly, there is within the approach an implicit success strategy that requires employees to become inexpensive, thoughtless, single-skilled or single-purpose instruments, who immediately respond to simple rewards. And finally, there is the assumption that technology is the industrial savior. Through machines and engineered jobs, the unreliable element in the production system—the human factor—could be controlled. Whatever success the future held for the Industrial Revolution could be found through technology. In effect, workers became mere servants to machines and methods.[2]

Early Reaction: The Human Relations Movement

Even with scientific management, the early industrial scene was not without its problems. Many organizations experienced inefficiency, employee dissatisfaction, and labor unrest. Since technology was infallible and jobs had been appropriately engineered to fit the machine, the source of difficulty must lie with the human factor.

In search of remedies to these problems, management turned to the scientific investigation of factors in the physical environment of the worker. The most widely reported of these explorations was conducted at the Hawthorne Works of the Western Electric Company near Chicago. With the cooperation of the National Research Council of the National Academy of Sciences, in 1924 the company began to study the relationship between the efficiency of the worker and illumination levels in the workplace.

Since the procedures and results of these illumination experiments are well reported elsewhere [see for example, Brown (1954), Cass and Zimmer (1975), Kelly (1969), Landsberger (1958), Roethlisberger and Dickson (1939)], let me simply reiterate that the researchers were surprised to discover that the level of illumination was not a predictor of productivity. Output went up as illumination intensities were increased; however, they rose as well when illumination intensities were decreased. Productivity also increased in the control group where illumination was maintained at a constant level. Obviously, there were other variables in the work situation which were not being held constant or under control. The serendipitous findings of the illumination experiment provided the impetus for subsequent studies of yet other environmental factors: number and length of rest pauses, pay schemes, free meals, length of work day, length of work week, etc. In the second experiment, the Relay Assembly Test Room, the effects of thirteen such variables were tested. The results of these various changes, each of which continued for a test period of four or twelve weeks, have been summarized by Brown (1954) as follows:

(1) Under normal conditions with a forty-eight hour week, including Saturdays, and no rest pauses, the girls produced 2,400 relays a week each.

(2) They were then put on piece work for eight weeks, and output went up.

(3) Two five-minute rest pauses, morning and afternoon, were introduced for a period of five weeks, and output went up once more.

(4) The rest pauses were lengthened to ten minutes each. Output levels went up sharply.

(5) Six five-minute pauses were introduced, and output fell slightly as the girls complained that their work rhythm was broken by the frequent pauses.

(6) Return to the two rest pauses, the first with a hot meal supplied by the company free of charge. Output went up.

(7) The girls were dismissed at 4:30 p.m., instead of 5:00 p.m. Output went up.

(8) They were dismissed at 4:00 p.m. and output remained the same.

(9) Finally, all the improvements were taken away, and the girls went back to the physical conditions of the beginning of the experiment: work on Saturday, forty-eight-hour week, no rest pauses, no piece work, and no free meal. This state of affairs lasted for a period of twelve weeks, and output was the highest ever recorded, averaging 3,000 relays a week.

Overall, output had increased more-or-less steadily over the two-and-one-half years that this series of experiments continued, despite the numerous changes to which the workers were subjected. Morale had improved steadily and attendance irregularities were reduced.

The results of these experiments have been variously interpreted: (1) a new supervisory relationship had developed, i.e., "friendly supervision"; (2) the workers had achieved elevated status as a result of their participation; (3) monotony and fatigue had been reduced through various rest-break arrangements; (4) the group wanted to help the researchers achieve the results they were seeking; (5) new social relationships had been formed among the participants.

The general conclusion that "social satisfactions arising out of human association in work are . . . important determinants of work behavior in general and output in particular" became the cornerstone for the development of the human relations movement.[3] What followed from this conclusion, however, could hardly be said to be "humanistic." The early approaches adopted by management to "satisfy" workers' social "needs" on the job were essentially manipulative (Leavitt 1965). This orientation, perhaps, may be best represented by the question, "How can we get people to do what we want them to do?" There was little, if any, concern for the well-being of the worker for his own sake. Workers were still regarded as problems rather than as persons, and social research and discussion focused around questions such as "How to *overcome* resistance to change?"

As a result, human relations training courses were developed and/or purchased by organizations to instruct their managers in the techniques of "friendly supervision" and how to make employees "feel" accepted. First published in 1936, Dale Carnegie's *How to Win Friends and Influence People* epitomized many of these early approaches. Carnegie proposed that one changes others (e.g., gets workers to produce more) by first developing a relationship valuable to the other person and then by using that relationship as a lever for bringing about the change sought. Thus, the emergent human problems of the workplace received but cosmetic attention. Workers received supportive attention from management *not* because management wanted to help them develop their abilities more fully, *not* because they were genuinely appreciated for their work effort, *not* because of any genuine concern for the problems of the worker, *not* because they were valued as human beings. Rather, they were given instrumental attention of the "if I'm nice to you, you'll produce more for me" variety.

Despite the exploitation of the Hawthorne findings by many management practitioners, the early work of Mayo, Roethlisberger, and others did open the door to the assessment of the social or human dimension of workers and work. These studies were truly, if only for the controversy and debate they have generated, the foundation for the growth of the behavioral sciences as a legitimate discipline in business. What is different about today's focus, however, is that the "benefit of the company" or the "benefit of management" is less a single criterion for investigation and experimentation. The present "human potential" movement is equally concerned with the growth and well-being of the worker in his own right and with the effects of maladjustment at work upon society.

Enter Max Weber and Bureaucracy

Proponents of precision, reliability, and efficiency received new support in the 1940s with the popularization of the work of Max Weber, the German sociologist, by Talcott Parsons and R. K. Merton.[4] While business and governmental organizations of that day already exhibited many of the characteristics of the bureaucratic form described by Weber, his work provided a new justification for the structures which had evolved and an impetus for their expansion and refinement.

Although any list of the characteristics of bureaucracy identified by Weber (1947) is likely to differ somewhat among writers, they are essentially the following:

(1) The regular activities required for the purposes of the organization are distributed in a fixed way as official duties. The clear-cut division of labor makes it possible to employ only specialized experts in each particular possible position and to make every one of them responsible for the effective performance of his duties.

(2) The organization of offices follows the principle of hierarchy; that is, each lower office is under the control and supervision of a higher one. Every official in this administrative hierarchy is accountable to his superior for his subordinates' decisions and actions. Authority flows "down" this chain-of-command; accountability flows "upward."

(3) Operations are governed by a consistent system of abstract rules that are applied to individual cases. This formalistic system is designed to assure uniformity of performance. Explicit rules and regulations define the responsibility of each member of the organization and the relationships between them.

(4) The ideal official conducts his office in a spirit of formalistic impersonality. The exclusion of personal considerations from official business is a prerequisite for impartiality as well as for efficiency.

(5) Employment is based on technical qualifications and is protected against arbitrary dismissal. It constitutes a career.

(6) Experience tends universally to show that the purely bureaucratic type of administrative organization is, from a purely technical point of view, capable of attaining the highest degree of efficiency.

Weber's concept of bureaucracy found significant appeal among businessmen because, as Merton (1957) concludes,

[its] structure is one which approaches the complete elimination of personalized relationships and nonrational consideration (hostility, anxiety, affectual involvements, etc.).

In other words, the bureaucratic structure exerts pressure upon the personality of the official to be "methodological, prudent, and disciplined." Essentially, persons are to be impersonal functionaries conforming to patterned obligations.

Aside from the dehumanizing aspects of such an interpersonal arrangement (i.e., social alienation), bureaucracy affects the official's relation to his work as well. As Merton (1940) points out in his "Bureaucratic Structure and Personality":

Adherence to the rules, originally conceived as a means, becomes transformed into an end in itself; there occurs the familiar process of displacement of goals whereby "an instrumental value becomes a terminal value."

Thus, the bureaucratic form, in a manner akin to Taylor's scientific form of management, set the stage for the development of alienation from the work itself. Work loses a great deal of its potential for meaningfulness when one's role is simply to execute faithfully a rule, a procedure, or a process whose terminal value or effect is either unknown or unseen.

Changing Patterns of Alienation

The continued growth of organizational bureaucracy and the ever-increasing role played by technology continued to effect an overall increase in the level of alienation in work society between the 1900s and the 1950s. However, a significant shift also appeared to occur with respect to its nature and locus.

As a result of her analysis of both periods, Taviss (1969) concludes that between the 1900s and 1950s a slight decrease in social alienation was evidenced, concommitant with a significant increase in self-alienation. In Taviss's terms, social alienation occurs when individuals find the social system in which they live (e.g., the workplace) to be oppressive or incompatible with some of their own desires and they, therefore, feel estranged from it. On the other hand, self-alienation occurs when individuals lose contact with any inclination or desire that is not in agreement with prevailing social patterns, manipulate themselves in accordance with apparent social demands, and/or feel incapable of controlling their own actions. In other words, self-alienation may be said to result from inauthenticity in attempting to conform to social structure. The self-alienated engage in self-manipulative behavior to reduce or eliminate social distance between themselves and others.

The social alienation which occurred in the 1900s as people rejected and maintained an isolation from oppressive and incompatible work systems yielded in the 1950s to conformity to these systems and to a subsequent rejection of one's own needs, feelings, and identity. Rather than escaping undesirable obligations through voluntary physical or mental isolation, the employee of the 1950s reacts more with malaise and half-hearted involvement, or with overconformity in which he denies his personal feelings, values, and desires. As Taviss (1969) points out, "Whyte's (1956) 'organization man' bespeaks of a new self-society relationship in which social alienation is no longer relevant." The employee of the 1950s, rather than rejecting others who are at odds with his position, becomes instead "other-directed," not only seeking to please others, but also deriving one's identity from these encounters (Riesman 1950). But these developments were not restricted to individuals. Etzioni (1968a, 1968b) has observed that post-World War II industrial societies devote a significant part of their endeavors to "front activities." Indicators of this phenomenon include the rise of technologies of mass communications devoted primarily to escapist communication, increased investment in mass advertising and public relations, etc. Etzioni's concern with inauthenticity is shared by Seeman (1966) who considers one of the two main results of inauthenticity to be role inversion. That is, he feels that man's impulses are turned into "coolness," whereby expression and release are prevented.

In addition to changes in the nature of alienation during this period, its locus has also shifted. In the 1900s, much of the literature about alienation referred to manual workers, and the concerns were class-oriented, a la Marx. But in the 1950s, alienation found its way into the white-collar and managerial ranks as well. White-collar clerical workers, who previously had been a form of elite, found themselves to be the new "working class." Although the managerial ranks show less evidence of alienating characteristics, it is not without presence, and its prevalence in this arena appears to be expanding. As Fromm (1955) notes, alienation has "become the fate of the vast majority of people . . . it pervades the relationship of man to his work, to the things he consumes, . . . to his fellow man, and to himself."

According to Fromm (1955), these shifts (both as to the nature and locus of alienation) have their roots in the process of individuation which results from the breakup of medieval social structure. He feels that modern man has become free of the constraints of small-group society and fixed economic and political orders. The home is no longer the focal point for work activity; families no longer live within close physical proximity; the concept of "neighborhood" means little as apartment dwellers fail to know even those who live next door; work mobility patterns uproot employees frequently.

The price of this new-found freedom, according to Fromm, is a loss of security of fixed identity in a stable social order. In the 1900s, values and norms are more clear and strongly adhered to, whereas in the 1950s, they are more flexible and are adhered to less strictly. For example, "the commitment to honesty in the 1900s is inflexible and independent of rewards or punishments, whereas in the 1950s it is clearly of instrumental value only" (Taviss 1969).

The liberalization of society which has taken place over this time frame has led to a shift from social alienation to self-alienation. For as Taviss (1969) concludes, "It is easier to reject society when society represents a harsh constraining force than when it exhibits flexibility." However, in a flexible, diverse, cosmopolitan society, self-definition becomes more difficult and those who are unable to develop and maintain a firm sense of self become estranged. Not only are they uncomfortable about much of what they do, but soon they may even lose a sense of what their own needs, feelings, and beliefs are.

Birth of Empirical Interest

The focus on alienation in the 1960s and early 1970s differs from earlier treatments of the subject in three significant ways (Lystad 1972): it involves (1) a concerted effort to clarify the meaning of the term; (2) a broader conceptualization of the causes and consequences of alienation; and (3) considerable empirical research on its prevalence and effects in society.

Work to clarify the meaning of alienation has led to the abandonment of the tendency to view alienation as a uniform or unidimensional experience or construct. Seeman (1959), for example, proposes that alienation be analyzed along five independent psychological dimensions: powerlessness, meaninglessness, normlessness, isolation, and self-estrangement.

Powerlessness refers to the degree to which a person feels unable to influence his own destiny in the social system to which he belongs. Elaborating upon Seeman's work, Blauner (1964) further identifies four modes of industrial powerlessness: (1) the separation from ownership of the means of production and the finished products (a condition frequently cited in the works of Marx); (2) the inability to influence general managerial policies; (3) the lack of control over conditions of employment; and (4) the lack of control over the immediate work process.

Meaninglessness refers to the degree to which the individual no longer understands the functioning of the social organization of which he is a part. As a result, the individual can no longer predict with certainty the consequences of his own actions, or he fails to understand the meaning of his actions. As Blauner (1964) points out, meaning in work depends largely on three aspects of the worker's relationship to the product, process, and organization of work: (1) the character of the product itself; (2) the scope of the product worked on; and (3) the sphere of the production process involved.

Normlessness, a dimension in many respects similar to Durkheim's (1964) concept of anomie, refers to the degree to which a person feels unable to reach socially acceptable and desirable goals through those channels which are accepted by society, or by the social organizations to which the individual belongs. In a somewhat related sense, it refers to the extent to which a person feels that there are few, if any, norms to serve as a guide for his behavior within the social system of which he is a part.

Isolation refers to the degree to which an individual feels the absence of a sense of membership in the community. In the work setting, isolation means that the worker feels little or no sense of belonging and is unable to identify or is uninterested in identifying with the organization and its goals.

Self-estrangement, for Seeman, refers to the extent to which various activities of the individual are no longer a goal in themselves, but are carried out to achieve other secondary rewards (money, prestige, etc.). That is, self-estrangement results when an individual experiences a kind of deper-sonalized detachment rather than an immediate involvement or engrossment in job tasks. This lack of present-time involvement means that the work becomes primarily instrumental, a means toward future considerations, rather than an end in itself.

Despite the attempts of Seeman and others to dimensionalize the concept of alienation, there is yet no clear-cut consensus regarding its definition. Even more perplexing, however, is the diversity of measurement or scaling methods employed to quantify and operationalize the concept. The reader should keep these two points clearly in mind in reviewing the empirical research which follows.

Alienation and bureaucracy

A great deal has been written in organizational literature concerning the potentially alienating effects of bureaucracy, particularly with regard to the feature of division of labor. Argyris (1964), for example, posits a basic incongruency between human needs and organizational requirements. He notes that as man develops from infancy, he undergoes development along several dimensions:

(1) From being passive as infants, humans grow toward activeness as adults.

(2) From being dependent on others, an individual grows toward being relatively independent of others.

(3) From only a few types of reaction or behavior, he develops many.

(4) He moves from the shallow, brief, and erratic interests of his in-fancy to the intense, long-term, and coherent commitments of his adulthood.

(5) He begins to want long-term challenges that link his past and future, in place of the old brief and unconnected jobs which typically were engaged in by him as a child.

(6) He begins wanting to go up the totem pole, instead of staying in the low place a child has.

(7) He develops from being not very self-aware and impulsive to being both self-aware and self-controlled, and this lets him develop a sense of integrity and self-worth.

However, Argyris continues to argue, if we use the principles of formal organization (bureaucracy) as ideally defined, employees will be working in an environment where

(1) they have little or no control over their workaday world;

(2) they are expected to be passive, dependent, and subordinate;

(3) they are expected to have a short time-perspective;

(4) job specialization asks them to perfect and value only a few of their simplest abilities; and

(5) they are asked to produce under conditions (imposed by the principle of unity of direction) ideal for psychological failure.

And, he concludes, it appears that the incongruency increases (1) the greater the maturity of the employee; (2) the more the formal structure is tightened in search of efficiency; (3) the more one moves toward the lower levels of the chain of command; and (4) the more jobs become mechanized.

Even Max Weber came to recognize and criticize the potentially dehumanizing effects of bureaucratic structure and its attendant division of labor which, in his words, "makes the individual but a cog in a giant wheel."

Few authors have empirically researched the relationship between alienation and various characteristics or dimensions of bureaucracy. Aiken and Hage (1966), however, in a comparative study of sixteen welfare organizations found two types of alienation—alienation from work and alienation from expressive relations—to be strongly related to two features of bureaucratic structure—centralization and formalization. Their results indicate that highly centralized and highly formalized organizational structures are characterized by greater feelings of (1) disappointment with career and professional development, (2) disappointment over the inability to fulfill professional norms, and (3) dissatisfaction in social relations with supervisors and fellow workers. More specifically, these forms of alienation are related to the absence of staff opportunities to participate in decisions concerning organizational policies and individually assigned tasks, and they are manifest where there are strict rules governing jobs and where rules are rigidly enforced.

Using five dimensions of alienation similar to those suggested by Seeman (1959) and five bureaucratic characteristics similar to those suggested by Weber (1947), Bonjean and Grimes (1970) tested the hypothesis that a direct relationship exists between bureaucratization and alienation. Their findings suggest that some dimensions of bureaucracy are more closely related to alienation measures than are others, and that these relationships are stronger among certain occupational categories than others. They conclude that among managers and independent businessmen no specific dimension of alienation seems to be more closely related to bureaucratization than any other. Among blue-collar workers, however, self-estrangement is significantly related to the bureaucratic features of authority, procedures, specialization, and impersonality. Powerlessness, normlessness, and anomia were also significantly related to the authority dimension of bureaucracy for blue-collar workers, while anomia was further associated with the procedural dimension. Indeed, these findings support the hypothesis that bureaucratic dimensions vary independently and are differentially related to various forms of alienation. In addition, they emphasize that as organizational positions become more bureaucratic along any of the dimensions suggested by Weber, those at lower levels of the organization are likely to be more significantly affected.

Alienation and technology

Much early empirical research on alienation relates to the effects of technology upon man—a characteristic which stems directly from the influence of Marx. That a direct relationship exists between the level of technology employed in the production process and the level of experienced alienation (particularly powerlessness and self-estrangement) has long been proposed, and a number of subsequent empirical studies support this contention (Lipsitz 1964; Neal and Rettig 1963; Pearlin 1963).

Blauner (1964), however, suggests that the relationship between technology and alienation may not be related in simple linear fashion. In a study of manual workers in four factory technologies (the craft industry of printing, the machine-tending industry of textiles, the mass-production assembly-line industry of auto manufacturing, and the continuous-process industry of chemical production), Blauner showed that while alienation (measured in terms of powerlessness, meaninglessness, isolation, and self-estrangement) increases as we move from a craft technology to mass-production assembly-line operations, alienation declines as the more mechanized assembly-line gives way to more automated, continuous-process technology.

Subsequent support for Blauner's findings has been reported by Shepard (1971). Compared on Likert-type scales of powerlessness, meaninglessness, normlessness, self-evaluative involvement in the work role, isolation from organizational goals, and instrumental work orientation, alienation among blue-collar workers was lowest in the craft sample, reached a peak among workers on the mechanized assembly-line, and declined among control room operators in an automated oil refinery.

Other studies have presented similar evidence. In its most advanced form, automated technology introduces basic changes in the man-machine relationship which may reduce the alienating effects experienced with earlier stages of industrial technology. As Lystad (1972) concludes, "The machine alone ... is not a crucial variable in alienation. Man's opportunity to act intelligently in his use of the machine and to gain respect and dignity in the work-group situation are also crucial." Nevertheless, while continuous process technologies may afford some opportunities for work improvement, their applicability to many work settings is restricted (e.g., by cost, by the nature of the product, by technical feasibility, etc.). Thus, process technologies should not be looked to as a form of technological "invisible hand" that will inevitably alleviate problems of worker alienation. To advance such a line of reasoning is to return to the assumptions of scientific management, i.e., the view of technology as the industrial savior.

Personal and organizational consequences

Manheim (1965) contends that the reaction of individuals to alienating situations can take a variety of forms: (1) fatalism, (2) withdrawal in protest, (3) the revolutionary impulse to conquer and reshape social order, and (4) involvement in change. Although the 1960s and early 1970s saw some attempts to combat societal alienation with protest and involvement (e.g., student strikes and involvement in political activities), these actions were narrowly based and for the most part short-termed. In general, the more dominant response could be characterized as fatalistic or noninvolving. Seeman (1962, 1963, 1967), for example, in a number of separate research studies, found individuals with higher levels of alienation to have inferior knowledge in areas of their experience over which they did have some real control. In his view, the alienated person not only feels powerless, but is less able than the nonalienated person to mobilize himself to manage his objective situation. Similarly, Valecha (1972) has found individuals who score higher on feelings of powerlessness to be less well informed about their occupations.

Conducting studies within a number of business organizations, Gemmill and Heisler (1972) found managers with greater feelings of powerlessness to experience significantly higher levels of job strain and job dissatisfaction than managers who feel less powerless. Those feeling most powerless were found more prominently in lower management levels.

Supporting the relationship between powerlessness and job satisfaction are the findings of Organ and Greene (1974). Scientists and engineers scoring higher in feelings of powerlessness were found to show less overall job satisfaction and less satisfaction with the specific content of their job. In findings similar to those of Seeman and Valecha cited above, scientists and engineers reporting greater feelings of powerlessness also reported higher levels of role ambiguity (feelings of uncertainty about one's organizational role obligations and/or the means to fulfill them). A number of researchers (Broedling 1975; Gemmill and Heisler 1972; Heisler 1974; Sims et al., 1975) have also found tendencies for persons higher in reported feelings of powerlessness to experience lower levels of effectiveness on the job, as measured by such performance indicators as promotions, salary increases, supervisory ratings, and the like.

Although there have been few, if any, empirical studies of other dimensions of alienation and their consequences in the work situation, or which empirically examine the other reactions to alienation suggested by Manheim, there is certainly no dearth of nonempirical evidence in this regard. One need only examine what workers say about their jobs to obtain a grasp of the extent and depth to which feelings of alienation persist. The following comments presented by Studs Terkel (1974) in his book *Working* should illuminate the issue:

> *Phil Stallings* (spot-welder): I don't understand how come more guys don't flip. Because you're nothing more than a machine when you hit this type of thing. . . . You really begin to wonder. What price do they put on me? [self-estrangement]

> *Steve Carmichael* (government project coordinator): The most frustrating thing for me is to know that what I'm doing does not have a positive impact on others. I don't see this work as meaning anything. . . . I doubt seriously if three years from now I'll be involved in public administration. One reason is each day I find myself more and more like unto the people I wanted to replace. [meaninglessness]

> *Larry Ross* (ex-president of conglomerate; consultant): Fear is always present in the corporate structure. Even if you're a top man, even if you're hard, even if you do your job—by the slight flick of a finger, your boss can fire you. . . . The executive is a lonely animal in the jungle who doesn't have a friend. . . . He can't confide and talk with the guy working under him. He can't confide and talk to the man he's working for. To give vent to his feelings, his fears, and his insecurities, he'd expose himself. This goes all the way up the line until he gets to be president. The president really doesn't have anyone to talk to, because the vice-presidents are waiting for him to die or make a mistake and get knocked off so they can get his job. [isolation]

To be sure, not all persons are alienated in their work to the extent to which these individuals are. In fact, opinion polls of workers frequently show only a small percentage of "dissatisfied" workers, even in occupational settings which might easily be defined as having high alienation potential.[5] But these findings may, in themselves, be cause for concern. Through many years of doing what they "must" do instead of what they *want* to do, and behaving as they "must" behave instead of as they would *like* to behave, most people come to accept the "natural order" of things. It is possible that under these conditions workers are alienated, but that their alienation is unconscious. And as Lindenfeld (1968) points out

The alienation of men from their work and from themselves, which is a hallmark of modern industrial society, is perhaps most dangerous precisely where it is unconscious. . . . There may be a connection between the repressed, unconscious frustration of modern employees and their being a willing part of a destructive system. Some employees, of course, do not take their work seriously and they good humoredly trade their labor for pay. In many others, however, there may be a basic aggressiveness lurking just below the level of their awareness. This aggressiveness, stemming from a feeling of frustration or alienation at being powerless to control the course of their work or their lives may lead to . . . vicarious pleasure from [observing aggression and destruction in other quarters, e.g., war, sports, etc.] . . . people who do not consciously face their feelings of alienation and hostility may become the unthinking apologists and supporters of the politics of totalitarianism (in its democratic or autocratic guises), war, and destruction.

The Current Scene

The problem of alienation facing today's work organizations has much of its roots in American society itself. Heightened mobility, urbanization, population density, poverty, religious decay, family decay, etc., all influence the alienated condition of today's citizen. While disquieting, there is little that today's organizational manager personally can do to alter these states of affairs. However, there are numerous company-specific factors, conditions, and actions which can magnify or abate some of these societal influences.

For example, in the selection of an overall organizational design criterion, many would opt for "efficiency," and would foster the development of more mechanisitic (Weberian) organizational structures, tighter controls, and closer supervision. But these organizational characteristics lead only to alienation enhancement for most workers and further reduce their sense of personal worth and well-being. Further, such practices restrict the total contribution an employee can make to the firm. Although highly specialized jobs may enhance "technical efficiency"—the optimum utilization of material resources—they fail to take into account the virtually untapped (yet purchased) mental capabilities of the human resource.

Further, as higher educational attainments become common for a larger portion of the population, less and less of the total potential of the human resource will be tapped by traditionally structured jobs and work organizations. However, because of various deficiencies (e.g., lack of operational human resource accounting systems) many of these corporate inefficiencies with regard to the human factor go unnoticed and ignored. They surface only when the level of alienation created by person-system incongruities becomes so great as to lead to some other visible cost outcome such as turnover, absenteeism, drug use, decline in technical efficiency, strikes, etc. Even then, however, attention is principally cosmetic and short-termed.

In Europe, a number of systematic and substantive efforts are being initiated to deal with the psychologically alienating characteristics of work. Legislation now in the final stages of passage through the Norwegian parliament will place companies under legal pressures to improve work environments through changes in the psychological aspects of work organization. Specifically, Article 12 of the proposed law states that "technology, work organizations, working hours, and pay systems" should not "subject workers to unhealthful physical *or psychological conditions*..." (emphasis mine). In the words of commentary prepared by Norway's Labor Ministry, there is "little doubt" that the following are unhealthful factors (Work in America Institute, 1976):

> Authoritarian management; jobs so narrow that they prevent workers from using all their abilities; jobs that require little knowledge, responsibility, or initiative; jobs that give workers little or no opportunity to influence planning of the work; jobs in which workers have no control over pace or methods; and jobs that give little or no contact with others involved in the work.

In Germany, similar activity is under way. Although the 1972 German Works Constitution Act requires the "tailoring of jobs to meet human needs," an even more important milestone in that country was the contract secured by the metalworkers' union (IG Metall) in response to a strike in 1973. The workers secured a package of improvements which included a minimum ninety-second task cycle on all new moving assembly lines, worker approval of all group arrangements, and opportunities for workers to press for job enrichment and job enlargement. This is believed to be the first time in the history of collective bargaining that a major strike was called, and a contract was signed, exclusively on work-humanization issues.[6]

In the United States, however, there is little evidence of more than microcosms of concern and action. The principal focus of government remains the *physical* safety and health of the worker. Unions, with few exceptions (e.g., Irving Bluestone of the United Auto Workers), remain concerned with "more basic" bread-and-butter issues of pay, hours of work, etc. Innovative management experiments have been sharply reduced or curtailed. There is yet even a lack of consensus as to the extent to which work alienation permeates our society. Neither is there agreement as to the nature or significance of its effect.[7]

But to deny alienation in work as a problem in our society today is to ignore personal and societal changes which have been superimposed upon what are for the most part archaic and unyielding organizational forms and practices. To be sure, they were efficient in the technical sense and appropriate to satisfy the exponentially growing needs of a young and poor nation. However, whether the externalities generated by such organizational forms and practices remain acceptable, or are indeed necessary, in an affluent, highly educated, and socially concerned society remains a vital and controversial question for the decades ahead.

NOTES

1. One recent bibliography of alienation literature (Geyer 1972), covering basically the decade of the 1960s, cites nearly 700 article references and over 250 book references.

2. One should question, however, if criticism for this effect should be directed at Taylor or at the misapplication of Taylor's theories by an eager management. Taylor himself had cautioned: "The mechanism of management must not be mistaken for its essence, or underlying philosophy. Precisely the same mechanism will in one case produce disastrous results and in another the most beneficent. The same mechanism which will produce the finest results when made to serve the underlying principles of scientific management will lead to failure and disaster *if accompanied by the wrong spirit in those using it.* Hundreds of people have already mistaken the mechanism of this system for its essence." (Taylor, 1911, emphasis mine)

3. Despite the more popular "social" interpretations of the Hawthorne evidence, it should be noted that not all persons share this interpretation. Alex Carey (1967), for example, who made a detailed comparison between Hawthorne conclusions and Hawthorne evidence, has concluded that "The evidence reported by the Hawthorne investigation is found to be consistent with the view that material, and especially financial, reward is the principal influence on work morale and behavior."

4. Although Weber was a contemporary of F. W. Taylor, his work was not translated and published in this country until the 1940s.

5. For an excellent discussion of this point, refer to Stanislav Kasl's article "Work and Mental Health: Contemporary Research Evidence," presented elsewhere in this volume.

6. For an elaboration of the events taking place in Europe, refer to Ted Mills' article "Leadership from Abroad: European Trends in Industrial Democracy," presented elsewhere in this volume.

7. Irving Kristol, for example, questions in a *Wall Street Journal* editorial (January 18, 1973), if we indeed have "alienated workers" or merely "alienated sociologists."

REFERENCES

Aiken, M., and J. Hage. Organizational Alienation: A Comparative Analysis. *American Sociological Review,* 1966, 31:497–507.

Argyris, C. Being Human and Being Organized. In *Current Perspectives in Social Psychology,* E. P. Hollander and R. G. Hunt, eds. New York: Oxford University Press, 1967, pp. 573–578.

Blauner, R. *Alienation and Freedom.* Chicago: University of Chicago Press, 1964.

Blood, M., and C. Hulin. Alienation, Environmental Characteristics, and Worker Responses. *Journal of Applied Psychology,* 1967, 51:284–290.

———. Job Enlargement, Individual Differences, and Worker Responses. *Psychological Bulletin,* 1968, 69:41–55.

Bonjean, C., and M. Grimes. Bureaucracy and Alienation: A Dimensional Approach. *Social Forces,* 1970, pp. 365–373.

Broedling, L. Relationship of Internal-External control to Work Motivation and Performance in an Expectancy Model. *Journal of Applied Psychology,* 1975, 60:65–70.

Brown, J. A. C. *The Social Psychology of Industry.* Baltimore: Penguin Books, 1954.

Carey, A. The Hawthorne Studies: A Radical Criticism. *American Sociological Review,* 1967, 32:403–417.

Carnegie, D. *How to Win Friends and Influence People.* New York: Simon and Schuster, 1936.

Cass, E., and F. Zimmer. *Man and Work in Society.* New York: Van Nostrand Reinhold Co., 1975.

Davis, L. Socio-Technical Designs for Alternative Organizations. Paper prepared for the Workshop on Organizational Design, American Institute for Decision Sciences, Cincinnati, Ohio, November 5, 1975.

Durkheim, E. *The Division of Labor in Society.* Translated by G. Simpson. New York: The Free Press, 1964.

Etzioni, A. *The Active Society.* New York: The Free Press, 1968.

———. Basic Human Needs, Alienation and Inauthenticity. *American Sociological Review,* 1968, 33:870–885.

Fromm, E. *Escape From Freedom.* New York: Farrar and Rinehart, 1941.

———. *The Sane Society.* New York: Holt, Reinhart, and Winston, 1955.

Gemmill, G., and W. Heisler. Fatalism as a Factor in Managerial Job Satisfaction, Job Strain, and Mobility. *Personnel Psychology,* 1972, 25:241–250.

Geyer, R. F. *Bibliography Alienation.* Amsterdam: SISWO, 1972.

Heisler, W. A Performance Correlate of Personal Control Beliefs in an Organizational Context. *Journal of Applied Psychology,* 1974, 59:504–506.

Kelly, J. *Organizational Behavior.* Homewood, Illinois: Richard D. Irwin, 1974.

Kristol, I. Is the American Worker "Alienated"? *Wall Street Journal,* January 18, 1973.

Landsberger, H. A. *Hawthorne Revisited.* Ithaca, N.Y.: New York State School of Industrial and Labor Relations, Cornell University, 1958.

Leavitt, H. Applied Organization Change in Industry: Structural, Technological, and Humanistic Approaches. In *Handbook of Organizations,* J. G. March, ed. Chicago: Rand McNally, 1965, pp. 1144–1170.

Lindenfeld, F. Work, Automation, and Alienation. In *Radical Perspectives on Social Problems,* F. Lindenfeld, ed. New York: Macmillan, 1968, pp. 207–218.

Lipsitz, L. Work Life and Political Attitudes: A Study of Manual Workers. *American Political Science Review,* 1964, 58:951–962.

Lystad, M. Social Alienation: A Review of Current Literature. *Sociological Quarterly,* 1972, 13:90–113.

Manheim, E. Reaction to Alienation. *Kansas Journal of Sociology,* 1965, 1:108–111.

Marx, K. *Economic and Philosophic Manuscripts of 1844.* New York: International Publishers, 1964.

Merton, R. K. Bureaucratic Structure and Personality. *Social Forces,* 1940, 18:560–568.

———. *Social Theory and Social Structure.* Glencoe, Ill.: The Free Press, 1957.

Neal, A., and S. Rettig. Dimensions of Alienation Among Manual and Non-Manual Workers. *American Sociological Review,* 1963, 28:599–608.

Organ, D., and C. Greene. Role Ambiguity, Locus of Control, and Work Satisfaction. *Journal of Applied Psychology,* 1974, 59:101–102.

Pearlin, L. Alienation from Work: A Study of Nursing Personnel. *American Sociological Review,* 1962, 27:314–326.

Riesman, D. *The Lonely Crowd.* New Haven, Conn.: Yale University Press, 1950.

Roethlisberger, F., and W. Dickson. *Management and the Worker.* Cambridge, Mass.: Harvard University Press, 1939.

Seeman, M. On the Meaning of Alienation. *American Sociological Review* 24: (1959):783–791.

———. Alienation and Social Learning in a Reformatory. *American Journal of Sociology,* 1963, 69:270–284.

———. Status and Identity: The Problem of Inauthenticity. *Pacific Sociological Review,* 1966, 9:67–73.

———. Powerlessness and Knowledge: A Comparative Study of Alienation and Learning. *Sociometry,* June 1967, pp. 105–123.

Seeman, M., and J. Evans. Alienation and Learning in a Hospital Setting. *American Sociological Review,* 1962, 27:772–780.

Shepard, J. *Automation and Alienation.* Cambridge, Mass.: MIT Press, 1971.

Szilagyi, A., and H. Sims. Locus of Control, Role Dynamics, and Job Behavior in a Health Care Institution. *Proceedings, 18th Annual Conference, Midwest Division Academy of Management,* 1975, pp. 104–115.

Taviss, I. Changes in the Form of Alienation: The 1900s vs. the 1950s. *American Sociological Review,* 1969, 34:46–57.

Taylor, F. W. *Principles of Scientific Management.* New York: Harper, 1911.

Terkel, S. *Working.* New York: Avon, 1974.

Valecha, G. Construct Validation of Internal-External Locus of Reinforcement Related to Work-Related Variables. *Proceedings, 80th Annual Convention of the American Psychological Association,* 1972, 7:455–456.

Weber, M. *The Theory of Social and Economic Organization.* New York: The Free Press, 1947.

Work in America Institute, Inc. *World of Work Report.* March, 1976, pp. 7–8.

Whyte, W. *The Organization Man.* New York: Doubleday, 1956.

Work and Mental Health: Contemporary Research Evidence

by Stanislav V. Kasl

IT WOULD BE DIFFICULT TO FIND WRITERS WHO HAVE NOT DESCRIBED the work role as a critical one in our society, as a central life activity. It takes up a large part of the worker's time, effort, and energy and is the major source of income. For the individual, it is probably the chief source of contact with the society at large (Friedman and Havighurst 1954) and is a major influence on his self-concept or self-identity (Erikson 1956; Miller 1963; Super 1951). From a cross-cultural perspective (Triandis 1973), it would appear that in almost all cultures work has significance beyond economic compensation, though individual cultures vary a good deal in the extent of valuing work. In modern American society, work is described as having certain "universal" functions: it provides money, regulates life activity, offers status or social identification, permits association with others, and makes available a meaningful life experience (e.g., Tausky and Piedmont 1967/68).

These sweeping observations lead directly to the concept of humanistic work or "humanization of work." We can do no better than to quote from Robert Kahn (1974) in elucidating this concept:

> We can define the humanization of work as the process of making work more appropriate, more fitting for an adult human being to perform: (1) Work should not damage, degrade, humiliate, exhaust, stultify, or persistently bore the worker; (2) It should interest and satisfy him; (3) It should utilize many of the valued skills and abilities he already possesses and provide opportunity for him to acquire others; (4) It should enhance, or at least leave unimpaired, his interest and ability to perform

85

other major life roles—as husband or wife, parent, citizen, and friend and (5) It should fulfill the instrumental purpose of getting a living, in terms acceptable to him.

In one sense, then, humanization of work means no more—and no less—than taking the theoretical writings on the importance of work in our society and making them into a reality for millions of low-skilled or unskilled blue-collar workers. Suggestions for humanizing work have included the creation of new reward systems (Porter 1973), putting greater emphasis on communication and participation in decision making (Likert 1967), improving the fit between the worker and his environment (French 1973), and altering various aspects of job design known to be associated with high job dissatisfaction (Sheppard and Herrick 1972). In general, the problem is not a paucity of plausible and worthwhile suggestions, but rather how to overcome the obvious barriers which stand in the way of implementing each suggestion and how to evaluate their effectiveness.

It is not the objective of this discourse to enter the ongoing debate on humanizing work with yet another suggestion for change or yet another idea of how to bring about implementation. Rather, the purpose of this paper is to provide substantive background for this current debate. Specifically, I wish to deal with one broad question: *"What do we know about the link between the work environment and mental health?"*

In examining the empirical evidence which bears on this topic, certain cautions should be observed. For example, with issues of profound social significance, one frequently finds an undesirable polarization of viewpoints: On the one hand, one may have the visionary but exaggerated extrapolation from meager or doubtful evidence which seeks to alert one's audience to some possible dangers or some possible undesirable consequences; on the other, we may see such a rigorous examination of the empirical evidence, such a sophisticated dissection of methodological weaknesses, that every single finding is questioned and a conclusion of "There is no good evidence that . . ." becomes inevitable. It is relatively easy to take this second stance since most studies on human beings, which deal with socially significant issues and are conducted in realistic settings, do not permit experimental manipulation and control, and thus do not allow clear-cut causal inferences.

In the context of the present review, neither of these polarized viewpoints is particularly useful. The first one is no longer necessary since it would appear that enough attention has been drawn to this social problem. Moreover, exaggeration of possible adverse effects may backfire if such a stance becomes the basis for intervention or social action: such intervention will appear to have failed because it was based on an attempt to correct a nonexistent cause-effect relationship. The second polarized viewpoint fails to make the distinction between a demonstrated absence of an effect and a mere lack of conclusive data (one way or another); it also fails to recognize the obvious fact that much of ameliorative social action takes place in muddy scientific waters. This review, then, will seek a balanced evaluation of the evidence, its limitations, and the uses to which it can be put.

Conceptual and Measurement Problems

One of the early barriers which must be confronted in the exploration of this area of inquiry is the conceptualization and measurement of *mental health* itself. This is a troublesome variable, and variations and differences in approach, definition, and measurement are the rule rather than the exception. Over the years, certain problems have been clarified but there has been no theoretical or methodological convergence of viewpoints (French and Kahn 1962; Jahoda 1958; Mechanic 1969; Scott 1958; Sells 1969; Smith 1961). It would appear that multiple definitions and multiple measures are necessary if we are going to cover all the major aspects which have been identified as relevant to mental health.

It is possible, however, to organize the different approaches under four generic headings:

(1) Medical-Psychiatric. The relevant measures here are specific diagnoses (such as schizophrenia, depression); global ratings (such as of psychiatric impairment); treatment-based indices (hospitalized, in- or out-patient treatment); and the presence of various psychiatric signs and symptoms (such as hallucinations).

(2) Sociological. The basic orientation of this approach is to view health and illness as states of the person which are relevant to the capacity to perform institutionalized roles, such as that of breadwinner, parent, or spouse (Parsons 1958). Measures focus on quantifying the extent to which the person is unable to perform usual duties and activities, especially those connected with the primary social roles which the person is expected to fulfill. Hospitalization, absence from work, quitting a job, deserting a spouse, etc., are some examples of this class of mental health criteria.

(3) Psychological. Emphasis within the psychological school is on numerous indicators of *personal well-being*. This would include the various measures of affect (e.g., depression, resentment, anxiety) of a whole range of psychophysiological symptoms (e.g., tense, jittery, insomnia, loss of appetite), and the various areas of evaluation and satisfaction (e.g., self-esteem, marital satisfaction, job satisfaction, specific need satisfaction).

(4) Positive Mental Health. A more recent focus of inquiry may be placed under the general label of positive mental health. It represents a distinctly humanistic orientation and emphasizes concepts of "mastery" and "competence." Measures of this state would include growth, development, self-actualization, adequacy of coping, use of valued skills, attainment of valued goals, etc.

All of the above concepts and measures appear indispensable, but none is preeminent. We should stop searching for the *one* index of mental illness–mental health. It would seem that any single measure which might be chosen (such as hospitalization in a mental institution or a psychiatrist's rating) will always be too narrow and too broad; too narrow because it will not reflect all of the underlying dimensions which have been proposed as indicative of mental health, and too broad because it will be "contaminated" by other influences as well—reporting biases in questionnaire measures, readiness for self-referral in treatment based indices, and so on. We might consider, then, the four categories or indicators or criteria presented above as a working definition of mental health. This multiplicity specifically implies that one index is *not* generated by averaging all the separate indices. However, what is implied is that we should be interested in the empirical association among these diverse indices. For example, there are several community follow-up studies of discharged mental hospital patients (Brown 1959; Freeman and Simmons 1958; Marks et al., 1963) which indicate a very low correspondence between symptomatology and psycho-social functioning. This multiplicity of criteria should also alert us to difficulties of interpreting some of the traditional behavioral measures. For example, absenteeism from work may be seen as an indication of inadequate role performance; however, it may also reflect coping with some job stress and may thus positively contribute to well-being.

A second troublesome issue involves the behavioral validity or significance of *measures of job satisfaction,* an indicator frequently used by investigators of the psychological and sociological camps as a generalized measure of well-being. A few illustrations of the problems involved with this indicator should clarify the nature of the difficulty. In two national samples of employed men and women (Quinn et al. 1971; Quinn and Shepard 1974), for example, about 12 percent indicated they were dissatisfied ("not too satisfied," "not at all satisfied") when answering the question "All in all, how satisfied would you say you are with your job?" However, in answering the question "If you were free to go into any type of job you wanted what would your choice be?", about 48 percent appeared dissatisfied ("Would prefer some other job") and another 6 percent preferred not to work at all. From other studies we also know that it is the latter question which shows much greater fluctuations across different occupations. For example, 93 percent of professors at urban universities would choose the same work if given the option to begin their careers over again, in contrast to only 16 percent of unskilled auto workers (Robinson 1969).

Another illustration can be drawn from studies investigating the "meaning of work." In one national sample of employed men (Morse and Weiss 1955), 80 percent of the respondents said "Yes" to the hypothetical question:

"If by chance you inherited enough money to live comfortably without working, do you think you would work anyway?" This would seem to reflect a strong commitment to the work role. However, when they were asked a follow-up question: "Why would you still go on working?" only 9 percent said "Because I enjoy work," and another 10 percent felt work contributed to their health or self-respect. On still another follow-up question: "What would you miss if you didn't work?"—only 9 percent indicated they would miss feeling doing something worthwhile, in contrast to 31 percent who would miss contact with friends, and 25 percent who would just feel restless. These additional probes suggest a weak attachment to the work role.

The above illustrations do not suggest that measures of job satisfaction are invalid. Rather they indicate that interpretations will be more complicated and that data from different questions and different sources must be brought to bear on the interpretation. And we must avoid interpretations which suggest absolute (rather than relative) levels of satisfaction. It is possible to gain a deeper understanding of job satisfaction measures if we invoke two old familiar concepts from general psychology: level of adaptation and level of aspiration. Stated simply, measures of job satisfaction reflect, to a great extent, what the person is used to and what his (her) goals and hopes for the job are. Stated another way, job satisfaction measures are rather static, insensitive measures reflecting only the end result of the whole process of a person's adaptation to his (her) job and of coping with its shortcomings.

A third difficult problem will be mentioned only briefly. Since much of the evidence on work and mental health comes to us from cross-sectional or correlational studies, there is always the *problem of making proper causal inferences* from such associations. Two issues are particularly troublesome: (1) We must be on the lookout for situations where the causal influence is from prior mental health status to some subsequent work-related variable, rather than from work to mental health; (2) We must also try to disentangle the separate influences of correlated variables, such as effects on an interesting and challenging job from effects of earning a higher salary. The whole topic of the role of financial compensation in industrial motivation is a relatively neglected area of research (Opsahl and Dunnette 1966) and a critical reexamination of the original Hawthorne studies (Carey 1967) suggests a long history of a bias toward underestimating the possible importance of financial rewards.

Importance of the Work Role and the Meaning of Work

As was noted in the introduction, most theoretical writings accept without hesitation the proposition that the work role is a central and critical one in our society. Only relatively recently have writers come to question and qualify this broad proposition. Kahn (1972), for example, has suggested that the traditional definition of work may be increasingly inapplicable in an affluent, technologically advanced society. What may be needed, perhaps, is a greater fusion of the work role and the leisure role (Sayles and Strauss 1966; Wrenn 1964). Along similar lines, Dubin (1973) has noted that while good citizenship previously was defined largely by the work a person performed, we now have increasing emphasis on an additional dimension of evaluation—a good citizen is a healthy active person who *consumes* a wide variety of goods and services.

If, instead of the theoretical writings, we consult the results of various studies, we will get the impression that among blue-collar workers, the diminishing importance of the work role is a process well on its way. In addition to the findings of Morse and Weiss (1955), discussed in the previous section, the conclusion of a tenuous attachment to the work role is supported from other investigations (e.g., Dubin 1956; Orzack 1959; Taylor, 1968) which present the respondent with a number of alternative activities and ask him which he would miss the most. Those choosing the alternative "a day's work" are considered to be job-oriented. The typical finding is that no more than 25 percent of industrial workers can be called "job-oriented." In addition, such studies find that job-orientation (or work involvement) increase with the status of the job and is high among professionals.

Another set of studies has investigated the role of work from the perspective of *retirement*. The results of one poll (Harris 1965) revealed that respondents (especially the younger ones) *desire to retire at an earlier age than they actually expect to retire.* Moreover, among those already retired, 39 percent indicated that retirement failed to fulfill their expectation, but less than a quarter of these dissatisfied retirees gave "miss work" as the reason. In another study which focused on retirees only (Loether 1965), the question "What do you miss most about not working?" was answered by an overwhelming majority of respondents with either "nothing at all" or "my work associates." The Barfield and Morgan (1969) study, using both a national random sample and a sample of older workers (sixty and up) in the automobile industry, has clearly shown that financial considerations are of paramount importance in plans for early retirement and that any attachment to the "work ethic" plays but a very small role. When given the opportunity to retire early, one third of the automobile workers did so and yet another third were planning to do so.

What are the implications of these studies for the meaning of work? Overall, it would appear that *lower-skilled industrial workers have a rather tenuous attachment to the work role.* This may be particularly true for industrial workers in large cities (Turner and Lawrence 1965). However, we have also seen that most would continue working in the absence of financial needs—not because of any intrinsic satisfaction in work but because society has not provided any meaningful alternatives. As Strauss (1974) points out, blue-collar workers still "accept the necessity of work but expect little fulfillment from their specific job."

Elsewhere, Sayles and Strauss (1966) have suggested that much of the writing on the meaning of work in our society may be applicable to workers who do highly skilled or creative work, and that for workers who must perform jobs which are difficult to make intrinsically interesting, one may need a reemergence of a leisure-based culture.

These tentative conclusions lead to the following question: "If we are saying that for low-skilled blue-collar workers work has become a more peripheral, less-important life activity, then does it not follow that various aspects of the work environment have a diminished potential for influencing mental health?" "If work is not important, how can it have an important influence on mental health?" This is an important, perhaps paradoxical, question. At this point, a tentative answer can be provided: It depends on what concept and what measures of mental health one is talking about. If one is talking about psychiatric signs and symptoms, psychophysiological symptoms of anxiety and tension, about depression and anger—then the answer is "Yes"; for a vast majority of blue-collar workers work is not a major influence of these factors. However, if one is talking about what we called "positive mental health" (i.e., growth, development, self-actualization, competence, etc.) then, of course, the very process of disengaging from the work role powerfully maleffects mental health.

This conclusion can be illustrated in more concrete terms. In 1955, Chinoy published a study entitled *Automobile Workers and the American Dream*. This book vividly describes the process of adjustment to dull, monotonous work on the assembly line. Initially, many of these workers looked upon their job as only temporary, and they fantasized about the day when they would be able to quit the factory and establish their own small business or engage in some other independent occupation. But as time went on, they lost their dreams and even their ambitions regarding the more realistic goal of becoming a foreman. Their chief notion of a better job was off the assembly line, but was now only a low level blue-collar job in the same plant. Only in their hopes for their offspring (i.e., a white-collar job) could one see an expression of their own aspirations, albeit dwarfed and displaced. "Job security" now expressed all of their "mobility" aspirations.

Ten years later, Kornhauser (1965) published his book *Mental Health of the Industrial Worker*, in which he echoes some of the same themes. What is this process of coping and adaptation to a dull, monotonous job? It is coping by limiting one's aspirations and, ultimately, killing them. As he reports, "The unsatisfactory mental health of working people consists in no small measure of their dwarfed desires and deadened initiative, reduction of their goals and restriction of their efforts to a point where life is relatively empty and only half meaningful.'' Kornhauser goes on to discuss the two dead-end options for the automobile worker: maintain high expectations from work, which leads to constant frustration, or limit one's expectations, which leads to a drab existence. Keeping these general conclusions in mind, let me now turn to a systematic investigation of some of the evidence linking the work environment to mental health.

Job Status and Indices of Mental Health

Initially, it would seem rather easy to establish a causal linkage between work and mental health. Numerous studies have repeatedly shown that members of the lowest social class are more likely to be hospitalized (Dohrenwend and Dohrenwend 1969; Fried 1969) and rehospitalized (Myers and Bean 1968) for severe psychiatric illness, and to score somewhat higher on interview-based psychiatric symptom checklists in population surveys (Gurin et al. 1960; Srole et al. 1962).

However, a convincing interpretation of the negative association between social class and mental illness which also implicates the work environment is not easy. For example, social class is a composite index usually consisting of such components as education, occupation, income, and place of residence or rental value. It is difficult, therefore, to isolate the effect of the occupational dimension alone. When the association with mental illness is examined separately for the various components of social class, occupational level reveals more exceptions to this association than any other component (Fried 1969). A more general difficulty is that it has not been possible to reject the alternate hypothesis that persons with prior mental health problems experience downward mobility (Dohrenwend and Dohrenwend 1969; Fried 1969; Srole et al. 1962). In short, *the general literature on social class and mental illness fails to tell us anything specific about the influence of the work environment*.

If we turn to one specific indicator of well-being, job satisfaction, we find a surfeit of evidence for a positive association between prestige or status level of a job and general job satisfaction (Blauner 1960; Gurin et al. 1960; Kahn 1972; Kornhauser 1965; Langner and Michael 1963, Porter and Lawler 1965; Quinn et al. 1971; Robinson 1969; Vroom 1964 and 1969; Wilensky 1964; Zander and Quinn 1962). Among the components of job satisfaction, those which deal with self-esteem, self actualization, autonomy, and pay are more closely related to job level than are job satisfaction components dealing with work conditions and relations with co-workers or supervisors (Argyris 1960 and 1964; Blauner 1964; Kasl and French 1962; Porter 1962; Quinn et al. 1971).

There are also several studies which have related occupational level to more general indices of mental health (Gurin et al. 1960; Kornhauser 1965; Langner and Michael 1963; Quinn et al. 1971). Again we find good agreement that individuals in higher status level jobs have slightly better mental health, as measured by diverse indices of well-being and indices of freedom of symptoms.

However, these studies of correlates of job status deserve several comments. First, the correlations between job level and job satisfaction or symptomatology are rather weak, seldom of a magnitude greater than 0.3 (Gurin et al. 1960; Langner and Michael 1963; Quinn et al. 1971). Thus, job level as a variable accounts for less than 10 percent of the total variation experienced in measures of job satisfaction. Second, finer breakdowns of occupations often reveal interesting exceptions: male clerical workers appear to have unduly poor mental health (Gurin et al. 1960) and engineers have unduly high alienation (Wilensky 1969), given their respective job levels. Third, the higher job satisfaction among respondents in higher status occupations should not blind us to the fact that these respondents also report more problems at work or more frequently state that they worry about work (Gurin et al. 1960; Langner and Michael 1963). Thus job involvement may be a factor more closely related to job level than job satisfaction or some other index of mental health. Fourth, much needs to be done to explicate and document the various possible links between job level and mental health. Specifically, we need to know what dimensions of the work environment are associated with job level and how they may influence mental health. Also, the role of financial compensation remains rather obscure. Finally, let me also note that we desperately need longitudinal studies in order to better pin down the presumed causal relationships between these variables.

Mental Health and Other Dimensions of the Work Environment

In addition to job status, many other dimensions of the work environment have also been examined. In order to avoid blurring the picture with regard to different mental health correlates, the literature will be summarized separately for job satisfaction and for the other mental health indicators.

The extensive findings on job satisfaction (e.g., Alderfer 1969; Blauner 1960; Caplan 1971; Caplan et al. 1975; Gross 1970; Indik, 1963; Kahn 1972;

Mott et al., 1965; Porter and Lawler 1965; Quinn, et al. 1971; Vroom 1964 and 1969; Zander and Quinn 1962) can be summarized very briefly as follows. *Low job satisfaction is related to the following factors:*

(1) *Conditions at work:* presence of health and safety hazards, and unpleasant work conditions, such as fast-paced and physically demanding work; long hours of work (if this is forced on the worker); afternoon and night shifts; unclear tasks; lack of control over work, such as pacing.

(2) *Work itself (job content):* inability to use skills and abilities; highly fractionated, repetitive tasks involving few diverse operations.

(3) *The work group:* lack of opportunity to interact with co-workers; work groups which are too large and lack cohesiveness; nonacceptance by co-workers.

(4) *Supervision:* no participation in decision-making; inability to provide feedback to supervisor; lack of recognition for good performance; supervisors who are not considerate or understanding.

(5) *The organization:* large organization with a "flat" organizational structure (relatively few levels in the organization); having a staff position (vs. a line position); discrimination in hiring.

(6) *Wages and promotion:* low financial reward levels or perceived inequities in wages; lack of promotional opportunities.

The additional literature linking the work environment with other indicators of mental health will be summarized in a comparable way to emphasize the many similarities in results (Caplan 1971; Caplan et al. 1975; Kahn and Quinn 1970; Kahn et al. 1964; Kornhauser 1965; Mott et al. 1965; Neel 1955; Quinn et al. 1971; Zander and Quinn 1962). *Poor mental health has been shown to be related to the following factors:*

(1) *Conditions at work:* exposure to health and safety hazards, and unpleasant work conditions; necessity to work fast and to expend a lot of physical effort; excessive and inconvenient hours.

(2) *Work itself:* lack of use of skills and abilities; perception of job as uninteresting; repetitious work, especially on a constantly moving assembly line; role overload, both qualitative and quantitative, involving generally a discrepancy between resources (time, worker's training and skill, machinery, organizational structure, etc.) and job demands.

(3) *Shift work:* fixed afternoon and rotating shifts, which affect time-oriented body functions and lead to difficulty in role behavior (e.g., role of spouse or parent), if these role activities are normally performed during the time of day when the worker is on the shift.

(4) *Supervision:* job demands which are unclear or conflicting (role ambiguity and role conflict); close supervision and lack of autonomy; lack of feedback from supervisor; reports of problems with supervisor.

(5) *The organization:* working on the boundary of the organization (e.g., salesman, customer service representative, etc.).

(6) *Wages and promotion:* inadequate income; perception of promotional opportunities as unfair or too slow.

In the above studies, the obtained relationships are generally stronger for mental health indices reflecting life satisfaction, self-esteem, tension, and the like, and are generally weaker for mental health indicators based on psychiatric symptom checklists.

Because of the attention which job enlargement and automation have received, it is worthwhile to treat these two aspects of the work environment separately. The relevant studies (Alderfer 1969; Faunce 1958 and 1965; Hulin and Blood 1968; Mann and Williams 1962; Marcson 1970; Shepard 1971; Vroom 1969) suggest that job enlargement leads to increased job satisfaction particularly in the following areas: use of skills and abilities, opportunity to learn new things, perception of work as meaningful (reduced alienation), and amount of responsibility and autonomy. However, we must distinguish *job enlargement* (which allows the worker to set his own pace, to inspect his own work, to set up and repair his own machinery, and so on) from mere *job extension,* which only adds similar elements to the job without altering job content (Hulin and Blood 1968); there is no evidence that job extension has any effects on job satisfaction.

To the extent that automation brings about job enlargement, the above-listed consequences of job enlargement will also hold for automation. However, sometimes early stages of "automation" (or, more properly called, mechanization), especially as exemplified by the introduction of new equipment in offices for clerical workers, really represent increased functional specialization and thus lead to decreased job satisfaction. We must also note that automation, even when accompanied by sizeable job enlargement, may have some undesirable consequences: need for closer supervision and a resultant lower satisfaction with supervision; reduced opportunity for social interaction because of need for constant and close monitoring; greater work pressures because of higher performance standards more rigidly enforced; reduced (perceived) job security; and increased perception of management as impersonal and disinterested.

In evaluating the findings described in this section, several points should be kept in mind. First, in many studies the dimensions of the work environment are measured subjectively, i.e., using the worker's self-reported perceptions. To the extent that the objective work environment and workers subjective perceptions of it may be tenuously related, an improvement in (objective) work conditions might not have the desired effects on job satisfaction if workers' subjective perceptions remain unaltered. For example, in the Kahn et al. (1964) study, the objective measure of the role conflict (the sum of pressures to change behavior as reported by organizational members who had some degree of formal influence over the respondent) correlated very poorly with the subjective measure of role conflict (intensity of experienced conflict as reported by the respondent himself).

Second, most of the studies reviewed are correlational in nature and often causal interpretations of the data are far from self-evident. For example, in the Mott (1965) study, workers on the rotating shift reported having fewer friends. But does this mean that working this shift interferes with the development of friendships, or does it mean that workers who are social isolates frequently volunteer for this kind of shift? Third, many of the dimensions of the work environment are correlated with each other (and with job level), and more sophisticated, multivariate analyses are needed in order to establish which dimensions are crucial and which others may "wash out" when statistical controls are applied. Finally, most of the observed correlations in the reviewed studies are not very high. For example, Quinn et al. (1971) found that workers' reports of the presence of problems in eighteen areas of Labor Standards concern (certainly one good general measure of the work environment) correlated in the low .30s with two indices of job satisfaction, and even less with several mental health indices. Thus, there are several methodological and statistical concerns which must be kept in mind in any attempt to evaluate studies reporting the association of job satisfaction and mental health to a variety of factors found in the work environment.

Intercorrelations among Mental Health Indicators

Given that the majority of studies of the work environment have used job satisfaction as the only indicator of mental health, we also need to examine the linkages which can be made between job satisfaction and other mental health indices.

Numerous studies have examined the association of job satisfaction with absenteeism, turnover, and job performance—a triad falling into the category of indices of "functional effectiveness" (Athanasiou 1969; Kahn 1972; Lawler 1969 and 1970; Martin 1969; Vroom 1964 and 1969). Reasonable agreement exists that *job satisfaction is negatively correlated both with absenteeism and with turnover, but bears no uniform relationship to performance or productivity.* Because of these findings, job satisfaction has been interpreted as primarily an index of motivation to come to work. Its potential causal influence (if any) on performance appears too complex to lead to a general, replicable association. More likely, performance may have causal influence on job satisfaction if good performance is followed by extrinsic (pay and promotion) or intrinsic (use of valued skills) rewards.

Even though the triad of turnover, absenteeism, and performance have been the dominant indices of vocational adjustment, in the perspective of this review they have no unique status. They are merely a partial reflection of functional effectiveness in one social role and, moreover, they put an exclusive emphasis on compliance with job demands. That vocational adjustment, thusly measured, can paint a misleading picture about the person's total life is dramatically illustrated in a longitudinal study (Hinkle 1959) of women employees of the Bell Telephone System. Women who were especially well adjusted, as measured by sickness absences, company dispensary data and psychiatrist's ratings, were those who were unmarried and were living a routine, dull, withdrawn existence, refusing to get involved with other people.

The literature on the interrelations among job satisfaction and other diverse indices of mental health (Bradburn 1969; Brayfield et al. 1957; Crites, 1969; Kasl and Cobb 1967; Kornhauser 1965; Langner and Michael 1963; Quinn et al. 1971; Seeman 1967; Super and Crites 1962; Veroff et al. 1962; Wilson 1967) suggests the following:

(1) Correlations between job satisfaction and indices of personal happiness and life satisfaction average in the low .40s and are lower for women.

(2) Correlations between indices of vocational adjustment (such as absenteeism) and personal adjustment run somewhat lower, and correlations between job satisfaction and symptom-based indices of mental health are still lower (ranging in the mid .20s). Among older respondents these correlations are especially low.

(3) Personal happiness is more closely related to satisfaction with family relationships than with job satisfaction.

(4) Alienation at work does not seem to generalize to other areas of life, such as intergroup relations or political events.

(5) There is no evidence that lack of satisfaction in one area of life is compensated for by particularly strong enjoyment or satisfaction in another—at least in the sense that none of the studies have shown negative associations between pairs of satisfaction or mental health indices. For example, a person who is satisfied with his supervisor will unlikely be dissatisfied with some other aspect of his job situation (i.e., pay, the work itself, etc.)

To be sure, the above correlational literature permits only limited causal inferences, and when such inferences have been made they are often in the opposite direction. For example, Super and Crites (1962) conclude that (prior) personality problems are the most common cause of discharge from work. The safest conclusion, given the relatively weak associations, would be that various aspects of the work environment could have a strong impact on job satisfaction without having much impact on symptoms or other areas of satisfaction. This conclusion should be further tempered by the suspicion that shared "method variance" (Campbell and Fiske 1959) and differences in the generalized tendency to complain or to be defensive have inflated the "true" association between job satisfaction and other mental health indicators also measured by self-report.

The Role of Individual Differences

In our search for general conclusions we frequently ignore individual differences which, when taken into consideration, may strikingly influence the overall effects. Furthermore, it would seem that given the lack of rapid progress in implementing various methods for humanizing work, paying attention to individual differences in the relevant characteristics of job occupants may at least lead to better selection procedures which would minimize adverse interactions between specific job characteristics and specific characteristics of the person.

Age is one of the demographic characteristics most frequently examined for its role in work and job satisfaction (Back and Gergen 1966; Meltzer 1965; Robinson 1969). Older workers (1) are more satisfied with their jobs, have a better attendance record and less turnover, and are more strongly identified with management and its policies; (2) are less concerned with advancement and are less worried about keeping the job; and (3) have a less positive attitude toward retirement, since work takes on more significance while spare time decreases in significance. The best interpretation of the higher job satisfaction among older workers is probably in terms of a process of gradual retrenchment of goals and aspirations. *Older workers are likely more satisfied because they have fewer expectations and they have come to terms with the limitations of their jobs*—somewhat like the process of "disengagement" described by social gerontology (Neugarten 1968).

There is evidence that individual differences in achievement motivation and aspirations play a crucial role. For example, Veroff and Feld (1970) have concluded that *individuals with high needs for achievement will be more dissatisfied, regardless of how high a job level they have reached.* Along similar lines, there is good evidence (e.g., Form and Geschwender 1962; Zander and Quinn 1962) that the association between job level and job satisfaction is modified by the workers' aspirations and that men who fail to achieve the occupational levels of their fathers or brothers have lower satisfaction. Kleiner and Parker (1963) have proposed a general theory which links frustrated aspirations to mental disorder. Their findings from a later study of urban Negroes (Parker and Kleiner 1966) further support this theory. The discrepancy between a high educational level and a relatively low occupational level has been interpreted as one indicator of frustrated aspirations and has already been linked to poor mental health (Jackson 1962; Kasl and Cobb 1971).

A number of studies have been concerned with the role of various personality variables in modifying the effects of the work environment. Vroom (1960) has shown that the effects of participation in decision making on satisfaction and job performance depend very much on the worker's need for independence and the degree of his authoritarianism. The Kahn et al. (1964) study revealed that the effects of role conflict and role overload on tension and job satisfaction are modified by differences in flexibility-rigidity and the resultant differences in the amount of communication with others. Hulin and Blood (1968) suggest that individual differences in susceptibility to monotony and boredom play an important role in effects of job enlargement on satisfaction, absenteeism, and turnover, and *the beneficial effects of job enlargement can be expected only for workers who are not alienated from middle-class work norms*. Rural and small town workers are apparently less alienated from middle-class work norms than are large city workers. The former reveal greater job satisfaction on jobs which are personally involving while the latter are more satisfied on jobs which are less personally involving (Turner and Lawrence 1965). Vroom's reviews (1964, 1969) offer many other excellent examples of studies in which individual differences in personality characteristics play an important modifying role.

Complex interactions such as between differences in occupational setting and individual differences in worker characteristics and personality, may sometimes be also present. For example, Quinn (1972) reports that the association between job satisfaction and mental health is stronger among those who are "locked into" their jobs (i.e., those who do not see much of a chance of finding better employment) than among those who are not. Neff (1968) has listed a number of differences in occupational settings which he feels may affect the generality of statements about work: (1) the degree to which output is under the control of the individual worker (or, what other writers have more broadly described as the effectiveness and visibility of goal-path linkages in an organization); (2) the relative amounts of horizontal and vertical mobility which are realistically possible; (3) differences in objectivity and scope of standards of performance; and (4) the differential importance of various norms, such as achievement.

Summary and Implications

There is a good deal of suggestive and indirect evidence linking work and mental health: low socio-economic status is related to high rates of psychiatric hospitalization and symptomatology; conditions of work, the nature of the work itself, opportunities for promotion, etc., can all contribute to poor mental health; positive associations are found between job satisfaction and other indices of mental health. However, a precise causal interpretation of this evidence is difficult; and the more convincing evidence comes from focused comparisons of mental health of men in different jobs and findings of relatively poorer mental health among workers in low skilled and unskilled jobs. This is more true of some indices of mental health (e.g., low job and life satisfaction, poor self-concept and self-evaluation) than others (e.g., psychiatric signs and symptoms). In addition, there appears to be good evidence that men in these low level jobs adapt by limiting their aspirations and their expectations and that, in effect, the greatest mental health deficit suffered by these men is in the area of job involvement and, consequently, self-actualization.

Thus, while low job status and all the associated work conditions remain our best lead, much more remains to be learned before we can pinpoint the particularly noxious elements in these low skilled jobs. For example, while many writers have emphasized the adverse effects of mechanically paced, repetitive work, Kornhauser (1965), in a more intensive multivariate analysis of data, concluded that these aspects of work do not really affect mental health, except perhaps in a symbolic way when the men equate being on such a job with failure. We have also seen that the effects of individual differences can also be strong, in particular with respect to alienation from the work norm (Hulin and Blood 1968; Sexton 1968; Turner and Lawrence 1965), which makes repetitive work satisfying for some persons. And we must not forget that low level jobs also have poor pay and generally lower job security, and that while the influence of these variables is not yet clear, it is probably powerful (viz., the evidence that financial circumstances are crucial in influencing the impact of unemployment or retirement).

In addition to our inability to pinpoint precisely the noxious elements in low status jobs, we also have the issue of the extent to which various elements of the work environment are modifiable. In general, it would appear that the variables which Herzberg et al. (1959) call "dissatisfiers" (e.g., working conditions, salary, job security, supervision, company policy, etc.) are more easily modified than those called "satisfiers" (e.g., achievement, growth, the work itself, etc.). For example, physically hazardous conditions, such as those encountered by mine workers, have documented consequences for mental health (Zaleznik et al. 1970) and are, in principle, correctable. Similarly, low status jobs are more frequently associated with various stressful life changes (e.g., layoff, unemployment, plant relocation, mechanization and automation, lateral job reassignment) and there is an increasing documentation about the health consequences of such changes (Dohrenwend and Dohrenwend 1974; Gunderson and Rahe 1974). Public policy needs to be directed toward ways of buffering the individual from such changes and preparing him for dealing with them in a more functional way.

On the other hand, it is difficult to see how routine, repetitive, dull work can be made intrinsically more interesting, challenging, or satisfying. Job enlargement may occasionally be a solution, but more frequently only job extension will be feasible and the latter does very little for improving job satisfaction or other aspects of mental health. Perhaps the only reasonable solution is to acknowledge the existence of individual differences, i.e., select those who "like" routine work.

Thus, it appears reasonable to suggest that Herzberg's "dissatisfiers" are more closely linked with some aspects of mental health (e.g., indices of well-being and symptoms) while the "satisfiers" are more closely linked with other aspects (e.g., job involvement, growth, self-actualization, and competence). The implication of this discussion for beneficial organizational change is that we may expect to make some improvement in workers' mental health in the former area but not in the latter.

The tentativeness of these comments stems from large gaps which exist in our knowledge and from the lack of a comprehensive theoretical framework within which to integrate the available evidence and to formulate new researchable issues. Perhaps the more appropriate framework is a field-theoretical one (e.g., Deutsch 1968) which places particular emphasis on the Person-Environment (P-E) Fit Model (Dawis et al. 1964; French 1973; French et al. 1974; Lofquist and Dawis 1969). This model integrates several elements and processes: (1) the dimensions of the work environment which are job demands (requirements) and those which are resources (need satisfiers); (2) the dimensions of the person which are his abilities (resources) and those which are his needs; (3) the relation, in particular the discrepancies, between the demands and the resources in the environment, and the needs and the abilities of the person; and (4) the consequences of these discrepancies, including attempts to alter them. Furthermore, within the P-E model, it is useful to make two distinctions: the first is between objectively measured and subjectively perceived (or misperceived) dimensions of P and E; the second between coping which alters dimensions of E (environment) and coping which alters dimensions of P (self).

The P-E Fit model is only a very general and rather abstract statement of perspective from which to view the issue of work and mental health. One consequence of adopting this perspective is the realization that while the dimensions of job requirements (demands) and the dimensions of the corresponding abilities in the person have been frequently studied in the traditional vocational fitness literature (especially for selected low skill, blue collar jobs), those dimensions of the person which represent his needs and the dimensions of the job environment which represent resources (potential satisfiers of needs) have been neglected. Most of the effort has gone into trying to establish the dimensions of job satisfaction (e.g., Herzberg et al. 1957; Katz 1951; Quinn et al. 1971; Smith et al. 1969; Vroom 1964), and there is reasonable agreement on a "basic" list of job satisfaction areas: pay and material rewards, work itself and working conditions, immediate supervision, company and management, promotion, and co-workers.

In contrast, the writings on human needs relevant to the work environment are largely speculative (Centers and Bugental 1966; Herzberg 1966; Levinson 1971; Lichtman and Hunt 1971; McLean and Taylor 1958; Schaffer 1953). Some of the empirical studies of work motivation have been involved in sterile controversies, such as the Herzberg two-factor theory of motivation (Friedlander and Walton 1964; Herzberg et al. 1959; King 1970) and the relative role of economic rewards vs. work content in affecting overall job satisfaction (Fein 1973).

Another consequence of the P-E Fit perspective is the recognition that job satisfaction measures are interaction measures and do not reflect the dimensions of either the person or the environment alone. They do not allow the person to indicate separately what his needs are and how well these needs are met by the work environment. Interestingly, both studies (Argyris 1960; Wilensky 1964 and 1969) in which there was a separate measurement of personality variables (needs or valued dimensions of self-image) and of the work environment (satisfaction of needs or congruence with self-image), failed to replicate the most stable finding we have—the link between occupational level and job satisfaction. Since men at different occupational levels appear to have different needs and expectations (Armstrong 1971; Kilpatrick et al. 1964; Taylor 1968), it is likely that measures which reflect the relative discrepancy between strength of needs and satisfaction of needs will relate much less to occupation level than the traditional job satisfaction measures, and that what primarily differentiates high and low status occupations is the degree of ego-involvement or commitment to work.

The P-E Fit perspective also forces us to pay more attention to the time dimension and to the process of coping with various types of P-E "misfits."

Job satisfaction measures are too static and tend to disguise and distort the whole process of man's adaptation to, and his coping with, the discrepancy between his needs and the satisfaction of these needs by the work environment. For example, in the studies which suggest that even highly repetitive and routine work can be satisfying, there is a suggestion of almost limitless plasticity and adaptability by some workers. Apparently, some workers prefer mechanically paced, highly structured jobs and find some satisfaction in their very rigidity and mindless, but predictable, triviality (Hulin and Blood 1968; Sexton 1968).

The need for additional studies to fill in the many gaps is fairly obvious. In particular, two lines of future research seem apparent. One line involves the conduct of a greater number of longitudinal studies covering three major areas of investigation: (1) life cycle studies, including studies of socialization into the work role and early career (Super 1963), mid-career changes and entrances into the labor force (such as mothers of growing children returning to work), and retirement studies; (2) before-and-after studies of various "naturally" occurring events which may be beneficial or stressful, e.g., job enlargement, promotion and demotion, automation, job-reassignment, plant relocation, layoff, and plant closing (unemployment); and (3) before-and-after studies of the effects of a particular program, such as special hiring of the "hard core unemployed," or job retraining.

A second area in which research is badly needed are studies specifically concerned with the interrelationship among life roles, or which study effects of events and changes which cross several life roles. It has been noted (Rapoport and Rapoport 1965) that research on work and the family has been quite segregated and, indeed, it is quite rare to find a study which focuses on more than one role. What we have at the moment are only a few correlational studies which relate job satisfaction to general life satisfaction and to satisfaction in other life roles, such as marriage. These studies show modest, positive correlations which are not very illuminating. Yet, we badly need to understand what effects lack of job involvement and lack of fulfillment (self-actualization) in the work role may have on performance and well-being in other life roles. Also, we need to know more about how we may be able to narrow the gap between the work role and the leisure role.

REFERENCES

Alderfer, C. P. Job Enlargement and the Organizational Context. *Personnel Psychology*, 1969, 22:418–426.

Argyris, C. Individual Actualization in Complex Organizations. *Mental Hygiene,* 1960, 44:226–237.

———. *Integrating the Individual and the Organization.* New York: Wiley, 1964.

Armstrong, T. B. Job Content and Context Factors Related to Satisfaction for Different Occupational Levels. *Journal of Applied Psychology,* 1971, 55:57–65.

Athanasiou, R. Job Attitudes and Occupational Performance: A Review of Some Important Literature. In *Measures of Occupational Attitudes and Occupational Characteristics,* J. P. Robinson, R. Athanasiou, and K. B. Head, eds. Ann Arbor: Institute for Social Research, University of Michigan, 1969, pp. 79–98.

Back, K. W., and K. J. Gergen. Personal Orientation and Morale of the Aged. In *Social Aspects of Aging,* I. H. Simpson and J. C. McKinney, eds. Durham, N.C.: Duke University Press, 1966, pp. 296–305.

Barfield, R., and J. N. Morgan. *Early Retirement: The Decision and the Experience.* Ann Arbor: Institute for Social Research, University of Michigan, 1969.

Blauner, R. Work Satisfaction and Industrial Trends in Modern Society. In *Labor and Trade Unionism,* W. Gelenson and S. Lipset, eds. New York: Wiley, 1960.

———. *Alienation and Freedom: The Factory Worker and His Industry.* Chicago: University of Chicago Press, 1964.

Bradburn, N. M. *The Structure of Psychological Well-Being.* Chicago: Aldine Press, 1969.

Brayfield, A. H., R. V. Wells, and M. W. Strate. Interrelationships Among Measures of Job Satisfaction and General Satisfaction. *Journal of Applied Psychology,* 1957, 41:201–205.

Brown, G. W. The Experiences of Discharged Chronic Schizophrenic Patients in Various Types of Living Groups. *Milbank Memorial Fund Quarterly,* 1959, 37:105–131.

Campbell, D. R., and D. W. Fiske. Convergent and Discriminant Validation by the Multitrait-Multimethod Matrix. *Psychological Bulletin,* 1959, pp. 81–105.

Caplan, R. D. *Organizational Stress and Individual Strain.* Ann Arbor: Unpublished Doctoral Dissertation, University of Michigan, 1971.

Caplan, R. D., S. Cobb, J. R. P. French, Jr., R. Van Harrison, and S. R. Pinneau, Jr. *Job Demands and Worker Health.* Washington, D.C.: HEW Publication No. (NIOSH) 75–160, 1975.

Carey, A. The Hawthorne Studies: A Radical Criticism. *American Sociological Review,* 1967, 32:403–416.

Centers, R., and D. E. Bugental. Intrinsic and Extrinsic Job Motivations Among Different Segments of the Working Population. *Journal of Applied Psychology,* 1966, 50:193–197.

Chinoy, E. *Automobile Workers and the American Dream.* Garden City, N.Y.: Doubleday, 1955.

Cobb, S., and S. V. Kasl. Some Medical Aspects of Unemployment. In *Employment of the Middle Aged,* G. M. Shatto, ed. Springfield, Ill.: C. C Thomas, 1972, pp. 87–96.

Crites, J. O. *Vocational Psychology.* New York: McGraw-Hill, 1969.

Dawis, R. V., G. W. England, and L. H. Lofquist. *Minnesota Studies in Vocational*

Rehabilitation, Vol. XV: *A Theory of Work Adjustment.* Minneapolis: Industrial Relations Center, University of Minnesota, 1964.

Deutsch, M. Field Theory in Social Psychology. In *The Handbook of Social Psychology Vol I, Historical Introduction,* G. Lindzey and E. Aronson, eds. Reading, Mass.: Addison-Wesley, 1968, pp. 412–487.

Dohrenwend, B. P., and B. S. Dohrenwend. *Social Status and Psychological Disorder: A Causal Inquiry.* New York: Wiley, 1969.

————. *Stressful Life Events: Their Nature and Effects.* New York: Wiley, 1974.

Dubin, R. Industrial Workers' Worlds: A Study of the "Central Life Interests" of Industrial Workers. *Social Problems,* 1956, 3:131–142.

————. Work and nonwork: Institutional Perspectives. In *Work and Nonwork in the Year 2001,* M. D. Dunnette, ed. Monterey, Cal.: Brooks/Cole Publishing Co., 1973, pp. 53–68.

Erikson, E. H. The Problem of Ego Identity. *Journal of the American Psychoanalysis Association,* 1956, 4:56–121.

Faunce, W. A. Automation in the Automobile Industry: Some Consequences for In-plant Social Structure. *American Sociological Review,* 1958. 23:401–407.

————. Automation and the Division of Labor. *Social Problems,* 1965, 13:149–160.

Fein, M. The Real Needs and Goals of Blue Collar Workers. *Conference Board Record,* February 1973, pp. 26–33.

Form, W., and J. Geschwender. Social Reference Basis of Job Satisfaction: The Case of Manual Workers. *American Sociological Review,* 1962, 27:228–237.

Freeman, H. E., and O. G. Simmons. Mental Patients in the Community: Family Settings and Performance Levels. *American Sociological Review,* 1958, 23:147–154.

French, J. R. P., Jr. Person Role Fit. *Occupational Mental Health,* 1973, 3:15–20.

French, J. R. P., Jr., and R. L. Kahn. A Programmatic Approach to Studying the Industrial Environment and Mental Health. *Journal of Social Issues,* 1962, 18:1–47.

French, J. R. P., Jr., W. Rodgers, and S. Cobb. Adjustment as Person-Environment Fit. In *Coping and Adaptation,* G. V. Coelho, D. A. Hamburg, and J. E. Adams, eds. New York: Basic Books, 1974.

Fried, M. Social Differences in Mental Health. In *Poverty and Health: A Sociological Analysis,* J. Kosa et al., eds. Chicago: Aldine Press, 1969.

Friedlander, G., and E. Walton. Positive and Negative Motivation to Work. *Administrative Science Quarterly,* 1964, 9:194–207.

Friedman, E. W., and R. J. Havighurst. *The Meaning of Work and Retirement.* Chicago: University of Chicago Press, 1954.

Gross, E. Work, Organization and Stress. In *Social Stress,* S. Levine and N. A. Scotch, eds. Chicago: Aldine, 1970, pp. 54–110.

Gunderson, E. K. E., and R. H. Rahe. *Life Stress and Illness.* Springfield, Ill.: C. C Thomas, 1974.

Gurin, G., J. Varoff, and S. Feld. *Americans View Their Mental Health.* New York: Basic Books, 1960.

Harris, L. "Pleasant" Retirement Expected. *The Washington Post,* November 28, 1965.

Herzberg, F. *Work and the Nature of Man.* Cleveland: The World Publishing Company, 1966.

Herzberg, F., B. Mausner, R. Peterson, and D. Capwell. *Job Attitudes: Review of Research and Opinion.* Pittsburgh: Psychological Service of Pittsburgh, 1957.

Herzberg, F., B. Mausner, and B. Snyderman. *The Motivation to Work.* New York: Wiley, 1959.

Hinkle, L. E., Jr. Physical Health, Mental Health, and the Social Environment: Some Characteristics of Healthy and Unhealthy People. In *Recent Contributions of Biological and Psychosocial Investigations to Preventive Psychiatry,* R. G. Ojemann, ed. Iowa City: State University of Iowa, 1959, pp. 80–103.

Hulin, C. L., and M. R. Blood. Job Enlargement, Individual Differences, and Worker Responses. *Psychological Bulletin,* 1968, 69:41–55.

Indik, B. P. Some Effects of Organization Size on Member Attitudes and Behavior. *Human Relations,* 1963, 16:369–384.

Jahoda, M. *Current Concepts of Positive Mental Health.* New York: Basic Books, 1958.

Jackson, E. F. Status Consistency and Symptoms of Stress. *American Sociological Review,* 1962, 27:469–480.

Kahn, R. L. The Meaning of Work: Interpretation and Proposals for Measurement. In *The Human Meaning of Social Change,* A. A. Campbell and P. E. Converse, eds. New York: Russell Sage Foundation, 1972.

————. The Work Module: A Proposal for the Humanization of Work. In *Work and the Quality of Life,* J. O'Toole ed. Cambridge, Mass.: The MIT Press, 1974, pp. 199–226.

Kahn, R. L., and R. P. Quinn. Role Stress: A Framework for Analysis. In *Mental Health and Work Organizations,* A. A. McLean, ed. Chicago: Rand McNally, 1970, pp. 50–115.

Kahn, R. L., D. M. Wolfe, R. P. Quinn, J. D. Snook, and R. A. Rosenthal. *Organizational Stress: Studies in Role Conflict and Ambiguity.* New York: Wiley, 1964.

Kasl, S. V., and S. Cobb. Effect of Parental Status Incongruence and Discrepancy on Physical and Mental Health of Adult Offspring. *Journal of Personality and Social Psychology Monograph,* 1967, 7 (whole No. 642):1–15.

————. Physical and Mental Health Correlates of Status Incongruence. *Social Psychiatry,* 1971, 6:1–10.

Kasl, S. V., and J. R. P. French, Jr. The Effects of Occupational Status on Physical and Mental Health. *Journal of Social Issues,* 1962, 18:67–89.

Katz, D. Survey Research Center: An Overview of the Human Relations Program. In *Groups, Leadership, and Men,* M. Guitzkow, ed. Pittsburgh: Carnegie Press, 1951, pp. 68–85.

Kilpatrick, F., M. Cummings, and M. Jennings. *The Image of the Federal Service.* Washington, D.C.: The Brookings Institution, 1964.

King, N. Clarification and Evaluation of the Two-factor Theory of Job Satisfaction. *Psychological Bulletin,* 1970, 74:18–31.

Kleiner, R. J., and S. Parker. Goal Striving, Social Status, and Mental Disorder. *American Sociological Review,* 1963, 28:189–203.

Kornhauser, A. *Mental Health of the Industrial Worker.* New York: Wiley, 1965.

Langner, T. S. and S. T. Michael. *Life Stress and Mental Health.* New York: The Free Press, 1963.

Lawler, E. E. Job Design and Employee Motivation. *Personnel Psychology,* 1969, 22:426–435.

————. Job Attitudes and Employee Motivation: Theory, Research, and Practice. *Personnel Psychology,* 1970, 23:223–237.

Levinson, H. Various Approaches to Understanding Man at Work. *Archives of Environmental Health,* 1971, 22:612–618.

Lichtmann, C. M., and R. G. Hunt. Personality and Organization Theory: A Review of Some Conceptual Literature. *Psychological Bulletin,* 1971, 76:271–294.

Likert, R. *The Human Organization.* New York: McGraw-Hill, 1967.

Loether, H. J. The Meaning of Work and Adjustment to Retirement. In *Blue Collar World,* A. B. Shostak and W. Gomberg, eds. Englewood Cliffs, N.J.: Prentice-Hall, 1965, pp. 525–533.

Lofquist, L. H., and R. V. Dawis. *Adjustment to Work.* New York: Appleton-Century-Crofts, 1969.

McLean, A. A., and G. C. Taylor. *Mental Health in Industry.* New York: McGraw-Hill, 1958.

Mann, F. C., and L. K. Williams. Some Effects of the Changing Work Environment in the Office. *Journal of Social Issues,* 1962, 18:90–101.

Marcson, S. *Automation, Alienation, and Anomie.* New York: Harper & Row, 1970.

Marks, J., J. Stouffecher, and C. Lyle. Predicting Outcome in Schizophrenia. *Journal of Abnormal Social Psychology,* 1963, 66:117–127.

Martin, A. R. Morale and Productivity: A Review of the Literature. *Public Personnel Review,* 1969, 30:42–45.

Mechanic, D. *Mental Health and Social Policy.* Englewood Cliffs, N.J.: Prentice-Hall, 1969.

Meltzer, H. Mental Health Implications of Aging in Industry. *Journal of Genetic Psychology,* 1965, 107:193–203.

Miller, D. R. The Study of Social Relationships: Situation, Identity, and Social Interaction. In *Psychology: A Study of a Science,* S. Koch, ed. New York: McGraw-Hill, Vol. 5, 1963, pp. 639–737.

Morse, N. E., and R. S. Weiss. The Function and Meaning of Work and the Job. *American Sociological Review,* 1955, 20:191–198.

Mott, P. E., F. C. Mann, Q. McLaughlin, and D. P. Warwick. *Shift Work.* Ann Arbor: University of Michigan Press, 1965.

Myers, J. K., and L. L. Bean. *A Decade Later: A Follow-up of Social Class and Mental Illness.* New York: Wiley, 1968.

Neel, R. Nervous Stress in the Industrial Situation. *Personnel Psychology,* 1955, 8:405–416.

Neff, W. S. *Work and Human Behavior.* New York: Atherton Press, 1968.

Neugarten, B. L. Adult Personality: Toward a Psychology of the Life Cycle. In *Middle*

Age and Aging, B. L. Neugarten, ed. Chicago: University of Chicago Press, 1968, pp. 137–147.

Opsahl, R. L., and M. D. Dunnette. The Role of Financial Compensation in Industrial Motivation. *Psychological Bulletin*, 1966, 66:94–118.

Orzack, L. H. Work as a "Central Life Interest of Professionals." *Social Problems*, 1959, 7:125–132.

Parker, S., and R. J. Kleiner. *Mental Illness in the Urban Negro Community*. New York: The Free Press, 1966.

Parsons, T. Definitions of Health and Illness in the Light of American Values and Social Structure. In *Patients, Physicians, and Illness*, E. G. Jaco, ed. Glencoe, Ill.: The Free Press, 1958, pp. 165–187.

Porter, L. W. Job Attitudes in Management: Perceived Deficiencies in Need Fulfillment as a Function of Job Level. *Journal of Applied Psychology*, 1962, 46:375–384.

————. Turning Work into Nonwork: The Rewarding Environment. In *Work and Nonwork in the Year 2001*, M. D. Dunnette, ed. Monterey, Cal.: Brooks/Cole Publishing Co., 1973, pp. 113–133.

Porter, L. W., and E. E. Lawler. Properties of Organization Structure in Relation to Job Attitudes and Job Behavior. *Psychological Bulletin*, 1965, 64:23–51.

Quinn, R. P. Locking-in as a Moderator of the Relationship Between Job Satisfaction and Mental Health. Ann Arbor: Institute for Social Research, University of Michigan, unpublished manuscript, 1972.

Quinn, R. P., S. Seashore, R. L. Kahn, T. Mangione, D. Campbell, G. Staines, and M. McCullough. *Survey of Working Conditions*. Washington, D.C.: U.S. Government Printing Office, Document No. 2916-0001, 1971.

Quinn, R. P., and L. J. Shepard. *The 1972-73 Quality of Employment Survey*. Ann Arbor: Institute for Social Research, University of Michigan, 1974.

Rapoport, R., and R. Rapoport. Work and Family in Contemporary Society. *American Sociological Review*, 1965, 30:381–394.

Robinson, J. P. Occupational Norms and Differences in Job Satisfaction: A Summary of Survey Research Evidence. In *Measures of Occupational Attitudes and Occupational Characteristics*, J. P. Robinson, R. Athanasiou, and K. B. Head, eds. Ann Arbor: Institute for Social Research, University of Michigan, 1969, pp. 25–78.

Sayles, L., and G. Strauss. *Human Behavior in Organizations*. Englewood Cliffs, N.J.: Prentice-Hall, 1966.

Schaffer, R. H. Job Satisfaction as Related to Need Satisfaction in Work. *Psychological Monographs*, 1953, 67 (whole No. 364), No. 14.

Scott, W. A. Research Definitions of Mental Health and Mental Illness. *Psychological Bulletin*, 1958, 55:29–45.

Seeman, M. On the Personal Consequences of Alienation in Work. *American Sociological Review*, 1967, 32:273–285.

Sells, S. B. *The Definition and Measurement of Mental Health*. Washington, D.C.: U.S. Government Printing Office, PHS Publication No. 1873, 1969.

Sexton, W. P. Industrial Work: Who Calls It Psychologically Devastating? *Management of Personnel Quarterly*, 1968, 6:2–8.

Shepard, J. M. *Automation and Alienation.* Cambridge, Mass.: The MIT Press, 1971.

Sheppard, H. L., and N. Q. Herrick. *Where Have All the Robots Gone?: Worker Dissatisfaction in the 70's.* New York: The Free Press, 1972.

Smith, M. B. Mental Health Reconsidered: A Special Case of the Problems of Value in Psychology. *American Psychologist,* 1961, 16:299–306.

Smith, P., L. Kendall, and C. Hulin. *The Measurement of Satisfaction in Work and Retirement: A Strategy for the Study of Attitudes.* Chicago: Rand McNally, 1969.

Srole, L., T. S. Langner, T. S. Michael, M. K. Opler, and T. A. C. Rennie. *Mental Health in the Metropolis: The Midtown Manhattan Study.* New York: McGraw-Hill, 1962.

Strauss, G. Is There a Blue-Collar Revolt Against Work? In *Work and the Quality of Life,* J. O'Tolle, ed. Cambridge, Mass.: The MIT Press, 1974, pp. 40–69.

Streib, G. Morale of the Retired. *Social Problems,* 1956, 3:270–276.

Super, D. E. Vocational Adjustment: Implementing a Self-Concept. *Occupations,* 1951, 30:88–92.

———. The Definition and Measurement of Early Career Behavior: A First Formulation. *Personnel and Guidance Journal,* 1963, 41:775–788.

Super, D. E., and J. O. Crites. *Appraising Vocational Fitness.* New York: Harper and Row, 1962.

Tausky, C., and E. B. Peidmont. The Meaning of Work and Unemployment. Implications for Mental Health. *International Journal of Social Psychiatry,* 1867/68, 14:44–49.

Taylor, H. C. *Occupational Sociology.* New York: Oxford University Press, 1968.

Triandis, H. C. Work and Nonwork: Intercultural Perspectives. In *Work and Nonwork in the Year 2001,* M. D. Dunnette, ed. Monterey, Cal.: Brooks/Cole Publishing Co., 1973, pp. 29–52.

Turner, A. N., and P. R. Lawrance. *Industrial Jobs and the Worker: An Investigation of Response to Task Attributes.* Cambridge, Mass.: Harvard University Press, 1965.

Veroff, J., and S. Feld. *Marriage and Work in America: A Study of Motives and Roles.* New York: Van Nostrand Reinhold, 1970.

Veroff, J., S. Feld, and G. Gurin. Dimensions of Subjective Adjustment. *Journal of Abnormal Social Psychology,* 1962, 64:192–205.

Vroom, V. H. *Some Personality Determinants of the Effects of Participation.* Englewood Cliffs, N.J.: Prentice-Hall, 1960.

———. *Work and Motivation.* New York: Wiley, 1964.

———. Industrial Social Psychology. In *The Handbook of Social Psychology,* Vol. V, *Applied Social Psychology,* G. Lindzey and E. Aronson, eds. Reading, Mass.: Addison-Wesley, 1969, pp. 196–268.

Wilensky, H. L. Varieties of Work Experience. In *Man in World at Work,* H. Borow, ed. Boston: Houghton-Mifflin, 1964, pp. 125–154.

———. The Problem of Work Alienation. In *Industrial Organizations and Health,* Vol. I, *Selected Readings,* F. Baker, P. J. McEwan, and A. Sheldon, eds. London: Tavistock Publications, 1969, pp. 550–567.

Wilson, W. Correlates of Avowed Happiness. *Psychological Bulletin,* 1967, 67:294–306.

Wrenn, C. G. Human Values and Work in American Life. In *Man in World at Work,* H. Borow, ed. Boston: Houghton-Mifflin, 1964, pp. 24–44.

Zaleznik, A., J. Ondrack, and A. Silver. Social Class, Occupation, and Mental Illness. In *Mental Health and Work Organizations,* A. A. McLean, ed. Chicago: Rand McNally, 1970, pp. 116–142.

Zander, A., and R. Quinn. The Social Environment and Mental Health: A Review of Past Research at the Institute for Social Research. *Journal of Social Issues,* 1962, 18:48–66.

PART 3

What Is the Current State of Organizational Art and Science, and What Is Its Potential for Effecting Work Humanization?

THE ARTICLES PRESENTED IN PART I OF THIS BOOK EXAMINE FROM PHILOSOPH-
ical and theological perspectives man's relationship to the activity commonly
referred to as work. In Part II, the authors traced a number of historical and
contemporary concerns for the dysfunctional outcomes which have emanated
from this relationship, observing that concern for and awareness of these
consequences parallel the revolutionary adjustments of the industrial age and
accelerate with the advancement of inquiry into the sources of man's behavior. These discussions have brought into focus the pressing issues of
worker alienation, job dissatisfaction, and diminished mental health. Having
identified the nature and scope of these effects, it becomes imperative to
examine ways of bringing about change in the relationship between man and
work so as to minimize work's dehumanizing aspects. While agreement as to
the sources, nature, extent, and impact of dehumanizing work is difficult to
attain, agreement regarding what should be done is equally elusive. Management, labor, government, and academia all offer diverse, and often contradictory, proposals based upon their own needs, motives, interests, values, and
concerns. The series of articles comprising this third section (1) offer and
examine a number of programs and proposals for work restructuring, having
as their central focus the humanization of work, and (2) evaluate the past or
potential effects of these change efforts.

In the first article, Ted Mills reviews current developments in the European movement toward ''industrial democracy.'' Although one aspect of the
movement (shop-floor democracy) parallels many American experiments in

work redesign, the other face of the movement (co-determination) is uniquely European and offers a startling contrast to the "American way of business." The impact of this movement is yet unclear: The only apparent certainty is its short history of phenomenal growth, an occurrence which has been for the most part ignored in the U.S. Much of the movement's growth can be attributed to its ability to secure the backing of all critical constituencies: government, labor, and management. In some respect it is clear that what has taken place in Europe has occurred there because of its predominantly socialistic character. Whether or not these advances in work humanization would thrive or even survive under different political perspectives and philosophies is uncertain. Nevertheless, these European developments offer a great deal of food for thought for American business practice.

In the second article in this section, William Sexton calls for work humanization through a program called "growth management." Sexton not only contends that work can and should be redesigned, but he proposes that the worker be an integral part of that redesign process. Joint cooperation in this regard will not only make work more meaningful to the employee, but will increase productivity by establishing congruence between the worker's developmental needs and the objectives of management. Additionally, Sexton sees the need for a greater legitimization of management if the worker is to accept management's objectives as his own. That is, managers must function in such a way as to demonstrate their expertise, intelligence, ability, ethics, etc. Episodes of unethical corporate conduct and gross mismanagement, Sexton concludes, are among the surest attacks upon the work ethic.

David Bowers, in the third presentation, examines a panorama of management efforts intended to improve the quality of work life and concludes that substantive efforts in this regard have come to a virtual standstill. Many attempts to humanize work via work redesign, de-statused organizations, socio-technically designed plants, innovative union-management efforts, etc., have either failed, evolved back into more traditional forms, or have been reduced or eliminated by short-run economic phenomena. He attributes the current state of affairs to several factors: (1) overstating the benefits which realistically could be derived from these programs (i.e., generation of unrealistic expectations), (2) failure to fit the program to the need (i.e., overapplication of single treatments), (3) inadequate sensitivity to organizational value structures, and (4) short-term management perspectives with respect to program financing. The view of work humanization as presented by Bowers need not lead one, however, to undue pessimism. For from these failures, Bowers points out, much was learned about designing and implementing planned interventions for change, particularly about the limits and constraints of change.

In the next article, Irving Bluestone delineates the role labor might play in effecting work humanization. Bluestone characterizes past and present management practices as paternalistic and authoritarian and places a great deal of the cause for this condition on the relativistic nature of management reporting and control systems. Recognizing the need for union-management cooperation to effect change, Bluestone describes a number of such efforts which have been initiated jointly by the United Auto Workers and General Motors. Although Bluestone is convinced that union interest and action in the area of organization development and work life quality is both warranted and necessary, his views are not widely shared among other union leaders. Even within the U.A.W., Bluestone suggests, "higher priorities" keep taking time away from these programs.

A number of the articles in this section criticize directly, or allude to, the inhibiting effects that current management reporting and control systems have upon efforts to humanize work. The fifth article in this section, by Ken Milani, explores developments in alternative reporting and control systems which allow for the measurement and assessment of changes in the value of the human resource. Because of considerable disagreement and debate among academicians, accountants, managers, etc., over the definition, methodologies, and ethics of human resource accounting (HRA) systems, Milani concludes that HRA to date has had little impact upon managerial decision making and work humanization efforts. Nevertheless, he suggests that the coming generation of accountants will be more interested in and equipped for integrating traditional accounting goals and practices with the goals of work humanization.

In the postscript, Gary Gemmill examines the repressive and stultifying characteristics and effects that are exhibited by contemporary organizational structures and processes. Efforts to resolve these conditions, Gemmill points out, have been inhibited by the desire for simple, painless, magical solutions and by a lack of awareness of viable alternatives to our present way of organizing work. The author calls for a more systemic approach, having as its nucleus the concept of the "person-centered organization." This orientation does not suggest that organizational structure, technology, the economic system, the group, or the individual himself are no longer appropriate targets for change. Rather, Gemmill suggests that these factors must be considered as interdependent elements in a systemic effort to effect change which encourages the development of human potential. He calls, therefore, for expanded experimentation in employing combinations of change strategies and targets on a planned, system-wide basis. These efforts, however, if they are to be effective, must provide a basis for clarifying values and for raising into awareness the value decisions implicit in the actions which we undertake.

Leadership from Abroad: European Developments in Industrial Democracy

by Ted Mills

THERE IS OCCURRING IN EUROPE TODAY A MOVEMENT THAT PORTENDS AS significant a change in the economic structure of Europe as anything, perhaps, that has occurred in this century. The movement to which I am alluding is variously referred to, but in Europe it is called "industrial democracy." The events which have swept Europe over the last five years have been nothing short of phenomenal. Yet I believe that in the years ahead we will see a continuation of the almost exponential growth of this movement. I think, and most of the political observers in Europe agree, that by the end of the decade, or even before, every single country in Europe this side of the Iron Curtain will have some kind of obligatory legislation requiring corporate enterprises to practice industrial democracy in one form or another, from active worker participation on boards to workplace democracy on the shop floor.

Yet one of the most fascinating aspects of the exploding European absorption with industrial democracy is the near total American indifference to the entire movement. Even though what is transmuting European industry is attacking many of the bases of economic free enterprise and the classic notions of the separation of the representational and political democracy from economic structure, these swiftly mounting events have been almost totally unreported and totally undiscussed in this country. And given our traditional American views toward business organization and management, I believe you will be somewhat astounded by some of the things that are happening. No American press or media columnist, no pundit, no political observer in the United States, has even reported on the subject, let alone attempted to assay the significance of what is going on there. The counter-culture press, the so-called minnesingers of workers' rights, has not reported on the extent of the importance of what is happening. Nor has the extreme right press, the Bill Buckleys, cried out in horror over what is occurring. There has been a significant vacuum. And yet I think this movement is an important story of our times. History quite probably will accord far greater significance to the industrial democracy story than, for example, to American intervention in Viet Nam or to the Portuguese revolution. It is a bigger story—a story of capitalism in transition. In countries where it is occurring, it affects the nature, control, and even ownership of private enterprises; the nature, control, power, and bargaining areas of the labor unions; the role of the governmental intervention in hitherto private labor-management matters; the kinds of tasks human beings perform at work; the mix of man-machine functions; conditions, environment, and rewards of work; and the role and contribution and rights of the individual workers or voters in contemporary and future industrial society. I think that the reader will probably agree with me that this involves many aspects of our lives which are of a little more than minor importance. But it is not a story that is easy to tell.

The extent and intensity of the fast-breaking nature of industrial democracy often varies dramatically from one country to another. Political nuances, militants, and ideologies, the strength of the labor movement, the economic health of the industrial machine, the attitudes and power of the workers and the political parties vary enormously from Sweden, to Britain, to France, to other countries. Further, truly meaningful representation of what has happened, and what is happening, even in a single country would require more than could be developed adequately in a book.[1] Therefore, at the risk of leaving out much of interest and importance (such as, for example, examining the operation of works councils in Yugoslavia behind the Iron Curtain), I will attempt to sketch in as much detail as possible what is happening and some notions as to why. At best, what I am presenting is no more than a survey of a profound social, political, and economic upheaval which is occurring in the fabric of Western society, starting in Europe.

Signposts of Reform

Let us examine a few signposts of this movement. On December 28, 1975, Robert Sole, the Rome correspondent for Paris's *Le Monde,* the *New York Times* of Paris, reported an announcement made by Italy's large dominant one-and-a-half million member metallurgical union, the FLM, to change radically that union's position toward the public and private enterprises with which it bargains. Headlined ''Italian Union Proposes a Comanagement Program," Mr. Sole's story suggested that the union's new position or platform was "revolutionary in many aspects for all the thousands of managements with whom the union bargains, including a company named Fiat." Noting with French delicacy that the decision engendered a certain emotion among Italian management, Mr. Sole suggested that they perceived the decision would change significantly, if not destroy, the existing Italian economic structure. "To accept the union's new stand would," the Italian managers said, "be equivalent to suicide." What had the FLM decided? Only, said Mr. Sole (because he's French), such little things as worker participation in dozens of management decisions including (1) all corporate investments, (2) utilization of manual workers, (3) decentralization of production, (4) temporary layoffs, (5) internal mobility of jobs, (6) the impact of technological change upon workers, (7) the conditions and organization of work, and (8) job classifications and qualifications. "All programs of change of large enterprise of national character will henceforth be bargained, nationally and locally, and their effect on work, worker mobility, and qualifications will be included from now on, in the collective bargaining process." Knowing the tremendous power exerted by the FLM in Italian labor and politics, and seeing in the announcement that the union fully intended to use the strike and refusal to work overtime as weapons to get these new contracts, Italian businessmen, Mr. Sole said, were not hiding their uneasiness.

Just eight months earlier in Paris, the moderate-to-right new government of Valery Giscard d'Estaing, after months of preparation, issued its now famous in Europe, "Sudreau Report" on the reform of French capitalism, which they called *Reform de l'entreprise*. The startling sixty-nine proposition report, prepared by a tripartite commission, was a fulfilling of a Giscard campaign promise to the eternally suspicious French electorate. It generated an explosion of outraged, delighted, and pensive reaction in the volatile French press, in volume and shrillness not unlike the American press reaction to the Rockefeller Commission report on the CIA. Many of the areas examined in the report, which in France is clearly an invitation to new legislation, were not new in political life. The predecessor Pompedieu government had pushed through the legislature a multitude of reforms of business conduct. These reforms, for example, strengthened France's mandatory profit-sharing system (which had already been in effect for six years), required participation of workers and managers together in a law so loose that both management and labor decided to forget it, etc.

The proposals of the Sudreau Report, however, were more specific and encompassing, including such recommendations as the following: compulsory one-third employee representation on all corporate supervisory boards; compulsory management transmission to employees of information on working conditions; compulsory restructuring of management; tight, new political check reins by labor on management's right to manage; etc. This was new. Predictably, the French communists and their union confederation, the CGT (*Confédération Generale du Travail*), screamed "foul," because *reform* of the system they wanted to overthrow was obviously a dirty trick. Also predictably, most noncommunist labor unions, including the CFDT (*Confédération Française Democratique du Travail*), and most socialist politicians and commentators purred, but with the reservations the French feel are always necessary. But less predictably, a sizeable number of pin-striped French business leaders, who often run their companies like monarchies, as well as Giscard's equally pin-striped key ministers, seemed to feel (when willing to be quoted) that it was high time that this kind of thing take place in France. Pierre Sudreau himself, Giscard's minister of labor, stated, "The justification for the reform of business must be sought less in the deficiencies of businesses' current results, than in the movement of society itself. It is because of the rapid mutations of industrial society that we must speed the mutation of enterprise."

Ivon Chauntare, who is vice-president of the powerful employer's group, *Le Conseil National de Patronat Français* (CNPF), the equivalent of the National Association of Manufacturers, said pompously, "I find our CNPF position well represented in the Sudreau Report." Even the French prime minister chipped in to the approving chorus. "Participation," he said, "is the only key which permits a modern society of free men."[2]

Exactly two weeks before the Sudreau Report hit the headlines, a highly similar tripartite government commission, in the Ministry of Labor in Sweden, issued its even more surprising "Democracy at the Place of Work Report," which the London *Financial Times* in March characterized as "one which would seem wholly revolutionary in any other modern society." The Swedish All-Party State Commission, like the French Sudreau Commission, was comprised of representatives of management, labor, and government. And like the French report, the Swedish report was signed by the minister of labor. The Swedish report, even more certain to become law than the Sudreau Report, recommends historic legislation which will require all Swedish public and private managements to bargain with unions before making decisions of any nature in the management of Swedish enterprise. Even the Swedish press noted that not since 1938, when Swedish unions classically traded off management's right to manage for the union's right to collective bargaining, had so drastic a proposal been made in Sweden or anywhere in the world. Specifically, the proposed law gives workers (through the union) the right to negotiate over the "management and assignment of the work, the establishment of employment agreements, or other aspects of company management." A demand to negotiate on such matters must be made during regular wage talks. Employers must offer to negotiate on important company moves (e.g., shutdowns, expansions, sale of assets, etc.) before decisions are made. Although still under discussion, almost all observers, including Olaf Palme, Sweden's prime minister, expect that its precepts will become the law of the land sometime during 1977. In a recent interview in the *New York Times,* Palme (in what is perhaps one of the understatements of the year) said, "We are at just the beginning of major developments toward the rights of employees to influence decisions at work."

What I have presented are three random signposts—three 1975 events selected from the chronicle of industrial democracy on the rise in Europe. They are just three of innumerable similar and related stories which poured out of Sweden, Norway, Denmark, Britain, Holland, Portugal, France, Ireland, and even Luxembourg in just 1975 alone. Each month my office gets from a clipping service a packet of clippings in the category "worker participation." Our packet from France each month is about two inches thick. The same is true of clippings from Britain, from Germany, and from Scandanavia. (Incidentally, from the United States the packet is about a quarter of an inch thick.) As one example, throughout 1975 the German press was filled with stories of the political furor over "Mitbestimmung"—worker equality or participation. But the debate is not over whether they should have industrial democracy; rather it is over where they should have it—boardroom or workplace, or both—and how much of it there should be. The current debate is whether there should be 33 percent workers on all boards of directors or 50 percent.

The monthly British packet was consistently thick with reports and editorials about the mounting demand by leftist British union leaders (notably Jack Jones[3] of the Trades Union Congress, Britain's equivalent of our own AFL-CIO) for German-style legislation by the British Parliament assuring British workers 50 percent parity on all boards of all British enterprises, public and private. One clipping quotes a leading British industrialist who said, "British management is resigned to the inevitability of such legislation."

The packets from each of the other European countries told similar and different stories about various aspects of the mounting attention and clamor for the new workers' rights in today's industrial society and what Europeans are doing actively and reactively about it. One French clipping aptly described the rising phenomenon as the "new social frontier" of this century.

Early Catalysts of the Current Scene

If you move backwards in time from 1975, when interest and activity in industrial democracy really began to peak, and wade through the morass of political, industrial, and intellectual outpourings on the subject, you begin to discern some of the seminal events, movements and theories, and legislation and activities which lit the fire and fed its flames in this decade. Certainly one of these was the mid-1972 decision by Volvo, Sweden's largest company, with no government intervention whatsoever, to build its now famed automobile assembly plant at Kalmar. It was conceived and executed, with worker help incidentally, to make automobile production work no longer a dirty word among Swedish workers as it had become. It was, in fact, nearly impossible to get a Swede to work in an automobile plant (close to 45 percent of the employees of the car assembly plant were non-Swedes). Labor had to be imported from Finland, from Greece, or from Turkey. Volvo's $20 million investment in this new experimental plant was intended partially to entice Swedes back into Volvo's family, and hopefully reduce, or eliminate, absenteeism which had been running around 20 to 25 percent and worker turnover up to 30 to 40 percent annually.[4] The Kalmar story, however, was probably truly no more seminal, except in its publicity, than what has happened since in a dozen or more other similar undertakings across Europe. The Imperial Chemical Company in England is far more advanced in humanistic work design than many large corporations in the United States. So is Kockums Shipyard in Sweden, Olivetti in Italy, and Germany's Bosch and Volkswagen. They are all doing things which in this country would be considered revolutionary, all without government pressure or intervention.

Although many disagree, there seems to be little question that the research conducted during the 1960s by Einar Thorsrud of the tiny Norwegian Work Research Institute provided a profound pioneering influence for the quality of work life movement being evidenced throughout Europe today. Using theoretical notions about people at work in technological environments, many of which were developed by Eric Trist and Fred Emery of Britain's Tavistock Institute, this Norwegian research group, with labor-business-government sanction and funding, conducted in Norwegian industry a series of what now seem to be tiny labor-management experiments testing alternative organizational forms and their impact on employee participation.[5] But in many ways these experiments set the scene for the development of another face of the industrial democracy movement—shop-floor democracy. Only a few years later, aspects of this movement were to be adopted by as distant a sponsor as Detroit's United Automobile Workers in their 1973 bargaining with General Motors. But again, Thorsrud's contribution was only one of hundreds of other similar, if less publicized, intellectual and theoretical contributions from all over Europe.

However, the most significant and critical event or signpost of this decade was the Works' Constitution Act, passed by a very large majority of the German Bundestag in 1972. Many people in Europe today, and particularly a number in the European Economic Community (Common Market) believe that this act (and its many repercussions across Europe) was a major impetus to what has happened in Europe since. Its focus on works councils was nothing new or revolutionary. Works councils—employee meetings to discuss work problems—have been kicking impotently around Europe for five decades, with little power or significance of any kind. What was new in the law, and was to some critics revolutionary, was that the works councils were now *required* by federal law, a condition which had not existed previously. The new law was a key plank in the social platform of the Social Democratic Party (SPD), under Willy Brandt, and was in its content much influenced by the theoretical writings of France's Marxist (but anti-Stalinist) André Gorz. The act imposed a mandatory works council on every German enterprise with more than five employees. Each such council, comprised solely of employees, but presided over by a manager, was legally empowered among other provisions to (1) be both consulted and informed on any contemplated change in working hours, wages, and salaries; (2) be both consulted and informed on any issues relating to professional advancement and compensation policies, with full and open access to and disclosure of every employee's personnel file; (3) approve or veto all hirings, transfers, and promotions of employees, and in the event of veto, to demand the employer gain a labor court decision overriding the veto; (4) permit union officials open access to the company's premises and to participate in all works councils deliberations; and (5) establish an economic council in every company with more than 100 employees, whose members are not only allowed but required to be told about anything relating to planned mergers, curtailments, shut-down, change in economic policy, as well as the company's investment plans and financial status. This was quite an assemblage of factors. Although hailed by German management and the conservative Christian Democratic Union (CDU) as crippling, disastrous, communist, etc., the provisions were rigorously enforced, and are being so today. Yet curiously, the new law had no perceptible braking effect whatsoever on the soaring German economy and its productivity rate, which continued to rise without a single downward deviation from its upward curve. In addition, foreign investment in German industry increased by over $600 million from 1972 to 1975.

Underlying Forces for Work Reform

Examined in their totality, this multitude of signposts reflects a growing infatuation in Europe with industrial democracy. But even more importantly, they reveal four basic forces underlying the clamor. It is important to examine and understand these causal phenomena because many may be present in this country today.

One force was political in nature, pushed primarily by socialists and left-of-center (but always anticommunist) labor and political leaders. A second was an industrial or economic force, spurred by innovative and socially aware management, and occasionally by unions seeking to mutate with the times. A third was an intellectual and theoretical force, pushed by such research pioneers as Norway's Thorsrud, Britain's Emery and Trist, and from the United States: Maslow, McGregor, Herzberg, Argyris, and Walton. The shaping influence of these American researchers, particularly Herzberg, is probably greater in Europe than it is has yet been in the United States.

The fourth discernible force is the one that I want to focus on because I think it is the most important. American Daniel Bell has labeled it the "revolution of rising entitlements" throughout Western capitalist and democratic worlds. The French call it egalitarianism. But by whatever label it is known, it began to emerge in the third or postwar quarter of the twentieth century, with an almost equal growth surge in every society within the capitalist world. In Tokyo as in Stuttgart, in Lyons as in Detroit, in Hamburg as in Liverpool, its many-headed manifests are all too familiar: growing public distaste, disrespect, and disillusionment with traditional institutions and their leadership; growing aberrant social behavior, including crime and drug abuse, divorce, sexual deviance, alienation, loss of will to work (or what the French call *je mon feutism*); new demands for participative rights of every kind including women's rights, ethnic and minority rights, sexual and homosexual rights, workers' rights, and in France and Italy today soldiers' rights.

Some protagonists of the revolution of rising entitlements would wholeheartedly agree with critic John Simon, who wrote recently that we are laboring under the delusion that humanism has outlived itself, when in fact the only trouble with it is that it has not yet wholly caught on. Yet in both the United States and in Europe there is a growing angry reaction against this trend. Even in the liberal establishment, which a decade ago would have been cheering it on, many have begun to identify it as "humanism gone amuck," democratic permissiveness become license to steal, human selfishness gone out of control, and to some doom-singers, the appalling terminal unraveling of democracy. One observer has called it the "I want mine" revolution of our time.

Yet, despite the battering of economic downturn, inflation, energy shortages, and alarming unemployment in Europe during 1974 and 1975, which one might think would dampen popular European clamor for social change, it has grown in almost every European society. Like Mount Everest, it's there; but unlike Everest, it's growing.

Some French and British observers, watching the various socialist or labor or democratic parties subsume this clamor into their political platforms, have remarked that the identification of the industrial democracy movement with socialism is more nearly expedient than it is politically revelant to socialism. In many European countries one can perceive the anomaly of socialism preaching state ownership of enterprise out of one side of its mouth and advocating industrial democracy within existing capitalist structures out of the other side. Now this fourth force behind industrial democracy has a larger social impact than just its manifestation in the workplace. Or put conversely, rising new workers' demands that are occurring in every country in Europe for increased influence in economic decision-making are manifest of something larger in contemporary society, something which includes the new sexual, ethnic, family, class, and geographic freedoms we are witnessing. You might say that the "revolution of rising entitlements," with its clamor for increased popular participation in everything in Europe, from church to army, has finally turned its focus to battering at the doors of the last redoubt of European authoritarianism—the capitalist workplace. And in so doing, it has affected, if not infected, each of these other social areas I have cited.

The Two Faces of Industrial Democracy

You may note that I have not yet cited democracy as a force. The reason for this is that despite the increased use of the term "democracy" in almost every European country, real democracy in the workplace (or government of the people, by the people, and for the people of an economic institution) is nowhere an announced goal of even the most militant activists. Perhaps, in order to best understand what industrial democracy means, we should look toward its definition. If you asked a Norwegian or a Dutch or a Portuguese or a German worker, or a Danish labor leader, what industrial democracy is, means, and seeks, you would receive a mystifying assortment of contradictory answers. They would range from "humanization of work" to "shop floor participation in decision-making" to "worker membership on boards" to "outright worker ownership of enterprise," to the definition we heard earlier, "capitalist suicide."

Yet most would agree with some common aspects in that term. Most, for example, would agree that whatever semantic costume it might wear, its goals are more nearly social than economic. Its objective, quite unlike those of Marx, does not derive from economic misery; nor did the recession and inflation in Europe seem to have any direct correlation with that sudden surge of industrial democracy clamor in 1975. Another common notion with which most agree is that in whatever form it appears, increased worker participation, or voice, or involvement in the destiny of the economic organization is its essential end. Yet another feature is that in all its manifestations (outside of Yugoslavia at least) it is profoundly anticommunist. Yet, as perceived by almost all of its European protagonists and opponents as well, when stripped of all the persiflage, the term "industrial democracy" suggests one of two fairly definable structures, neither of which is truly new under the European sun.

The first meaning of the term, widely perceived throughout Europe, is active employee participation in the direction of public and private enterprises through employee representation on the boards of directors, ranging from 30 to 50 percent of all positions. This version of the term used to be called "codetermination," a view increasingly less descriptive of the emerging industrial democracy movement. The second meaning of industrial democracy is greater employee participation and influence in decisions affecting *their* work and its rewards in *their* workplace. This version is frequently characterized by the term "shop-floor democracy." Increasingly in Europe as in the United States, the term "quality of working life" is also being used as a descriptor of industrial democracy's multifaceted work reform objectives.

Codetermination (and I think this is fascinating), was introduced into Europe by the occupying powers in Germany following World War II. Afraid that the Nazis would regain strength in the coal and steel industries—which were symbolic of Germany's industrial and military power and which had especially close relations with Hitler—these industries were to be weakened as a safeguard against resurgence in their former role. The execution of this decision fell initially to the British, whose occupation zone included the Ruhr Valley, center of these industries. Hans Böckler, head of the newly established postwar labor movement, suggested, and the British occupation authorities agreed, that a system of worker comanagement would fit in nicely with these goals since the German workforce was largely anti-Nazi in its composition. Thus, workers were assigned to workers' boards, thereby becoming 50 percent "owners" of the critical coal and steel industries. The Allied occupying powers essentially gave birth to codetermination in Europe.

Many people in Europe still considered that experiment as totally cosmetic. But whatever its effect may have been (incidentally there is no research that I am aware of relating how this has affected the German coal and steel industries, except that it did not prevent German coal and steel enterprises from massive two-decade resurgence to world domination), it is probably safe to say that at least ideologically, codetermination poses more problems to labor than it does to management. For one thing, as you keep hearing in Germany, if half the board is composed of "brothers" from your union, who are you going to bargain with? For another, most unions in the world are understandably leery of assuming any responsibility for management of the enterprises with which they have contracts. They prefer the solid, traditional notion of "let management manage, and we'll grieve." Codetermination implies at least some kind of responsibility from those workers who are sitting on that board, directing the destiny of the enterprise, and as a result (as has happened in Germany), they "become" management and often become hated by their worker brothers.

Codetermination poses a number of other serious problems as well to both sides. One problem is how, by any stretch of the imagination, could six or seven or eight workers on a board really democratically represent a work force of ten thousand. In democratic terms it can be argued that that is absolute, sheer sham. Another problem occurs in companies dealing with perhaps ten, twenty, or thirty different competing worker units. Who is going to get those eight or nine positions on the board? Another cause of concern, voiced by both unions and management, is whether or not organizations can avoid turning the corporate boardroom into a new kind of bargaining table. Still another side of the issue, affecting particularly the multinationals in Europe, was recently voiced by Sir Reay Geddes, chairman of the multinational Dunlop Holdings Ltd. He asked, "If you have operations in a dozen countries, how do you select a worker, from what country, and who appoints them, and how are they... ?" This he concluded is absolute idiocy.

In answer to these and the many other problems posed by codetermination, and in response to mounting awareness of the critically accelerating demands in every country for industrial democracy, the Common Market has proposed that all European industry adopt what is called a two-tier system of management. Going on three years worth of the German and other experiences with this form, the two-tier approach suggests that all EEC companies move toward two governing boards. One is called the "supervisory board." It would be comprised of 50 percent workers' representatives and 50 percent representatives of ownership interests, like bankers, chairmen of other enterprises, etc. It would be in function very much like our own boards of directors. The other tier is called the "management board." It would be comprised entirely of management (no worker representatives) and would be responsible for the day-to-day management of the company. Under this arrangement, the supervisory board, like the U.S. board of directors, establishes policy, earnings goals, investments, allocation of resources, and the like, and then transmits these goals and policies down to the second, pure management board, for implementation and action. It should be noted, however, that despite a lack of direct representation on the management board, workers would not be without influence since, as proposed, each supervisory board (comprised of 50 percent worker representatives) would appoint the members of its respective management board. In both cases, members would be nominated to hold office for a period not exceeding six years.

It is felt by the codetermination advocates in almost every country that this face of industrial democracy should be *imposed* on industry. In other words, everywhere this first "face" appears as an issue, advocates are saying: "We have to pass a law. We can't get it any other way." So they legislate the form politically. However, this is not true of the second "face," or shop-floor democracy. One of the problems with this latter form is that it is extremely difficult to identify legislation by which it can be effected. This may be one of the reasons that with respect to shop-floor democracy the general role of government has been supportive and stimulative, rather than legislative.

To describe and elaborate upon what is meant by shop-floor democracy, I would like to cross the ocean back to this side and describe some of the experiments that are going on in the United States with which my organiza-·tion, the National Quality of Work Center (NQWC), is deeply involved. Although we do not call the process shop-floor democracy (that term would probably scare most American managements), what is being done here is very similar to what is happening in Europe, but only in this shop-floor democracy aspect. The NQWC is presently supporting seven highly diverse projects. For example, one is a hospital; one is a coal mine; one is a group of engineers in the Tennessee Valley Authority; another is a group of lumberjacks in a sawmill. They are intentionally quite different.

Basically what we propose, as they propose in Europe, is joint ownership of the projects undertaken by unions and by management. By joint ownership I mean that both union and the management are jointly responsible for, and involved in, what takes place. Second, we call the undertakings "experimental." Third, we try to have as diverse a group of organizations as we can. And fourth, we attempt to undertake the projects in places that will lead to a high degree of visibility, such as the Weyerhaeusers, the General Motors, etc. What we do, and all we do, in the case of my organization, is insist that workers and managers join together in labor-management committees and be allowed, *officially allowed,* by management and by labor, to investigate the problems of that workplace and ways by which a greater quality of working life can be provided. There are almost fifty different things that those committees have studied. The list includes, for example, eliminating supervisors and forming autonomous work teams, examining new technology and its impact on the work force, etc. They make these decisions jointly. And in my opinion, this is what industrial democracy really means to the people on the work floor, the people who are doing it. These meetings are held on company time. In our TVA project, for example, a participant in that project, which is about a year old, told me that approximately fourteen thousand man-hours were logged last year in this type of participatory activity.

Summary and Conclusions

In closing, I would like to return to a question I brought up earlier. We have been skimming over the topic of industrial democracy in Europe, and it is very important to ask at this stage, "Are they really talking about democracy?" John Dewey in defining political democracy, once said:

> The foundation of democracy is faith in the capacities of human nature, faith in human intelligence, and in the power of pooled and cooperative experience. It is not belief that these things are complete, but that if given a show, they will grow, and be able to generate progressively the knowledge and wisdom needed to guide collective action.

For all the robustious politicking of the Right and Left today in Europe and in this country, for all the so-called shackling codetermination legislation passed and to be passed, and for all the multinamed adventures in shop-floor participation, if the collective goal is really having faith in human nature and human intelligence in the workplace, and faith in "pooled and cooperative experience" to generate progressively the knowledge and wisdom required for the direction of economic enterprises, then what is happening in Europe is highly desirable. If the limited (not truly democratic) forms and structures developed to date are only a beginning, an opening, and if as structures they remain open and not closed systems, with stochastic potential for never-ending human evolution of those structures, based always on faith in human beings and their endless potential to learn and grow, then what is happening (so fast and perhaps so dangerously in Europe) could be the first, tentative, awkward step toward a new kind of democracy. It could be a democracy as newly valid and applicable in the economic sphere as we have considered it valid in the political sphere for a bicentennial of years.

However, these are strong "ifs." Certainly the reality is that, so far, most protagonists of the codetermination form in Europe are seeking not democracy, but naked power; not faith in human nature and intelligence, but greater entitlement; not pooled and cooperative human experience in learning, but status. They are fired, I think, less by faith in human beings, than by an angry reaction to the traditional power structure. And most protagonists of even shop-floor democracy seek relief from tedium, escape from work brutality, and a greater piece of the economic pie in the best "I want mine" tradition. There are many, however, like Thorsrud in Norway, who would define shop-floor democracy in nearly the exact terms that Dewey put down. Faith in the common man and his intelligence and ability, through cooperation, to contribute to economic performance underlies almost all the theoretical writings about shop-floor democracy. Yet in a world which has only imperfectly imbibed political democracy as a faith and not just a form, it is naive to believe that what is happening so fast in Europe is democratic in the sense that Jefferson or Dewey might perceive it. Wouldn't it be wiser to be skeptical and put it down as simply more entitlement hunting, a nice term to mask greed and lust for power? The answer, of course, is that I don't know, and I don't think anybody else knows. But perhaps, as John Simon has suggested, it just hasn't quite caught on yet. Perhaps all the furor in Europe over workers on boards and shop-floor democracy is European society beginning to catch on a little. Perhaps worker participation is an expression of European worker faith in the democratic process of growing and learning in "pooled and cooperative experience."

One thing is certain. There are profound portents for American society in what is happening so fast in Europe. True, in many respects, our system is different, our labor unions are different, our democracy is different, but for all our inequities, ours is really the most democratic society on earth. Most of us still believe a little of what we were taught to believe about human nature and human intelligence and the miracle of learning. It is not an accident that ours is the most educated society on earth; we venerate learning. We can probably say, with almost absolute certainty, that the American Congress will never legislate works councils or workers' representation on American boards, or require mandatory shop-floor participation. But I think we can also say, and maybe we should say, that even if industrial democracy goes sour in Europe, and does become rigidified into mere cardboard structures, there is certainly, underneath the posturings and the forms, a yearning in the people, perhaps even a faith in the people, with which we in the United States can easily identify. So perhaps the portents of industrial democracy in Europe in the 1970s is that someone over there has had an intriguing and quite American idea for us to contemplate right here at home.

EDITORS' NOTES

1. The Swedish "Democracy at the Place of Work Report" is, in itself, 950 pages in length.

2. In order to truly comprehend the profoundness of these proposals and endorsements, one must understand the traditional French perspective toward industrial management. To quote from one postmortem of the 1968 worker-student revolt: "The typical enterprise in France represents a structure not found in any other country: a sort of centralized dictatorship in which the president manages not only the business, but also the bodies which are supposed to act as a check on him, the board of directors and even the general assembly of shareholders." (Club Jean Moulin, *Que Faire de la Révolution de Mai?*, Paris: Editions du Seuil, 1968, p. 39.) David Jenkins (*Job Power*, Baltimore: Penguin Books, 1973) further notes that "the family-controlled company remains an extremely important feature of the industrial scene, and this fact contributes to the parochialism . . . of French managers. In this autocratic context, there is almost a paranoid concern for secrecy, and even so mundane a step as providing minimal information to employees or the public is regarded as exceptionally radical."

3. Next to the prime minister, Jones may well be the most powerful man in the

United Kingdom. His power stems from his enormous popularity among members of his union, prompted in large part by his continuing efforts to give workers a voice in union affairs in industry. Once viewed as a left-wing ideologue, Jones has become far less doctrinaire in recent years. In terms of political philosophy, he is today primarily a realist. He no longer shares many of the views held by such Marxist labor leaders as Hugh Scanlon, head of Britain's second largest labor union.

4. Volvo's Kalmar plant goes a step beyond Saab-Scania's earlier team-based engine production facility in that it attacks directly the favorite object of most alienation literature—the line on which the automobile itself is assembled. Physically, according to Pehr Gyllenhammer, Volvo's managing director, the plant is "shaped like a star and on each point of the star you have a work group finishing a big share of the whole automobile—for example, the electrical system or the safety system or the interior." Assembly takes place along the outer walls, while component parts are stored in the center of the building. Workers are divided up into autonomous teams of 15 to 25 persons. Each group distributes the work among themselves and sets their own pace, subject to the requirement of meeting production standards. A second "experimental" plant—a $30 million engine factory—based on the team concept has also been placed in operation.

5. The socio-technical system approach used by Emery and Trist considers neither the technical nor the human dimension as paramount in designing organizations, but instead focuses on the interaction between the two, in conjunction with considerations of effectiveness. Socio-technical analysis provides a basis to determine the appropriate organizational boundaries for systems containing men, machines and information.

One of the experiments referred to was conducted at Nobø Fabrikker in Trondheim, a maker of heating equipment, steel office furniture, and other fabricated products. At the time the experiment began, operations in the trial department were organized along traditional scientific management principles: each worker had a single, relatively small, fixed job. Workers were reorganized into three groups corresponding to natural work divisions: simple working of steel sheets, surface treatment, and assembly. Within each group workers learned four jobs instead of one, so that they could shift from job to job according to circumstances. The groups were autonomous; there were no foremen or other supervisory personnel, and the workers met each morning to discuss problems, plan production, and assign jobs. Individual piece rates were abolished and a new pay system was established, splitting a group incentive equally among all workers. At the end of a seven month trial period, production of furnaces per man hour had risen more than 20 percent.

Perhaps a more well-known, but similar, undertaking was Nørsk Hydro, one of Norway's major companies with 8,000 employees and interests in power, chemicals, oil, metals, and other fields. Initial efforts were made at the company's fertilizer works in Herøya, which consisted of one established production facility and a new one under construction. Using a "Future Group" (composed of a foreman, a worker representative, a personnel officer, and a researcher) which operated as a liaison between workers, management, the union, and the researchers, a "model" of the ideal organization was developed. As with the Nobø experiment, it was decided that workers should be organized into small autonomous groups, that every worker should master several jobs, etc. A new pay system was again introduced based on the principle of pay for knowledge, not for production. All parties were pleased with the results and after only a few months of operation, reform projects were begun in a carbide plant and a magnesium plant. By 1971, department reorganizations had covered more than 10 percent of the company's employees.

Work Humanization in Practice: What Should Business Do?

by William P. Sexton

> To punish him atrociously, to crush him in such a manner that the most hardened criminal would tremble before such punishment—it would be necessary only to give his works the character of complete uselessness. . . . Let him be constrained in his work as to pour water from one vessel to another and back again, then I am sure that at the end of a short period he would strangle himself or commit a thousand crimes punishable with death rather than live in such an abject condition or endure such treatment.
>
> Dostoevski, *House of the Dead*

IT IS INTERESTING THAT DEHUMANIZATION THROUGH THE PERFORMANCE OF overly specialized work (i.e., work with a high degree of division of labor) was noted by writers such as Dostoevski nearly a century ago. If the cause to which antispecialization advocates are devoted is not realized, it will not be for lack of fervor. Rather, it will be for the lack of consistent evidence or the inability of philosophers, social scientists, and writers to state the case in terms compelling to the businessman. In the first instance, a great deal more empirical analysis must be done before we can state positively the specific manner in which individuals are malaffected by exposure to such work. Secondly, to prompt constructive action from business, antispecialization proponents are compelled to demonstrate the consequences of this malaffectance in terms of productivity, costs, and efficiency.

The Disadvantage of Full Mental Stature

In the first half of this century, a large number of experiments were undertaken to introduce the subnormal (i.e., mentally retarded) to industrial work.

(Davies and Williams, 1961). In the 1940s one major textile manufacturer engaged in a program to test the employment potential of mentally deficient persons whose mental ages ranged from six to ten years. The concern of management was not the mental readjustment potential of such employment; they were interested simply in productivity.

Within a short period of several days, the productivity of the subnormals *equaled* that of the veterans, their "normal" working companions. They were also extremely happy. Managers rated the behavior of the subnormals as superior to that of the "normal" workers: they were more punctual; they were quiet, respectful, well-behaved, and very obedient. To paraphrase the views of several top managers: "From a production point of view, in intellect and ability to perform their work, they were at least equal and in many cases better than our normal workers. We are surprised that these people are classed as subnormals." The point is that persons having a mental age of approximately eight years were as capable in industrial work as their "normal" co-workers. The main difference noted was that these "subnormals" were better adjusted to industrial work. To be sure, no one had anticipated these results. Those responsible for these experiments concluded that the subnormals had the opportunity to employ themselves fully in the tasks to which they were assigned. *They did not suffer the disadvantage of possessing full mental stature.*

The problem is painfully clear: If the mentally deficient can be fitted into industry on an immediate parity with normal employees, on whose level has this equality been achieved? Had the subnormal been uplifted to a higher plane of competence or had those operating "normally" been pulled down to a lower plane? If a boy with a mental age of less than eight years, who also has a severe lack of muscular coordination, can perform most conventional tasks in a manufacturing plant, what were the "normal" workers doing in this process before the crippled and retarded boy came along? I have asked this question of a number of manufacturing managers and all too frequently the response is something like the following:

> So what? We are not here simply to satisfy the employees. We're employed to do one thing, and that's to make a profit. The people who invest their money in our business have the right to the best return we can give them on their dollars. In return, I make a salary, you get products you need for a good life, and employees earn wages to make their lives what they wish. If you are talking about making my employees' work lives better, that's not enough. For one thing, I am not convinced they are unhappy. My people only become unhappy when you come around here telling them they are. Even if they are unhappy, this is not intended to be a recreation center.

Based upon the results of the study cited, the organizational design problem facing business today seems incredibly obvious and simple: Do something quickly and drastically. But to face the problem adequately and realistically will require a thorough and careful examination of several more fundamental questions: Are normal employees truly dissatisfied with highly specialized jobs? Is productivity affected adversely when persons are dissatisfied with highly specialized work? Will persons be more satisfied with enlarged jobs? Will this enlargement of task improve productivity?

If one were to stay strictly with the literature related to *job satisfaction,* one may be persuaded to conclude that most workers are not dissatisfied with their jobs and, therefore, there is no profound problem of design facing business organizations. Robinson and Connors (1963), for example, in a survey of a large number of studies, concluded that global assessments of satisfaction find an average of about 13 percent of respondents dissatisfied with their jobs. It seems to me that a much more reliable indicator of the problem may be the worker's *mental health.* In this regard, today's organizations fare less well. Kornhauser (1965), for example, found that among automobile production workers a mere 18 percent of those engaged in specialized jobs could be considered to have "good mental health." Equating satisfaction with good mental health would be equivalent to saying that all should be contented. But, in fact, the development of such a state might well cause serious performance difficulties. As Lawler (1975) has pointed out, satisfaction is more likely to reduce performance than to increase it. The "contented cow" may be quite difficult to energize. One might speculate that his activation level would be lower and thus the likelihood of his possessing a reasonable level of drive would also be low.

Finally, any good definition of a mentally healthy work situation should include some measurement of existing levels of challenge, stress, and tension. Contemporary views regarding the effects of tension should certainly compel us to take account of the possibility that a certain level of dissatisfaction may be fundamental to *personal growth.* Maslow (1943), for example, has pointed out that mentally healthy individuals are often motivated to seek personal growth and development as a result of *dissatisfaction* with their present state. Blauner (1964) further notes the possible distinction between satisfaction and psychological well-being by noting that "the typical worker in modern industrial society is probably satisfied *and* self-estranged." Perhaps when we consider the results of the Gallup polls of several years back in which 19 percent of all workers expressed dissatisfaction with their jobs, our concern should lie with those 81 percent who did not report being dissatisfied. Thus, if one considers the full implications of traditional work settings, one should reasonably conclude that job satisfaction does play a role in influencing organizational performance, but at best it is a mediating variable of questionable influence. There is a real need for greater attention to issues of mental health and personal growth. However, for a number of reasons, primarily pragmatic (e.g., traditional orientation, measurement development, lack of expertise in "mental health" areas), the principal focus of organizational investigations into areas of worker well-being is likely to remain "job satisfaction."

Psychological Success and Job Demands: A Basic Incongruency?

A popular thesis exists that there is a basic incongruency between a worker's growth and developmental tendencies and the characteristics required of workers for the performance of highly specialized work (i.e., work involving repetition, fixed procedure, a short work cycle, and few skill demands). A strong spokesman for this point of view, Chris Argyris (1957), has characterized such a work environment as "making demands which are at odds with the 'psychological success' of the worker." "Psychological success" is the process by which an individual experiences personal growth and wherein self-esteem is generated. The argument continues that for a person to realize a sense of personal growth—an acceptable level of psychological success—he must experience the *involvement* of himself more fully. He must experience a sense of *self-responsibility* and *self-control,* e.g., defining his own goals. He must enjoy a sense of *commitment,* e.g., perseverance to achieve these goals. He must feel a sense of *accomplishment* and the feeling that he has *utilized* his unique abilities. When these opportunities are denied him, he will become alienated. The ingredients of this alienation have been identified as: (1) powerlessness, i.e., no control of work processes; (2) meaninglessness, i.e., no impact on the nature of the product; (3) isolation, i.e., separation from the social aspects of work; and, (4) self-estrangement, i.e., a depersonalized detachment from the work activity (Blauner, 1964). In the face of this alienation, the worker protests (as in the often cited case of Lordstown) or he stays and makes the necessary adjustment to the unhealthy demands his work situation makes upon him. In this latter case, the worker's alienation reflects itself in absenteeism, increased numbers of grievances, turnover, and diminished productivity.

Empirical evidence to support the Argyrian thesis has been inconsistent at best. Some researchers have found support for the thesis; a like number have failed to find any evidence to support such a view; and a third group have even reported evidence to the contrary. Walker and Marriott (1951), in an exhaustive study of workers in the automobile industry, found 35 percent of the men complained of boredom with their work. In these assembly line plants, feelings ranged from resignation to considerable bitterness. In probably the most widely publicized study of these variables, Walter and Guest

(1952) found positive correlations between measures of turnover, grievances, and absenteeism. Kornhauser, in the study cited earlier, found that indications of poor mental health increased as job level decreased. In other words, the lower the job level (those tending toward simple repetitive activity), the greater was the likelihood of the worker experiencing poor mental health. The evidence from studies of the type cited leads to three conclusions: (1) there is invariably support for the proposition that highly repetitive, fractionated work leads toward increased absenteeism, grievances, and turnover; (2) there is some evidence that mental health is malaffected; and, (3) there is little evidence to support the contention that productivity necessarily is reduced.

There is, however, some evidence to indicate that the thesis may not be substantiated or which at least creates the impression that perhaps the thesis is too simply stated. Kennedy and O'Neill (1958) conducted a study of workers in a variety of job structures. At one end of the job structure continuum were assembly operators who performed highly repetitive, routine, deskilled, and mechanically paced jobs. At the other end were utility men who performed such varied jobs as relief, providing demonstrations for new employees, correcting faults, etc. It was expected that the assembly operators would have less favorable job attitudes than the utility personnel. This was not the case. There were no statistically significant differences in job attitudes between the two employee samples.

In a study conducted within a large firm in the communications and electronics industry, Sexton (1968) similarly investigated worker attitudes across a continuum of jobs of varying structural components. The jobs were classified into job categories from "most structured" to "least structured" based on the extent to which the following variables were present in the job: a prescribed method, repetition, short work-cycle, machine paced, and the absence of skill, challenge, discretion, or control over the pace of work. "Perceived structure" scores were also obtained for persons in the study, based upon their responses to a Likert-type questionnaire in which the worker judged various qualities of work situation. Significant *positive* correlations were found between the measures of structure and levels of felt satisfaction with respect to egoistic needs (i.e., affiliation, autonomy, recognition). However, effectiveness was not found to be related significantly to structure or to any of the egoistic need categories.

Argyris (1959), in a comparison of the attitudes of skilled, semiskilled, and unskilled workers, found that lower-skilled employees held lower estimates of their abilities and wanted to be left alone, to be passive, and to have routine. In a similar study, Turner and Lawrence (1965) noted that participants responded in quite different ways to the same set of conditions. Overall, these researchers found little support for the specialization-dissatisfaction thesis.

Potential Reconciliation: Cosmopolitan-Local
Orientations

Although Turner and Lawrence (1965) found no overall support for the Argyrian thesis, they found that by splitting their sample of workers on the basis of the factory's location they were able to sustain the incongruency hypothesis. Workers from small town settings appeared to be repulsed by the highly-specialized job, but workers from urban settings were not so affected. What their findings seemed to indicate is that if an employee has had the experience of small town or rural living, he is more likely to become alienated to highly ,specialized work. However, if a person has as his prior personal frame of reference a more urbanized setting, he is less likely to be alienated to that same structured job experience. A preliminary reexamination of the data from my own study (Sexton 1968) cited earlier tends to reinforce the conclusion that the town-city dichotomy may well be operating as a moderating variable in the individual's response to highly-specialized work.

What is there about these two different experiences (town-city) that account for the dramatically different reactions of these respective groups? Hulin and Blood (1968) have performed a rather elaborate examination of a number of the studies cited above and more recent experiments into the effectiveness of job enlargement. On the basis of their examination, they have theorized that workers from large cities, confronted with the extremely heterogeneous social cultures that these cities present, fail to develop strong group or subcultural norms and values because of the extreme size and diversity of the city environment. Therefore, they do not respond positively to middle class values related to work. They could be said to be alienated from the work ethic (i.e., positive affect for occupational achievement, belief in the intrinsic value of hard work, striving for attainment of responsible positions, and belief in the work-related aspects of the Protestant ethic).

To test their assumptions, Hulin and Blood studied workers from twenty-one plants whose employees were drawn from surrounding communities. The communities were classified using the Kendall (1963) criterion for community "integration." The principal components of this measure are the extent of urbanization, population density, slums, poverty, and the standard of living. It was hypothesized that workers from more integrated communities (small communities, few slums, etc.) would respond as the Argyris model would predict. That is, workers from integrated communities would be more motivated and would perform better in the large, varied job and would experience greater alienation when subjected to the highly-specialized job. This hypothesis was supported. They also hypothesized that workers from largely nonintegrated communities (large industrialized communities) would not perform well in the large, varied job. Rather, they could be expected to be more motivated and to perform better in the more specialized job. This hypothesis was also supported.

An interesting addendum to this line of thinking can be obtained from Whyte's (1955) earlier profile of the "rate buster." In his analysis of workers involved in a piece rate system, he found that the "rate busters" (those who produced above standards) tended to be from rural or small town backgrounds. Their parents were mainly entrepreneurs or were self-employed. They tended to look to their parents, who were usually Protestant and Republican, for authority sanctions, rather than to their peer group. In contrast to these findings, employees who worked to restrict quotas were more likely to have been reared in large cities and come from working class families who were predominantly Catholic, and Democratic in their political affiliation. They were also likely as a youth to have been a member of a boy's gang. As a consequence of these findings, it has been argued that the former group—those with rural or small town backgrounds—were not alienated from the work ethic and regarded management's norms as legitimate; whereas, the latter group—those from big city environments—rejected these norms and were more influenced by the peer group.

When we couple the results of these studies with some findings and insights from related studies (e.g., Kilbridge 1960; Turner and Michette 1962), we begin to see yet another explanation of the reaction of individuals to highly-specialized jobs which accomodates the consequences of different work value orientations. The individual whose prior community experiences have caused him to become alienated from the work ethic, will realize positive affect from specialized, structured work and will not experience lower levels of satisfaction or lower productivity in such work assignments. This value orientation, reinforced by his work experience in the specialized task, will set a climate in which the goals and methods of the organization and the authority of management will not be accepted as norms. He will be more susceptible to peer influence than those identifying with the work ethic. He will see work generally as having only instrumental value. Additionally, the work value alienated worker will tend to view problems of public concern (e.g., crime, corruption, social injustices, ineffectiveness of public services, etc.) as inevitable, regard himself as powerless in the face of these "realities," and resign himself to noninvolvement.

On the other hand, the work value identified worker is hypothesized to respond in the opposite manner. He will view work as possessing terminal value. That is, he will find personal fulfillment in the performance of the work itself, not solely in the external rewards he receives for its performance. He will value challenging, varied work experiences. He will tend to see management authority as legitimate. He will tend to take action in the face of what he sees as problems of social concern.

Extensions of Work Value Orientation Research

It is my belief, moreover, on the basis of some of these investigations, my own research, and, in particular, studies and experiences in other industries and institutions, that the impact of specialization and of work value orientation is not restricted to line workers in automobile assembly plants. If a job possesses a fixed method, little discretion, little control over performance, and little involvement of the whole person, whether the individual is a white-collar or a blue-collar worker makes little difference. If the individual has cultivated an alienation to the work ethic, wherever and at whatever he works, it may set into motion an unfortunate chain of events.

With the purpose of testing these hypotheses, Chang and Sexton (in a study not yet released) have investigated the effect of work value orientation on the job structure-satisfaction-productivity linkage. Tentative findings support hypotheses related to the role played by an individual's orientation to the work ethic. Specifically, higher levels of productivity were found to be related to (1) a varied, demanding job; (2) the degree of employee control over the work; (3) the employee's belief in the legitimate authority of management; *and,* (4) the employee's work value identification. Those with more personally demanding tasks, wherein they had a greater degree of personal discretion or control, were better performers if they identified with the work ethic and saw as legitimate the authority exercised by management. Work ethic alienation correlated positively with susceptibility to peer influence, the absence of control over the work, and the belief that getting ahead is dependent more on company politics than on performance. The work ethic alienated worker also saw himself powerless in the face of crime and corruption. Finally, those individuals who were alienated from the work ethic, who possessed a specialized job, and who viewed the company reward system as illegitimate, were less likely to take action when confronted with ineffectual actions of public officials or to participate in public affairs within the community. The opposite was true of individuals identifying with the work ethic. All of the findings cited above were magnified as the person's tenure in the specialized task lengthened. Correlations between major variables doubled in magnitude when the worker who had been in a highly-specialized job for two or more years was isolated for study.

The problem we are placing before business becomes clearer now after reviewing these findings and their tentative explanations. The inconsistent results obtained from some research on the impact of job enlargement on productivity can now be explained. We also have a sense of direction regarding potential solutions to what are in essence two problem areas: one related to the frustration and alienation of the work ethic identified person, and the other related to the apathetic maladjustment of the work ethic alienated person who sees work as having only instrumental value.

On the basis of the research presented and that which is currently in progress, I would conclude that the number of workers who are presently turned off to the work ethic are probably about one in four. If we consider the present movement of population in this country away from the inner city and the consequent decline in population density and poverty that may result from such movement, one might be tempted to conclude that in the future there will be fewer persons in this work ethic alienated group. However, if we look more closely at these population movements and density trends as Freedman (1973) suggests, we would likely find that it is the work ethic alienated who will have stayed behind. Nonetheless, I feel that we can conclude with relative safety that the worker's feelings toward management, its exercise of authority, and the operation of the organization's reward system, are at least as important in producing this value orientation as the demographic factors (i.e., town-city dichotomy) which have previously been cited. Certainly, it can also be concluded that workers' attitudes toward management, authority, and control will mediate the work ethic identified employees' efforts to realize personal development and productivity in the job-enlarged situation. In other words, *an enlargement of the job is a necessary but not sufficient condition to insure increased motivation and performance.* The individual must also be given a measure of control over his work, discretion in performing the task, and a belief in his management and its decisions (i.e., its legitimacy).

What Should Business Do?

Provided with the insights derived from studies of the town-city dichotomy and its effect on work ethic identifications, it would be relatively easy to view the problem facing business simply as a problem of selection. The argument could be made that companies with jobs which are quite specialized should go into densely populated urban areas and recruit those likely to be turned off to the work ethic. These employees may be apathetic and short-sighted about what they are doing, but at least they won't be frustrated, belligerent, or always asking questions about why things have to be done the way they are. Essentially, the strategy would be to find those people who will be quiet and obedient, do their job, ask no questions, and go home. To accept this recommendation, management must be as short-sighted as they are asking their workers to be. Everything about this arrangement says "treat work as a means to an end, not an end in itself." The work ethic alienated person comes to the job with that feeling, and the manner in which he is asked daily to perform his work reinforces that feeling.

Management cannot afford to employ a work force of this type. We need not refer to the argument that the mental health of these persons is jeopardized by this environment, nor must we point to the impact we foresee for a society composed of apathetic people who believe that crime and corruption are inevitable and who see no reason to fight it. (After all, Nixon was only doing what every other person in public office does. He just got caught. "Did his programs keep you in a job? That's what you should be concerned about, not how he did it.") We need only talk about costs. If management were to accept their employee's fixation with work as simply a means to wages, comfort, convenience, and status, it would amount to an acceptance of an increasingly hedonistic and increasingly apathetic partner in the enterprise.

It is very expensive to support a group which sees its work and work situation in a dominantly hedonistic way. As Herzberg (1966) has pointed out, if an individual is cut off from the opportunity to develop himself as a person and cannot engage in growth-producing experiences such as those that result from a varied, challenging task, he will turn to an APE strategy—that is, *A*void *P*ain from the *E*nvironment. When individuals are forced to accept this mode of adaptation they become extremely sensitive to their working conditions, their interpersonal treatment and, of course, their wages. Two rather uneconomical consequences thereby accrue to management. First, the effect of improvements in working conditions and in wages, as costly as they may be, will likely have only a *temporary* impact upon the satisfaction of the worker. In a short time, he will be back for more—more money, more time for breaks, more personal conveniences, etc. In addition, each time that management is forced to yield, a higher plane of expectations is established in which material and physical matters are dominant. These forces act to drive up direct labor costs and overhead, thereby squeezing the company's profit margin. To permit this cycle of events and consequent pressures to operate is mismanagement of the most absurd form, since it is economically disastrous in the long run.

Growth Management: A Plan for the Future

It is important to point out that we must believe that those individuals who are turned off on the work ethic, who do not want to be involved, who see themselves as powerless in the face of social "realities," are retrievable. It is obviously not possible to support this hypothesis by the research which has been cited here. To develop evidence of that type would require longitudinal investigations over a considerable period of years. However, we are not without experience on this matter. Texas Instruments (Roche and MacKinnon 1970) was highly successful in its implementation of a "meaningful work" program which developed the job content of workers who could not possibly be described as possessing positive feelings with regard to the value of work. The management of TI attributed the success of their action program to: (1)

the establishment of greater worker participation in problems which affect them; (2) the ambitious cooperation of first line supervisors in priming and maintaining the participative climate; and, (3) the commitment of top management to the value of this participation and cooperation.

To reverse the diseconomy and the inhumanity of the work ethic alienated will require the implementation of other such programs of "growth management." Growth management deals with an identification of the values of employees so that management and workers might gain a better sense of what is important to them, why it is important, and what can be introduced into the work place to make employment more developmentally rewarding. The attractive feature of the program is that it involves the work force in self-examination, self-development, and self-control in much the same fashion as management will later be asking the employee to operate in a job enlarged situation. This strategy for effecting change accents the reality that we cannot directly change others' values. However, we can involve them in self-examination to help them clarify their own desires, expectations, etc. This process must precede efforts at job redesign where work value alienated employees are involved. Without this preparation, the work value alienated group cannot possibly be responsive to more challenging tasks. Unfortunately, there have been many cases in which programs to upgrade job content have been introduced without such preparation. Of course they did not succeed. But what is worse, many used the results of these attempts as evidence that constructing meaningful jobs is not the answer to worker frustrations in specialized work.

What must management do for those who are not work value alienated—those who value challenge, variety, and discretion in their work. The answer is emphatically—much, much more than has been done to date. A recent survey (1975) indicated that 55 out of 100 jobs in the United States provide the job holder with some discretion as to the way in which he carries out his job. While there were other startling findings in this investigation, the most dramatic was the discovery that *from 1950 to 1970 there has been no change in the percentage of employed persons having discretion in their jobs,* even though the total number of such jobs have increased from 31.7 million to 41.2 million. Clearly, the redesign of a great deal of work is possible. Vertical loading of these jobs (e.g., combining jobs into "natural" sets of production) could create a climate of greater challenge, greater involvement, and greater opportunities for achievement as well as for personal growth and uniqueness. To reiterate, the job enlarged condition is not sufficient to assure the goals we profess through a humanization of work. As research indicates and experience dictates, greater worker self-control and participation and the legitimization of the exercise of management authority are nonnegotiable prerequisites for the success of this process.

It has been reported in a recent update on the Lordstown experience that a certain amount of job redesign is being done by the workers themselves (without management sanction). The practice is referred to as "doubling." In this practice, four workers might agree to form an informal team. Subsequently, they determine a period of time over which two of the four will do the work of the four while the other two workers do what they wish (this might involve coaching, checking, encouraging, and planning with others). Later, the roles are reversed. The workers claim that it improves morale by forcing them to concentrate on what might otherwise be boring monotonous tasks, by giving them a chance to rest and socialize, and by giving them a sense of control over their own actions. However, it was reported that doubling drives foremen within the assembly division "up the wall." When workers engage in doubling, managers have responded with discipline. The workers then file grievances and the sequence may conclude with a strike of several days' duration. Recently, in one six-month period, 5,000 separate grievances were filed at the Lordstown plant.

Work Humanization: What Is Truly Needed?

The doubling process at Lordstown is a somewhat simplistic step in the direction of implementing work redesign that secures a genuine humanization of work. The components necessary for that realization are many, but perhaps the first requisite element is *control*. Giving control to a group of line workers over the processes to which they would be collectively assigned may be the most difficult prescription for management to accept. It would involve a greater dependence on staff groups (e.g., production, quality control, and industrial engineering) to support small work groups which would be responsible for decision-making in areas previously the domain of first line management. Group members would decide their individual production methods. The group would decide the distribution of tasks, which additional tasks to take on, and when to work. In addition, the group would settle questions regarding internal leadership and group norms. The group would also set its own objectives and evaluate the quality of its production. The role of supervision and management under such a regime is drastically changed. Ironically, it may be that, in the last analysis, this schema might challenge management personnel to do the task of "management" instead of giving the task over to standard methods, machines, and conveyor belts which have been more traditional choices to date.

This challenge to management—to begin managing—goes right to the heart of the question of legitimization. What does it take for the worker to see his management's objectives and exercise of authority as appropriate, in keeping with his view of problems, and reflective of an understanding of performance problems? It occurs when the manager works with his subordinates to identify and solve work-related problems, when he helps subordinates set challenging goals for themselves, when he educates them to check their own performance, when he encourages his subordinates' development of new methods and induces their innovation. This prescription for role change is not restricted to first level management. O'Toole (1975) feels that probably the biggest stumbling block to our progress in work humanization is top management. Legitimization of authority rests on recognition by subordinates of the leader's greater expertise, skill, intelligence, charisma, or ability. If he cannot call upon this source of legitimacy, he must rely on force or manipulation to defend his position. Unfortunately for business, it is this form of control that is all too commonly used and is increasingly unacceptable to a well-educated work force. It has been said that one of the surest attacks upon the work ethic is the subjection of workers to gross mismanagement and unethical corporate conduct (e.g., Lockheed's illegal campaign contributions). At Lordstown there have been frequent complaints by workers of confused and pressured "crisis management" practices which caused work to come to a virtual standstill. In the absence of top management pursuit of corporate goals, through what are seen by workers up and down the hierarchy as legitimate means, we cannot look to the future of work humanization but with great concern. Thus, the *legitimization of management* is perhaps the second of our necessary elements in our matrix for greater humanization of work.

Although it may be necessary to make a case for this "total system redesign" on the grounds that productivity would likely increase and that net profits would rise as a result of predictable decreases in human resource wastes accruing from reduced absenteeism, accidents, scrap, grievances, and turnover, I would prefer to conclude with an appeal on moral grounds. It is my belief that we must continually lobby and speak out for the principle that corporations benefit from the resources of society, both human and natural, and that they have a responsibility to return them as they found them. As Peter Drucker has concluded, "It is not enough for business to do well—it is unrealistic to expect them to do good—but society must require of them that [at least] they do no harm."

REFERENCES

Argyris, C. *Personality and Organization.* New York: Harper & Row, 1957.
———. The Individual and Organization: An Empirical Test. *Administrative Science Quarterly,* 1959, 4:149–167.

Behling, O., and C. Schriesheim. *Organizational Behavior*. Boston: Allyn and Bacon, 1976.

Blauner, R. *Alienation and Freedom*. Chicago: University of Chicago Press, 1964.

Brown, J. S. How Many Workers Enjoy Discretion on the Job? *Industrial Relations*, 1975, 14:196–202.

Davies, W., and R. Williams. *Social Control of the Mentally Deficient*. New York: Sheed & Ward, 1961.

Dostoevski, F. *The House of the Dead*. New York: Dutton, 1911.

Drucker, P. *Management: Tasks, Responsibilities, Practices*. New York: Harper & Row, 1974.

Freedman, J. L. The Effects of Population Density on Humans. In *Psychological Perspectives on Population*, J. T. Fawcett, ed. New York: Basic Books, 1973, pp. 209–238.

Herzberg, F. *Work and the Nature of Man*. New York: World, 1966.

Hulin, C. L., and M. R. Blood. Job Enlargement, Individual Differences, and Worker Responses. *Psychological Bulletin*, 1968, 69:41–55.

Kendall, L. M. *Chronical Analysis of Job Satisfaction and Behavioral Personal Background, and Situational Data*. Ithaca, N.Y.: Cornell University Press, 1963.

Kennedy, J. E., and H. E. O'Neill, Job Content and Workers' Opinions. *Journal of Applied Psychology*, 1958, 42 (6):372–375.

Kilbridge, M. D. Do Workers Prefer Larger Jobs? *Personnel*, 1960, 37:45–58.

Kornhauser, A. W. *Mental Health of the Industrial Worker: A Detroit Study*. New York: Wiley, 1965.

Lawler, E. E. For a More Effective Organization—Match the Job to the Man. *Organizational Dynamics*, 1975, 4:19–29.

McGregor, D. *The Human Side of Enterprise*. New York: McGraw-Hill, 1960.

Maslow, A. A Theory of Human Motivation. *Psychological Review*, 1943, 50:370–396.

O'Toole, J. Lordstown: Three Years Later. *Business and Society Review*, 1975, 13:64–71.

Robinson, H. A., and R. P. Connors. Job Satisfaction Research of 1962. *Personnel and Guidance Journal*, 1963, 42:136–142.

Robinson, H. A., and R. P. Connors. "Job Satisfaction Researches of 1963," *Personnel and Guidance Journal*, 1964, 12:373–377.

Roche, W. J., and N. L. MacKinnon. Motivating People with Meaningful Work. *Harvard Business Review*, 1970, May-June:97–110.

Sexton, W. P. Who Says Work is Psychologically Devastating? *Management of Personnel Quarterly*, 1968, 6:3–8.

Turner, A. N., and P. R. Lawrence. *Industrial Jobs and the Worker*. Cambridge, Mass.: Harvard University Press, 1965.

Turner, A. N., and A. L. Michette. Sources of Satisfaction in Repetitive Work. *Occupational Psychology*, 1962, 36:215–231.

Walker, C. R., and R. Marriott. A Study of Attitudes Toward Factory Work. *Occupational Psychology*, 1951, 25:181–190.

Walker, C. R. Work Methods, Working Conditions, and Morale. In *Industrial Con-*

flict, A. Kornhauser, R. Dubin, and A. M. Ross, eds. New York: McGraw-Hill, 1954, pp. 345–358.

Walker, C. R., and R. H. Guest. *The Man on the Assembly Line.* Cambridge, Mass.: Harvard University Press, 1952.

Whyte, W. F. *Money and Motivation: An Analysis of Incentives in Industry.* New York: Harper & Row, 1955.

Work Humanization in Practice: What Is Business Doing?

by David G. Bowers

LIKE THE TERM "QUALITY OF WORK LIFE," THE TERM "HUMANISTIC WORK" has different meanings for different users. For a number of employers and their staff representatives it means attaining higher productivity and lower costs through some form of stimulation of more positive attitudes. For union leaders who have become involved in this area, it appears to mean attaining higher wage levels, better working conditions, shorter hours, and earlier retirements from work settings that are acknowledged (by the term itself) as onerous. Finally, academicians all too often tie the term to some muddy combination of satisfaction and performance called "effectiveness." Perhaps the best that can be said for the moment is that "humanistic work" refers to work activities and settings that are congruent with human needs and desires, and our concern with this problem reflects a feeling that in this day and age the alignment is not very good.

Let me elaborate a little on this. Clearly, at this particular juncture in our national life, the issues of worker alienation, dissatisfaction, restlessness, and quality of work life are critical and key problems. Along with them is the issue of productivity. As one looks at various national statistics over a period of recent years, it is clear that more and more of the materials used in production come from abroad, more and more of the energy we use to power our plants, our mills, our offices, our factories comes from abroad, and so on. It thus becomes more apparent that if there is a truly domestic resource it is the human resource, and to the extent that there is any national difference, it is attributable to the quality, character, motivation, willingness, and commitment of that resource.

Humanistic Work and Productivity

There is a dispute running through discussions about the issue of satisfaction, worker alienation, productivity and the like which takes a variety of forms. At the academic level, it takes the form of at least an implicit debate about whether the subjective quality of work life is a simple reaction to experience or a function of a discrepancy between what people expect and what they experience. On a more concrete, practical level, I think it takes the form of a debate about whether system efficiency is or is not contrary to human well-being. I believe that social scientists for a number of years have accepted on the basis of too little evidence and a great deal of faith the proposition that human well-being and system efficiency go hand in hand. But why they should go hand in hand is usually less well articulated. The whole resurgence of interest in humanistic work calls this into question.

Let us pick up one particular thread of this somewhat tangled mess and deal with it rather specifically. Several years ago, in the course of conversations with people from a major national industry, I heard some rather distressing news—news not intended for public consumption or to "scare anyone into anything." It was the simple, rather perplexing admission that executives in that industry previously had always been able to count on absorbing the increased costs of any new union contract settlement from technological improvements that would occur during the life of that contract. Although that capability had been declining for some years, they now found themselves, for the first time, no longer able to do so. What this meant (and what we've subsequently seen) was the beginning of an endless round of price hikes and inflation, with each industry and its companionate union jockeying for comparative advantage (which they gain only momentarily). The societal effects in the intervening years have been multiple: inflation, periodic currency crises, fears of economic collapse (probably unwarranted) and depression, and the frightening example of Great Britain, seen by some as predictive of what is in store for the United States.

For the moment, however, things seem to be better. Inflation has slowed; the dollar has been firming up; our trade balance looks more favorable, etc. How has this been done? Is it really a sign that the problems have been solved? In part it is, in that we have a respite at least, perhaps a time in which more intense examinations can be undertaken. But we have achieved these seeming improvements by an induced (although unintentional) recession that forced marginal facilities out of production and added the marginally skilled employee to the unemployment rolls. The burden of supporting the latter is then passed on to—or perhaps more descriptively, wrung out of the remaining employed workers in the form of taxes, diverted services, lower quality goods and services, poor deliveries, and ultimately, higher prices. So, although what has occurred in the short run may have accomplished some useful purposes and may be a stop-gap measure, it is not a viable strategy for the long haul and it has not provided us with any necessary groundwork for solving the problems of humanistic work.

Returning to this broader issue, it is my opinion that if we do not tie concerns for humanistic work in some way to productivity (i.e., bringing the latter into our calculations), we run the risk of toppling the entire work structure down to a more primitive level. The prosperity, affluence, and development that we have experienced over the last couple of decades have lifted our society up a Maslowian-type hierarchy to a level where we begin to become concerned about issues in the upper regions of the hierarchy (e.g., self-actualization, self-realization, and the like). However, one thing that is implicit in a Maslowian hierarchy often escapes attention: it assumes that the satisfied lower-order needs remain satisfied. At least as commonly used there seems to be the notion that, as we grope to learn how to provide work which is truly humanistic, we may inadvertently initiate actions which plummet our society back down the hierarchy to the more primitive levels (which we feel we have left in the past ten years). Only by the deliberate searching for solutions that explicitly deal with productivity concerns can we hope to avoid this regression to levels where the predominate concerns are subsistence, security, and the like.

Let me take a different cut at the problem—one which I cited earlier: the idea that one way the debate is phrased is in terms of whether the subjective quality of work life is a function of what people experience or a function of a discrepancy between what they experience and what they expect. I think thoughtful scholars would probably say immediately that it cannot be anything other than some form of discrepancy between expectations and experience. If it were simply a matter of what people actually receive—what they experience in the work situation, people today would, I think, clearly not be alienated. In terms of material well-being, work hours, or the oppressiveness of labor or working conditions (defined as how hard one must work, how long, and what one receives for it), etc., people today are infinitely better off than their grandparents were. And people today in this country and in most of the Western world are infinitely better off than the rest of the world. But expectations have changed and it is the *discrepancy* between these expectations and the experience which counts.

If we can at least tentatively accept that proposition, let us think for a moment about the expectation component. Where does it come from? It comes, in a sense, from the aggregation of the other component—experience—over a period of time. That is, the experiences we have cumulatively influence our future states of expectation. Part of that experience comes in the very early years of life from youthful experiences (socialization processes) which influence the development of one's level of need for achievement, for sociability, for affiliation, for independence, etc. These experiences are modified, however, over the course of a lifetime, and they are modified at least to some extent in daily living. Thus, at least in some modest way the formation of expectations is influenced by current experience. The actual return (i.e., what people actually receive or experience) comes from the work role itself; that is, it comes from behavior in the organizational system context.

As I add this up, I come to the conclusion that the expectations component is probably more individually and less work-organizationally set (reflecting as it does what has uniquely happened to each of us), whereas the actual return component is much more organizationally determined (i.e., work setting related). The latter is also more immediate and more alterable than our expectations. If, therefore, the alienation problem is the result of a discrepancy between expectations and experiences (and I think it must be) that is too large today (and I think it is), then *the only humanistically acceptable alternative is to raise the level of return*.

This may seem rather self-evident, but I would like you to think for just a moment about the alternative, implicit perhaps, in a discussion à la Club of Rome. It seems to me that this alternative argument might go something like this:

> The output of the system must be held constant. Expectations exceed experience by too great a fraction. Therefore, some way must be found to manipulate people's expectations downward.

Not only do I believe that this alternative is highly unfeasible as a planned change strategy, I think that what it implies humanistically is totally unacceptable.

Granted then, that raising the level of return is the more humanistic alternative, it is important to note that the return level which exists in any work setting comes, in the end, from the efficiency of the system—a property which is defined as the ratio of the outputs from the system to the inputs coming into the system. The distribution of those returns is a totally different issue and, in any particular short segment of time, one might propose one or another of an infinite variety of mechanisms for the distribution of returns within a system. But over the long run, in the absence of growth and efficiency, distribution becomes a rather academic matter and consists largely of the sharing of dissatisfactions. From this emerges the notion that system efficiency in the long run must be a principal criterion, if not *the* principal criterion. And the more equitable or appropriate distribution of returns therefore becomes an issue whose resolution lies in the time frame of reference under consideration (i.e., the period of time for which the system is to be efficient).

There exists a great deal of evidence that system efficiency in the long run is tied to a number of concerns which appear at the heart of humanistic concerns in the management area: the motivation, commitment, involvement, and the feelings of well-being of system members. And there is also evidence that these characteristics tend to produce results in work settings that lag the conditions that caused them by anywhere from one to five years. As Rensis Likert (1967) noted in his own consultative-research studies, "time intervals between changes in causal variables and the related changes in the intervening variables (attitudes, motivations, etc.) and finally in the end-result variables took much longer than the investigators had expected" (p. 79).

Thus, in the short run we are able to effect any division of returns we desire. We can trade off one factor (favorable employee attitudes, for example) for another (increased productivity). However, the question becomes for the long run: "How long do we want the system to be viable?" Here we must face the time lag considerations cited above.

Let me briefly summarize at this point what has been said. I will put the summary in the form of four questions. The first question that I touched on was:

> Is the design of humanistic work an issue separate from the issue of enhanced productivity?

In my mind it is not. Humanistic work and productivity are inevitably intertwined and we cannot ignore the productivity side without risking retrogression back down some Maslowian-type hierarchy to lower order concerns. Workers are unlikely to be concerned about humanistic work design if there is an insufficient amount of work, if there is insufficient income, etc. At these points, security concerns overpower interests in self-actualization. However, it is also true that in an affluent society, humanistic concerns cannot be ignored in the long run without jeopardizing productivity.

The second question I posed was:

> Does the altered economic situation of the last several months indicate that our productivity problems have been solved, and that we can now turn (or return) our attention to other areas of interest that are more intrinsically satisfying to social science researchers such as myself, that is, designing jobs that are more enjoyable to workers, creating new interpersonal arrangements that are more satisfying and the like?

Once again I believe the answer is "No." All we have done is to hide the nonproductive part (unemployment and its concommitant costs) away in the national attic and doctor the statistics that the financial community uses.

The third question was:

> Is the subjective quality of work life a function of actual experience or a function of the discrepancy between actual experience and what is expected?

It seems highly likely that it is a discrepancy function and that the expectations in this arena cannot be effectively or ethically altered downward. Therefore, any attempt to improve the quality of work life must come from an improvement in the actual experience component, and that is an organizational problem.

Finally, I asked:

> What kind of problem is it?

It is a two-sided problem. One side amounts to sheer efficiency so that return levels can be maximized. The other side, however relates to the distribution of returns, and while in the short run the distribution can take on any form, in the long run it becomes a time-frame problem because of the lead-lag relationships that exist within the system.

Work Innovation: The Current Scene

With this lengthy setting of the stage behind us, let us now turn to what seems to be happening on the American business scene. *What, in fact, is business doing to enhance the humanistic character of its operations? The answer, right now, is very little, almost nothing.* True, there is, and there has been, a great deal of talk. Three or four years ago there was also a great deal going on. But the actions and the results, I'm afraid, have become sparse and much of what was going on has been quietly ended.

To be a bit more specific, the period 1968–1973 saw a major flurry of activity and effort in this field. Indeed, the whole preceding decade, roughly 1962–1972, was one of new and innovative thrusts. One of the first I would note centers on the entire area of *job redesign*. Innovative restructuring of the work itself was undertaken in a number of places. These efforts went in at least two directions. One was making the work more challenging, that is, some form of job enrichment.[1] The other direction that work restructuring took was making the work setting more interpersonally compatible with human needs. Action efforts in this regard included the formation of autonomous work or assembly teams rather than individual, fixed-position jobs along an assembly line. Under the "team concept," workers, operating as a unit, assemble a total product or some complete segment thereof.[2] Other forms of more compatible interpersonal arrangements that were tried included business teams (i.e., the "business within a business" or "office within an office" notion) and matrix organizations (i.e., organizations with a product or project structure superimposed over more traditional functional arrangements).

A second type of innovation that occurred was what one might call *de-statused organizations.* In a number of organizations, often small manufacturing plants, the traditional hierarchical authority relationship (the supervisor-subordinate relationship based on formal authority rights) was removed or at least minimized. In the late 1960s, no fewer than a dozen major corporations experimented with this status equalization mode.[3]

The third form of emphasis was on *socio-technically designed plants.* In a number of instances, ordinarily when the opportunity arose to construct new facilities, an attempt was made to design them with social, as well as technological, configurations in mind. The concept of a socio-technical system arose from the consideration that any production system required both a technological organization—equipment and process layout—and a work organization relating to each other those who carry out the necessary tasks. In other words, facilities were designed to more adequately match the organization's technological processes with the social and psychological properties of its members. And in certain instances, large and extremely expensive facilities were thusly designed and constructed.

During this period there were also *innovative union-management efforts* focused around the discovery of new ways for cooperative endeavor and new ways for solving organizational problems. A number of *public agency projects* were also undertaken. These organizational development efforts extended to extremely large systems and encompassed such major agencies as the Department of Defense, the Postal Service, and the Department of State.

Finally, as derivative efforts, a large number of *new supportive service units* developed. Research institutes, such as the Institute for Social Research at the University of Michigan, were set up to study issues related to job and organizational design and to encourage experimental activity aimed at the discovery of more satisfying and effective organizational properties. Consulting firms, a number of them small, went into business. Training programs were set up and new publications came into existance to disseminate information about the volume of activity that had begun.

Looking at all of this four years ago, one would have had to conclude (and many of us did) that things were finally on their way—that the work organization, the human organization and its functioning, was finally going to secure the attention that it deserved. But what has happened in each of these areas in the ensuing years?

A Look at the Evidence

Looking first at job redesign and in particular job enrichment, I think a number of persons began to realize that the evidence sustaining this approach was far from persuasive. While it is true that there were instances in which rather remarkable results were achieved, an undue proportion of the evidence came from highly technical settings (engineering firms and the like). In addition, many of the much-talked-about application cases were small, isolated, and very parochial. In many cases one was lead to believe that these successes occurred in large companies when in fact the experiment may have involved only an extremely low proportion of total company employees. One such effort that comes to mind received national television attention and was described, at least in that show, as a rather large effort. In fact, this job enrichment experiment involved about thirty people in one operation of a very large activity.[4] Thus, in many instances, there has been a certain nonmatch of evidence with the claims.

What of business teams, matrix organizations, etc.? Again the success rate has not turned out to be very high. For example, in one large plant an effort of a business team type was highly successful in one small operation. This was an operation in a large assembly activity. However, when the company attempted to extend that concept to another operational area of approximately the same size (but in this case a staff operation, specifically plant security), the effort failed. When they attempted to extend the concept to an operation very much like the first one, but one of a much greater size, again it did not work. Thus what appeared to work quite well in a small, confined setting, with perhaps a relatively high degree of functional differentiation, was a failure in a functionally different department and in a similar but much larger department.

What of de-statused organizations? One never hears of them anymore. One application that I am particularly familiar with deteriorated to a conventional form within a couple of years. The organization began, for example, with no foremen. Rather it was a group process that ran itself, and it functioned marvelously. But it was an indigestible element in the larger unit of which it was a part. The frictions between this unit and the rest of the organization were constant, and so, ultimately, it simply reverted to classical form.

What of socio-technically designed plants? Some of the early efforts in this regard were billed as "successes" in publicized accounts, and perhaps they were. But some of them at least were later disputed. Questions were raised as to whether they had been successful or not, or if success had indeed been achieved, whether it was attributable to the socio-technical design or some other causal factor. Of the later attempts, with which I am more familiar, many seemed unable to really cope with both the social and technical sides. Either the social organization was splendid but the hardware designers and suppliers were unable to provide a technical system that would function effectively in such a social configuration, or the hardware or technical side was fine but the personnel who were hired and recruited could never seem to achieve the levels of production that had been anticipated.

Most innovative union-management efforts failed as did the one we tried at the Institute for Social Research. At the top company and union levels there was a great deal of commitment, determination, and interest in effecting more cooperative union-management activities. At the level of the local plant management and the local shop committee there was similar interest and determination. But at the intermediate level—the level of the regional manager of the company and regional business manager of the union—there was no such interest. On neither side at this level could they tolerate any change which threatened to cut into their personal and bureaucratic power bases. Thus the effort failed and I suspect a great many others did also.

What of public agency projects? There are still some signs of continuing activity in this area, but many are more cosmetic than real. Change attempts in this sector at least seem to have been derailed by T, B, and P (Tradition, Bureaucracy, and Politics). As for the new support units that came into existence during this period, many of the newer consulting firms have had great difficulty and a goodly number of the smaller ones have gone under. Training programs have been drastically cut. The National Training Laboratories (NTL), which were pioneers and a major influence in at least part of this field for twenty-five years, all but went bankrupt. Others also have been forced into curtailed operations and reorganization. And finally, many "in-company" organizational development efforts, a good number of them widely known, have been either cut to the bone or eliminated completely.

The Rise and Fall of a Movement: A Potential Rationale

Let us pause again and take stock of the implications which these events may have for where we are today. Obviously, my view is that the concern for humanistic work or quality of work is an outgrowth of events of the last decade and a half, not a cause of them. Placed in this form, the sequence of events raises three simple, but critical questions: *Why did this flurry of activities and concern begin? Why did it decline? What lies ahead?* And as part of the latter question, are there specifically things that we learned from all this that we can build upon for the future?

Let us begin with the first question: Why this flurry of activity at this particular juncture in our history? Why in the 1960s? In part, I think because the 1960s were turbulent years. The customary structures and patterns within which decisions were made, problems solved, and objectives set showed signs of breaking down. It was an age that called for answers, that called for solutions and new ways of functioning, and that questioned old forms and old norms (i.e., customary ways of behaving). Consider all of the things that happened in that one short decade.

The fabric of society seemed to be torn early in the decade both with assassinations and with political polarization. There was a disruptive war which shredded a great deal of public confidence. The hyperactivity level of economic institutions, brought about by the "guns and butter" policy of the 1960s and early 1970s brought marginal producers into the workplace to fill needs and positions. Sputnik scared everyone and generated national concern about scientific stagnation. Finally, the end of this decade was capped off with a national political scandal that suggested the frailty of government organizational functioning, and trust in that institution began to decline. Sheer affluence had pushed a substantial segment of our society far up a Maslowian-type hierarchy to a point where people became concerned about such things as self-actualization and self-realization. The customary structures and patterns within which decisions were made and problems solved and objectives set showed signs of breaking down.

All of these events and changes created enormous "people" problems—dissatisfaction, grievances, rejection of authority, resistance to direction, etc. In their frustration, institutional managers turned for solutions to a number of sources, including altered or redesigned work systems as perhaps one solution to their problems. In short, they were somewhat desperate; they were eager to try anything that might work. One thing they were willing to try was more humanistic work designs. But one must not forget that they tried other things too. Legal and quasi-legal mechanisms, bureaucratic controls, and "improvement by fiat" all received attention.

There appear to be several plausible reasons for why all of this organizational innovation failed in large measure. For one thing, the knowledge base was not up to the claims of the proponents. To use Noel Tichy's terms, there was overadvocacy: organizational managers were led to expect miracles where only modest improvements, if anything, were likely. Thus, many of these efforts built in the seeds of their own failure from the very outset by setting unreasonably high expectations. There was also excessive commitment to the application of single treatments, regardless of what the specific need of the organization might be. There was an inadequate sensitivity to the prevailing organizational value structure and the constraints which it placed upon what was acceptable within the system. This was, and continues to be, a major problem in organizational change efforts. Too often consultants or management personnel, rather than providing feedback about how to progress toward objectives with which organizational members can identify, try to impose their own directions and values upon the system. Thus, they frequently encounter resistance to their proposals. In short, you can tell people they're off target from where they want to go and they'll think you're helpful. But if you give them information telling them they're going in the wrong direction, that the place they want to go is not the place they should be going, they will reject you and your information. This is precisely what has happened in many of these change attempts.

Finally, there was, and there remains, a major flaw in the financial and economic thinking of organizational managers with regard to the human asset. Work in this field (i.e., any attempt at applicational efforts in humanistic work design, improvement of the quality of work life, or organizational development) is still expensed, rather than treated as an investment. As a result, implementational efforts are considered a luxury or frill, to be cut or canceled whenever there is a downturn in the business cycle. And this is exactly what has happened in the most recent recession. This last rationale covers a multitude of related reasons, but they boil down to a model of organizational functioning hailed by most managers which is not consonant with either the tenets of humanistic management or the facts of real-world life. It's a model of organizational functioning that says: "Most of our organizational success is attributable to the unimpeded operation of the hardware (i.e., capital equipment). Unfortunately, people are required to run the hardware. Our job as managers is to prevent their screwing up this efficient technical system." It is within this debilitating framework then, that many managers view efforts related to humanistic management.

What Lies Ahead?

Was the preceding decade a total loss? Is there some value in current practice and knowledge that has been retained and upon which we can build? Are there trends in society which must be taken into account if we're to move ahead in this field? I do not think the period of the late 1960s and early 1970s can be considered a total loss. Much was learned about designing and implementing "interventions for change." In particular, much was learned about the constraints or limits upon planned change. Another thing that was learned is that opportunities to design more humanistic work originate in the organization's environment and stem from the inability of customary practices and patterns of functioning to cope with those changes. It is therefore a systems adaptation problem. Another learning that will probably emerge from this whole era is that *no one method of attempting to design humanistic work will work in all settings in the face of all problems.* No one method will work everywhere. Instead successful efforts—and there have been some—have tended to use a more eclectic or mixed bag of action steps, and they have been applied only after some sort of systematic diagnosis of need has taken place.

Yet a fourth thing that has been learned is that this whole process is not unique in human experience. It's been played before in other settings such as medicine, and I think we can learn a great deal from those other disciplines. It is interesting to me to look at the extent to which the arguments, the difficulties, and the conflicts in this field (work humanization) very closely resemble the kinds of problems and conflicts they had in medicine nearly a hundred to a hundred and fifty years ago. Perhaps we can learn more quickly from their experiences. Finally, I think it has been learned that no attempt to humanize the workplace, to develop the organization, or to improve the quality of work life can be carried out successfully without some form of quantitative evaluation and feedback. The reason for this is that systems without feedback cannot exist. It is through feedback processes that their adaptation potential is realized.

A number of things I've just said are illustrated in three successful change efforts with which I am personally familiar. One of these took place about twenty-five years ago in a pajama factory (Coch and French 1948). In brief, it represented an acquisition by a major competitor of a relatively unproductive plant and the attempt to restore that plant to higher levels of productivity and profit. More than a dozen different interventions were attempted, some with most or all employees, some with certain specific groups, but all of them in a carefully sequenced developmental program. One thing interesting to note about this particular effort was that the direct dollar cost of the change effort on the human organization side was about as large as the direct dollar cost of improvements made to the physical plant. Furthermore, what was done was rather consistently tied to real problems being experienced on the job, not simply focused upon some sort of abstract socio-emotional space. So, for example, while the organization used sensitivity training as a part of their total package, they related that technique to problem-posing and problem-solving efforts involving all employees in their work tasks. The variety of outside resources they brought to bear on this set of problems were carefully selected for their relevance, not simply purchased because of their persuasive pitch. Throughout the entire endeavor there was a careful imparting of knowledge to those involved in the change effort and continual demonstrations of the ways in which that knowledge could be used. The results of this undertaking are, I think, fairly well known. Not only did satisfaction and the perception of organizational conditions improve rather dramatically during the three year study, but productivity also improved by 43 percent. Operator turnover, which had been phenomenally high prior to the change effort declined by nearly 90 percent. Absenteeism was reduced by 50 percent. The rate of manufacturing defects was reduced 39 percent; customer returns dropped 57 percent; and the company moved from a loss of 15 percent on investment to a profit of 17 percent. Not only that, but the improvements held, at least as long as we tracked the company (seven years after the initiation of the study).

The second case occurred in an experimental project in heavy industry, specifically in assembly-line manufacturing. Resources were again provided in fairly abundant measure. There was a staff of fourteen on-line consultants, sixteen researchers and measurement personnel, and a clerical and support staff. The study involved the initiation of a three year project in which there was an initial thirteen month standardized survey-feedback activity, followed by an eleven month coordination period in which local teams in each of the locations decided what interventions they wanted to implement (the central staff simply coordinated their efforts). This, in turn, was followed by a twelve month autonomous period during which the central staff monitored what was happening. There was a fairly rigorous evaluation of the whole effort. Passing over a lot of detail, let me simply say that by the end of the third year direct labor efficiency in this extremely large plant had improved by 14 percent, indirect labor efficiency had improved 23 percent, the grievance rate had dropped 60 percent, and there was evidence in employee survey responses of substantial gains in employee satisfaction and improvement in their perception of their work conditions. Not only this, but the money saved at this particular location, in that one year, outweighed all the costs of the entire project in all locations, in all years, by a factor of five.

Let me take the third case—a clerical operation in a large insurance company. This project was undertaken about three years ago, using a survey-guided development effort.[5] Internal consultants and supervisors were given intensive and extensive conceptual and skill training prior to the initiation of the action steps that were subsequently included in the program. The consultants spent hours both privately and in joint staff sessions digesting and analyzing each group's survey data to determine its problems and identify its strengths and weaknesses. Not only did the consultants not set exaggerated claims in undertaking this effort, they took on the project precisely because they wanted to avoid some of the worst aspects of the commercial offerings they had encountered. Scientific knowledge, and measurement and evaluation, played a very large role in the entire activity. They also ensured that they paired (and I think this is an innovative, interesting, and seemingly productive twist) the social and technical consultants in each of these efforts. The results again were quite persuasive. After one-and-a-half years, measured productivity showed an improvement of 22 percent, a gain that persists to the present time. Manpower turnover, which had been a large problem, declined by 10 percent, a decline which was felt to be substantial for that location. And, as in the preceding instance, the improved productivity outweighed the total cost of the change effort, direct and indirect, by a factor of five to one.

Several key factors stand out in these successful cases. In none of them did the companies economize on resources made available to the effort; more efforts of a humanistic kind have starved to death than have received the resources they needed to be successful. In all three cases, those who designed the effort went to great care to make certain that their proposals meshed with the existing structure of positions, roles, values, tasks, and persons. This does not mean that they did not undertake restructuring; rather, it means that they did not go in with a program of activities that was at odds with the structure they were encountering. That is a very different issue. In each instance the effort was carefully introduced, with success perhaps in some degree proportional to the extent to which realistic expectations were established. In each instance a great deal of resources, time, and importance were given to the evaluation activity. In each instance, the successful consultative style was one which emphasized successful knowledge transmission, not simply emotional and personal confrontation. In each instance, there was some form of survey-feedback activity, but that may be less important than the fact that there was a built-in program of feedback about the operation and its progress. It could have been in survey form or otherwise. Finally, in each instance, the substantial performance improvements which subsequently occurred took two to three years to appear. These then, are the things I think we have learned personally out of what we have done.

Frankly, these are not small learnings, and to have gained them may well turn out to have been worth the price that has been paid. Perhaps, realistically, we who are eager to see work organizations attempt anew to modify practices and conditions toward more humanistically desirable and effective forms must be patient. Hopefully, in the future the things which we have learned will help us to construct sounder interventions, and the success rate will be higher.

Some Trends for the Future

A number of people have been asking recently if there are new trends emerging in the work place. One potential area for exploration in this regard concerns whether there are emergent changes in what people want from a job. In a recent study, researchers at the ISR asked a number of questions of a representative cross-section of the employed population, aged sixteen and older. The results of this investigation indicated that Americans of all ages and in all types of organizational settings (a major attribute of the study was a civilian-Navy comparison) want, or at least say they want, substantially the same things out of a job—despite the fact that they live with drastically different events, under different working conditions, and with quite different returns.

What these people have stated is that there are two kinds of things that are most important to them as human beings in their work setting. It is most important, for example, that their job provides them with *personal independence* in the form of an opportunity to control their personal lives themselves. They wish to avoid bureaucracy, that is, to avoid "red tape," endless referrals, and unexplainable rules and regulations.[6] That workers wish to avoid these conditions is no doubt indicative of bureaucracy's rising presence on the business scene. Indeed, one major criticism leveled at today's organizations by social scientists is that they are over-defined or over-structured. The second factor employees cited as being most important to their well-being was *economic success*—that is, economic well-being in the form of salaries, fringe benefits, etc. These two factors—an opportunity to have a say in things that affect you on the job and economic success—stood at the head of everyone's list (civilian as well as Navy). These results are not unlike the findings of earlier studies of a similar nature or even what might have been found in classical texts on American values eighty or one hundred years ago. These two factors have always been important and the findings of the present study suggest that they are still important.

If there is this degree of constancy in American work expectations, are there any emerging changes? In this same national survey a series of questions were asked to ascertain worker beliefs in autocratic work principles. Questions were phrased in terms of autocratic versus democratic, domineering versus cooperative, etc., and people were asked to indicate their degree of endorsement. The results of this aspect of the survey indicated that the willingness on the part of workers to endorse autocratic (or domineering) management values rises with age and declines with level of educational attainment. Age and education are of course related to one another with younger segments of the work force generally having higher levels of education than older workers. Changes in this regard over the recent decades has been phenomenal. What these findings suggest is that workers who are more willing to endorse (or accept) more autocratic management values or styles are those who are older and have little formal education. Those least willing to support these principles or values are younger and have higher educational levels.

Aside from the question of whether you can manage today's (or tomorrow's) complex organizations primarily with people with little formal education, there remains the question of what happens along the age curve. Of those current employees who are willing to accept a more autocratic style of management, half will exodus from the labor force within the next ten years and virtually all will be out of the labor force within the next twenty. Thus, *organizational managements of the future, if they are to adapt to emerging societal changes, will have to seek and adopt methods and styles more compatible with cooperative or democratic alternatives.* This may once again open up new avenues for humanistic work alternatives.

Summary

I think we have seen an amazing period come and go in our national life, a period focused around this issue of the quality of work life. It began in the turmoil of the 1960s and produced a tremendous volume of activity, much of which was unprofitable. However, there is some residue, some learning, some set of principles, that we have gotten out of this period that will remain with us. I look forward to a new period, sometime in the years immediately ahead, when there will be another surge of activity of this kind, hopefully based on a little more knowledge and a little less pure advocacy. I think such a resurgence is important and necessary because some of today's societal trends suggest that the configuration of values with which organizations must cope are shifting. Because of trends away from the endorsement of more autocratic management practices (as older employees exit the work force) and rising patterns of national affluence and increased job options (particularly for those workers with higher educational levels), tomorrow's managers must be more willing and more able to design organizational forms, develop organizational practices, and implement training and other action interventions that will increase the personal independence of workers. However, these efforts must also provide the levels of productivity necessary to permit good, solid economic returns to employees (and other claimants) for the contributions they make. Anything less will fail to meet employees' economic expectations and will ultimately result in a less than optimum quality of work life.

EDITORS' NOTES

1. Early enrichment experiments at IBM and AT&T soon led to the proliferation of a number of similar experiments around the country. Typically, when a job was experimentally enriched, employees would be given responsibility to set up and inspect their own work, to make decisions about methods and procedures to be used, and within the framework of output objectives, to set their own work pace. As Porter, et al. (1975),

have noted, by the early 1970s job enrichment showed all the signs of turning into a national fad. One survey of *Fortune's* 500 largest firms indicated that at least 20 percent of the firms had a job enrichment program. Among these were Texas Instruments, Corning Glass Works, Polaroid, United Airlines, Travelers Insurance Company, and other industrial giants.

2. For examples, refer to the discussion of the Saab-Scania or Volvo production methods cited in the previous article by Ted Mills, "Leadership From Abroad: European Developments in Industrial Democracy."

3. In the new (1971) General Foods Pet Food Plant in Topeka, Kansas, for example, traditional status differentiations were minimized by opening parking lot positions to all regardless of rank, and providing a common office-plant entrance, and providing common decor throughout office, cafeteria, and locker room.

4. A number of instances of this kind can be cited. For example, the Corning Glass Works study (1965) in which workers were allowed to assemble entire electrical hot plates affected only six employees. One Texas Instruments study (1967) involved only 120 maintenance personnel who were organized into nineteen-member cleaning teams. Similarly a number of the European successes cited in the previous article by Ted Mills ("Leadership From Abroad: European Developments in Industrial Democracy") were extremely modest in scope. Job enrichment activities at Nobø Fabrikker (1965), a Norwegian fabricator, involved fewer than fifty personnel as was also true of experiments at Nørsk Hydro (1966). Even those interventions that were plant-wide successes frequently represented but a small fraction of total corporate activity. It should also be noted with respect to these "successes" that participants in these experiments were usually volunteers. That is, these success studies frequently involved people who had self-selected themselves into the altered work situation; therefore, they may have been more suited to the work environment being tested and more committed to making the activity a success than would a typical employee working in the same organizational context.

5. Survey-guided development, as the term is used by Dr. Bowers, refers to an organizational development (OD) intervention which involves collecting survey data from all people in an organization, tabulating it, and then feeding it back to organizational members for their analysis and action recommendations. The data is presented to organizational participants through interlocking conferences made up of a supervisor and his immediate subordinates. The data is discussed with the help of a resource person and strengths, weaknesses, and problems of the unit are identified. Action plans are then formulated to improve unit operations.

Survey-feedback processes originated in the late 1940s at the Institute for Social Research and grew out of the fact that managers at that time paid little attention to the survey results that were compiled and presented to them. They paid for the study, they were instrumental in its conduct, but they paid little heed to the findings. Researchers at the ISR concluded that the problem lay in the format by which the findings were presented. Therefore, they established the form of interlocking conferences, first as simply a means of discussion. It was found to be profitable and was subsequently expanded to a more elaborate form called survey-guided development. In this latter form the survey data are used not only as a vehicle for discussion and the dissemination of information, but as a diagnostic tool to help the group determine what direction it wishes to go in terms of the design and implementation of specific interventions (e.g., job enrichment, management-by-objectives, skill training, etc.) to improve the unit's functioning.

6. It is interesting to compare the responses of today's workers in the United States with comments made by teenagers in Sweden when asked to define a bad job.

Twelve-year-old Malin Löfgren, for example, defined an undesirable job as follows: "A bad job is one where others make all decisions, and where you have to do what others say." Fifteen-year-old Miklas Hellberg agreed: "It wouldn't be so bad to be a dishwasher, as long as you could take part in making the decisions on hours and pay and working conditions" (*Dagens Nybeter,* November 10, 1971).

REFERENCES

Coch, L., and J. R. P. French. Overcoming Resistance to Change. *Human Relations,* 1948, 1:512–532.

Likert, R. *The Human Organization.* New York: McGraw-Hill, 1967.

Porter, L. W., E. E. Lawler III, and J. R. Hackman, *Behavior in Organizations.* New York: McGraw-Hill, 1975.

Work Humanization in Practice:
What Can Labor Do?

by Irving Bluestone

We now know the difference between the way work is, and the way work can be.

Comments of some GM workers

THE SAME DRIVE WHICH HAS MOVED PEOPLE AND NATIONS THROUGHOUT HIStory toward political freedom, toward freedom of expression and religion, exists as well at the workplace between the employer and the employee. For two centuries, the owners of capital have assumed, in a sense, the same mantle of authority as was assumed by the "divine right of kings" principle which existed during the days of absolute monarchy. I think all of us who have done any reading at all are familiar with the oppressiveness, or I might say the *oppression,* that exists in the workplace today, that has existed in the workplace since the early days of the Industrial Revolution.

But to bring home to readers whose experience in factories is limited or perhaps restricted to an occasional summer job (certainly not an effective device for discovering the true character of work for workers in "perpetuity"), I would like to explore some of the work conditions of the past and the present. Let me start with a favorite example of mine: Zachary U. Geiger, who was the proprietor of the Mt. Cory Carriage and Wagon Works in Ohio, imposed the following rules and regulations on his employees.

1. Employees will daily sweep the floors, dust the furniture, shelves, and showcases. [Obviously, this is clerical help.]

2. Each day fill lamps, clean chimneys and trim wicks. Wash the windows once a week.

3. Each clerk will bring in a bucket of water and scuttle of coal for the day's business.

4. Make your own pens carefully. You may whittle nibs to your individual taste.

5. This office will open at 7:00 a.m. and close at 8:00 p.m. daily, except on the Sabbath, on which day it will remain closed. [A mere thirteen-hour day.]

6. Men employees will be given an evening off each week for courting purposes, or two evenings if they go regularly to church. [We can wonder how many readers would have gotten two evenings off.]

7. Every employee should lay aside from each pay a goodly sum of his earnings for his benefit during his declining years, so that he will not become a burden upon the charity of his betters.

8. Any employee who smokes Spanish cigars, uses liquors in any form, gets shaved at a barber shop, or frequents public halls, will give good reason to suspect his worth, intentions, integrity, and honesty.

9. The employee who has performed his labors faithfully, and without fault, for a period of five years in my service, and who has been thrifty and attentive to his religious duties, and is looked upon by his fellow men as a substantial and law-abiding citizen, will be given an increase of five cents per day in his pay, providing, of course, that just returns and profits from the business permit it.

This was corporate paternalism, 1872 style, the year these rules were dated. But matters (except for wages) did not improve quickly. It was nearly five decades later when tens of thousands flocked to Detroit to collect Henry Ford's five dollars a day, an unheard of wage for its time. These workers were put on the assembly line, with its minute division of labor and demanding tempo of the carrier system. It was a technological marvel for its time. It still is for plant tourists, but as I will later show, not for workers. Henry Ford said of it: "The assembly line is a haven for those who haven't got the brains to do anything else."

Ford also embraced a series of heavy-handed and suffocating personnel practices which were not much different than Zachary Geiger's. No women, for instance, were allowed to work in any Ford factory. He followed through on the famous German expression, *Kinder, Küche, und Kirche;* that is, women were to bear children, they were to remain in the kitchen, and they were to go to church. Moreover, men who failed to support their dependents would automatically be fired (the logic being, of course, that if they didn't support their dependents, he would deprive them of work so they couldn't support their dependents). Similarly, any man who was divorced, or in Mr. Ford's term "was living unworthily," would be fired, or at least would not be hired. And by living unworthily, he meant anyone who smoked cigarettes or who drank hard liquor.

In order to enforce these rules, he had a spy system, not only in the shop, but outside the plant to visit the homes of the workers. He called them "social workers" and they were on the Ford payroll. They would enter the worker's home and report on living habits. "Did the worker raise his own garden as he was instructed by Mr. Ford to do?" "Did his family house male boarders?" (That was taboo.) "Did the worker complain about his job and factory conditions?" (That was also taboo.) And if the answers were "wrong," according to Ford's standards, then a worker could be fired. On one occasion, they found a worker with a Polish surname who had violated one of these rules at home, but they couldn't pinpoint which worker it was. Consequently they fired every Polish worker with the same surname in order to be sure they got the right man.

Certainly some practices have changed since Mr. Ford's time. Management rarely attempts to control the worker's life outside the plant, especially in unionized plants. Still though there are some vestiges of this "off the job" paternalism. Today, however, second echelon management, not workers, are the ones more likely to be subject to Zachary Geiger's scrutiny and his 1872 rules. In some corporations, for instance, before a man is promoted, it is not unusual for the senior executives to have a look at his wife to find out if she will "fit in." And if she doesn't, no matter what his merit might otherwise be, he will be denied the promotion.

But what of "on the job" conditions fifty years after Henry Ford's heyday? I will let a worker, Dan Clark, answer this question by referring to his description (*Worker Alienation, 1972,* p. 12) of conditions at GM's relatively new (mid-1960s) Vega plant at Lordstown, Ohio:

> The problems that face the workers are monotony of the job, repetition, and boredom. We are constantly doing the same job over and over again. Where you have problems of hours, like right now—I am on sick leave, just had an operation, but before I left, 4 days ago, we were working 10½ to 11 hours, which you have no excuse to leave . . . you cannot leave in 8 hours unless you have an excuse to go to the doctor's, hospital, or emergency call if one of your kids are sick. That is the only way you are going to leave.

> You stay in that plant for 10½ to 11 hours of their choosing, and it may be maybe 95 degrees outside, but inside you can almost bet in the body shop it is a good 110. But that is not the warmest place in the whole plant. The warmest place in the whole plant is the paint shop. That is on the second level.

> When it is 95 outside, it is 120 or so in the paint shop, and your ventilation system, the air you are getting blown in on you, is supposed to be so cooled down—that is that 95 degree temperature outside that is coming on. You have no ventilation really at all. . . . Your job may be off

to the lefthand side and the ventilation is on the righthand side. They say there is nothing we can do about it, that is the way it was designed, and that is the way it is. There is nothing we can do.

There is the noise level in the plant. The body shop is worse. One man (supervisor) says . . . "I know there are problems there, it is above the noise level that it is supposed to be." He says (he) will take care of it. That is a year and a half now which has gone by and nothing has been done yet. There has been nothing provided unless you want to provide it yourself. I know. I put cotton in my ears because I cannot take it too much longer.

There is pollution in the plant. In the body shop that consists of, where you are welding, you are assembling the car together, and you are welding. You will have fumes like smoke or something that come on over, and dust and fumes and smoke coming out, and they do not have anything for that either. You put on your safety glasses and grin and bear it. That is about it.

You are going to find men today, who are younger—most of the men there are my age. I am 25 years old, and most of us agree that we do not want to spend all of our life in this plant working under these conditions.

Anyone who has not worked in an auto assembly plant probably can not relate to much of what Dan Clark has described. However, many who have worked in factories of other types probably have experienced a situation very much like the following: You got up, you dressed, you had breakfast, you went to work. You had to be there usually at 6:00 a.m. or 6:30 a.m., sometimes a little earlier, sometimes a little later. You parked your car if you drove to work. You walked into the plant, and the first thing you did was to punch a clock card. Having punched your clock card, you followed a particular pattern of walking to your job. You waited at your job until the bell rang. You then started to work. And you were told what you were to do; you were told in what order the job was to be done; you were told what the elements of the job were; you were told what tools to use; you were told how many pieces you had to do per hour; you were told where the water fountain was; you were told where the restroom was; you were told what your relief time would be; you were told what your lunch hour would be—actually a half hour is more common—and you did this precisely in the same fashion eight hours a day, five days a week or more, nearly every week of the year. You were following a specific set of rules and instructions handed down in the operation of your particular job. Now, in addition to that, someone, usually a supervisor, would have said to you, "There's a list of rules and regulations that you've got to take a look at concerning coming late, being absent, etc. You're not allowed to spit at the foreman; you can't use abusive language; you've got to do this;

you've got to do that. . . ." These are prohibitions, and there are typically twenty or thirty of these rules at any plant. If you violated any one of them, or if you violated any of the instructions which were given you in the method, means, and processes of performing your job, you would be subject to disciplinary action.

Worker Rights and Due Process under Collective Bargaining

I would ask the reader to think about the authoritarianism, the paternalism, that exists inside the typical factory even to this day. These are rules and practices governing *adults* through much of their waking day, and may I emphasize, in a society claiming the democratic ethic. To be sure, after many decades of collective bargaining, there have been many rights that workers have gained over and above wages and fringe benefits. Obviously, any worker who is being disciplined where there is a union contract will have the right to "grieve" (ultimately to go to arbitration) "to find out if management was right or wrong." The grievance procedure provides rights to the worker which previously rested solely in the hands of management.

Most industrial collective bargaining contracts deal with seniority rights, promotion rights, transfer rights, job-assignment rights, shift preference rights. Even the matter of receiving your pay check while you work on the job had to be negotiated. Years ago it was only after work that you went and got your pay. Of course that was on your time, not the company's. That had to be negotiated. Relief time, fair production standards, all of these things, now are matters which are negotiated, and which become in effect, the rights of workers. This extends to shop conditions as well. We have had to negotiate about how much oil can be on the floor. You can go into some shops today and you'll slop around in oil that will come up like little geysers as it pops up out of the wooden blocks on the floor when you step on them. We have had to negotiate the whole question of water fountains, of clean toilets and restrooms. We once had a strike against the General Motors Corporation because we insisted that there be doors put on the toilets, so that if a worker was in there, he just was not out in the open. The reason management took the doors off when the toilets were installed (they all came with doors) was that they did not trust the workers. They wanted to be able to see if the fella was sitting down on the toilet with his pants up or his pants down. Well, we've got doors on the toilets today. *It's a matter of plain human dignity.* I can recall some of the press blasting us at the time and making ridicule of the fact that workers would strike over *that* matter of simple dignity.

Health and safety conditions are also now a matter which is subject to coequal overview by the management and the union. And the union has health and safety representatives to see to it that healthful conditions and safe working practices are implemented and enforced in the plant. I could go on and on describing the changes that have taken place in working conditions, and yet I must go back to the description I presented earlier of the worker entering the plant in the morning and being subject to the autocratic or the authoritarian control of supervision by reason of an array of rules and regulations laid down by management. Now, what is this all about, this that I've been discussing in these descriptive terms? For one thing, it has to do with the establishment of decent jobs, and I guess the word "decent" is subject to definition. But fundamentally, it has to do with the dignity of the human being as a worker. Every human being has a worth just because he or she is a human being and *the worker expects the respect that goes with being a human being and the dignity that goes with the democratic concepts of human life*. That is what it is all about.

Achieving this kind of respect and dignity in the plant is not going to be easy, especially if we remember that authoritarianism has been the cornerstone of the factory system since its very inception. In fact it can be argued, union contracts notwithstanding, that reforms are more difficult to obtain today than they were in the past. This is true because of the internal competitive system that exists within large businesses, particularly within multiplant corporations like General Motors, about which I am most familiar. For example, within the Assembly Division of General Motors, there are eighteen plants. Each of these plants is audited daily and the auditing is done on the basis of what they term "efficiency," which I would consider to be unit costs on the one hand and quality on the other. This is a computerized system which provides reports to the general manager of the total division on a daily basis, and of course it is reviewed by him and by his staff. The report would indicate which among those eighteen plants are the least efficient and are putting out the poorest quality of work. The general manager of the plant which is eighteenth on the list, lowest on the totem pole, can expect a call from the central office to find out what is happening.

You must remember that the competitive system internally is quite sharp and that, in some measure, the bonus which the general manager receives at the end of the year is related to how well his plant has done. This is his incentive to do better. After some conversation I guess he realizes that something must be done so that his plant will not remain eighteenth on the list. Immediately he will call in his production superintendent and, in turn, superintendents over the various other departments. They in turn, will then talk to the foremen. The end butt of this system is the worker, the worker on the assembly line, on off-line operations, in materiel departments, all through the plant. The pressures are enormous.

Now suppose over a period of time this particular plant moves from eighteenth to, let us say, thirteenth place. Since there are eighteen plants, some other plant is now number eighteen. And the same pressures are applied to that general manager, that production superintendent, those superintendents and foremen, with the end of the line once again being the worker. This is an endless treadmill of competition within the corporation to increase efficiency, to reduce unit costs, and of course, to improve quality.

Now if a general manager is successful in moving his plant from number eighteen up to some midpoint among the eighteen, he is still not free of pressures because every department of the plant is audited similarly. If he happens to move his plant to number twelve on the list, it may be that his cushion room is still number eighteen, but the rest of the plant is doing well enough to bring him up to some higher average standing. The pressures then are on the cushion room to bring it up above number eighteen. And as soon as he has accomplished this, some other manager has a plant where the cushion room is number eighteen, and the treadmill of course then applies to him.

Given this sophisticated degree of internal control, the reader can envisage the pressures that grow inside the plant and what that means in the workplace is expressed by the workers in their attitude toward that workplace. This internal competition, this constant drive for higher production, for lower unit cost, for greater efficiency, and for higher quality—which of course from a consumer point of view is most meaningful—creates an environment in the plant which encourages resentment, absenteeism, lateness, and the general attitude of what we term "alienation" among the workers.

This attitude about "work being nothing more than a paycheck" can be illustrated by a favorite story making the rounds in the plants. There was this very good worker who would work only four days a week: He would not come in on the fifth day even though his foreman kept threatening him. Finally the superintendent spoke to the foreman about this employee; "How come you can't control your guys?" he asked. The foreman replied, "Well, if you think you're so good, you try it." So the superintendent walked over to the worker and said, "Hey Joe, I notice that you work four days, but you always take one day off. How come?" Joe looked at him and replied, "It's very simple. I can't afford to live working only three days a week."

In the 1960s and 1970s absenteeism began to rise markedly in the plants. There are few plants today in the industrial sector which can boast of having what was then a normal absenteeism rate of three or four percent. Absenteeism is bad for both management and the worker. A worker, by virtue of his seniority, can choose a particular job he likes only to find that he is forced by someone else's absenteeism to shift from job to job in order to maintain production quotas. Naturally he resents this, both because management is forcing him to do it and because his fellow workers are absent when they should not be. Absenteeism, as well as tardiness and labor turnover, is expensive for management. The quality of the product is affected. In addition, there is the cost of constantly hiring and retraining workers. Morale and motivation in the plant decline, and this can be felt all the way through to the customer who finally buys the product.

One thing we have learned is that absenteeism will not be solved by the authoritarian methods of the past. For example, the practice of laying-off a worker for a few days as punishment for excessive absenteeism proved an ineffective motivator. Management found that it had developed an untenable situation which might be characterized by the following anecdote. A supervisor goes up to a guy and says: "Why the hell were you absent yesterday?" "None of your god-damned business," comes the reply. "Okay, you're suspended for three days." "Thanks," says the worker, "can you make it a week?"

Signs of Change at the Workplace

I think both labor and management are going to have to re-think seriously the nature of the workplace, and I believe they are commencing to do this. For example, General Motors, the corporation I am most familiar with as director of the G.M. department for our union, set up a center for Organizational Development. Originally, it was directed toward managerial personnel and focused upon issues like "How do you motivate managers to become more innovative, creative, and more satisfied with their work?" But soon their activities were directed toward blue-collar workers as well, those represented by our union. At this point we became interested. Were these experiments designed toward holding down workers, or toward seeing to it that these efforts would expand workers' horizons and allow them to become more participative in the decisions that affect their jobs? We began a series of discussions with GM personnel to find out what their organizational development (OD) activities were all about. We subsequently informed them that we (the union) would like to join with them in a mutual endeavor to develop ideas, projects, and experiments with the goal of establishing meaningful, effective participation by the workers in all of this. We believed that this last point was critical, otherwise the program would fail—at least from the worker's point of view. It would still be the case of workers constantly getting their orders from above, being put in straitjackets, or simply being robots to the machine and cost accounting processes.

Eventually our discussions bore fruit. At the 1973 contract negotiations, we signed an agreement to establish a joint National Committee to "improve the quality of working life of the Auto Worker." We agreed that this committee was not designed to impose programs and experiments from the top, but rather to encourage both union and management people at the local plants to undertake programs of their own. The National Committee would be a monitoring and advisory agency.[1] For three years, we have devoted most of our effort toward developing programs; however, other "higher" priorities frequently keep taking our time away from this effort. Nevertheless, we have made progress that I can report.

One of our first experiments dealt with a plant in which we had a difficult collective bargaining relationship in the past, with a large number of grievances and strikes during the duration of the contract. It was just a bad, unsound collective bargaining relationship. The plant also had a history of producing poor quality products (this is an auto assembly plant), by GM's own internal audit standards. I guess we felt that we might as well tackle the difficult cases first. We decided that the first step should be to find out what would be achieved if we brought workers directly into the decision-making process. Could this improve the quality of product *and* the quality of work life? In August 1974, we (labor and management) jointly hired an outside consultant who was an expert in teaching problem-solving techniques. Thirty-six workers volunteered for the experiment from the glass area of Soft Trim, the department in which the windshield and side door glass is installed. It had a very poor record of scrappage, breakage, and work which later had to be repaired. These people went through a training program in which they were taught various problem-solving techniques. This training was paid for by the company and took place on company time. The workers were then asked to apply to their job what they had learned. They were given time, again paid for by the company, in which they could sit down together as a group and discuss what was wrong with the work that they were doing. They asked themselves why they achieved such poor quality, such heavy breakage, and such large quantities of scrappage.

This program has been in effect about a year now, and breakage is almost zero. Repair work has been reduced to a minimum, far below the norm for the plant. The workers are very pleased with what they have done because *they* made the decisions. *They* are the ones who dreamed up what ought to be done. They haven't increased their productivity in terms of so many jobs per hour (the line runs at a mechanically determined speed). There has been no one pressing them to do more work, but they themselves have improved the quality of the product they are producing. And as a result of all this, they have taken great pride in what they accomplished. They were not disciplined; they did not have a foreman standing over them day after day, hour after hour, minute after minute. They had the opportunity as a group to make decisions which previously were made only by foremen, by engineers, and by management.[2]

Workers in the area of the plant near the glass department began to take notice of what was happening. We began receiving requests for the expansion of the program from groups of workers in the vicinity. As a result, a survey was taken in which 700 additional workers volunteered to participate in a similar program. We are now in the process of training these new volunteers in problem-solving techniques. They work in all different kinds of jobs. It might be hard trim or soft trim; it might be chassis assembly. Any of the jobs in which these volunteers work will now be subject to the same participatory process.

What does all this mean? Fundamentally it means that we are tapping the creativity, the innovativeness of workers, *not* to do more work, *not* to work harder, *not* to work at a faster work pace, but to give them the opportunity to decide for themselves what ought to be done. I can envisage a situation where the workers will be told, "This is the volume of sales we need; here is the kind of product and the product mix that has to be produced. Now you sit down and figure out how many workers and production steps it takes to do it." We are a long way from management surrendering rights such as these. Right now, they decide the number of workers, then we fight with them. But I think in time management will recognize that workers know as much about these jobs as any of their management people, maybe more, and that they must begin to agree to let the workers make decisions which previously had been purely a management prerogative.

Let me cite another example which will relate to the discussion of absenteeism presented earlier. A few years ago GM and the union undertook an experiment which involved the building of a van. Five volunteers (one woman, one black, and three whites) of varying ages (twenties to the late thirties) formed a group to do a team exercise in assembling a van. They were given the blueprints for the assembly of the van plus the assistance of an engineer (when they needed him). For days they did nothing but read the blueprints and work out how they were going to build that van. (Now, I am not talking just about an engine or a chassis, I am talking about the van once the chassis has already been assembled.) They determined how to divide up the work among themselves and decided which operations would be performed by whom.

Over a seven-week period absenteeism became zero. Absenteeism had been very high among some of these volunteers, and one of them was on the verge of being discharged for excessive absenteeism. There was not a single accident during the seven weeks that required medical treatment, except for one scratch. There was no lateness. Now the first few times these workers assembled the van, it took them much longer than it does on the assembly line. But at the end of the seven-week trial period, the van was being assembled in exactly the same amount of time that a van is assembled on the normal assembly line. At this point the experiment ended. The workers were informed that they would have to go back to their original jobs on the assembly line, and we had a miniature revolt. I had to go up there and sit down and talk with them. What they told me was this: "We now know the difference between the way work is, and the way work can be." They were the ones who made the decisions as to how to assemble a van. They also had to test it. And now, knowing what it means to do something in which they were the decision-makers, they were unwilling to go back to their original jobs. In each case, we worked out transfers to put them on a job somewhat more satisfactory than the normal assembly line type jobs from which they had come. Nevertheless, one of them said he was going to quit, rather than go back. He could not follow through, however, because at that time the depression hit the auto industry and there simply weren't any other jobs to be found.

I would like to stress this last point because it bears on the question of job satisfaction. There have been a number of studies which supposedly tell us that the vast majority of workers are satisfied with their jobs. I believe the reason for this is that there is little else the worker can say. What are his alternatives? He has a job; it's a stinking job; it's a repetitious and monotonous job. It bores him to death—he has to be always thinking of something else while he is working or he'll go crazy. But also, he has to accommodate himself to it because that job is the only way he can earn a living and support his family. There is no point in knocking what one has to do, even for a survey questionnaire. But I believe that when we reach the point where workers can make a comparison between their present jobs and a more creative alternative, then we will find different results from these surveys. However, it is true that some workers do not like to think through a job in the way that our five workers did in the van assembly experiment. Apparently they prefer the repetitious in job design; they do not like to work with others, thinking through ideas and making decisions. They prefer to be isolated, and obviously that is the kind of job they ought to be put on. And I have no doubt that this kind of work will always be available.

There is another experiment that has received considerable publicity in which our union is cooperating with a company, Harman International, at a plant in Bolivar, Tennessee. Bolivar is a little town about sixty miles outside of Memphis in an agricultural community. If ever an experiment in improving the quality of work life had a less promising setting, it has to be this plant. It is an old plant consisting of two Quonset huts that are dilapidated and filthy. The work force is divided about 50 percent black and white and there are still some racial tensions in the area. This plant builds side view mirrors for most of the automobiles made in America. Given the miserable working conditions at the plant, they put out a very good product.[3]

Again the company and the union jointly initiated a quality of work life program in which workers volunteered to determine how they wanted "the job'' done. But this program not only attacked the job, it went to the plant facilities as well. It considered what color the workers wanted their machines to be painted, and what color they wanted the walls to be painted. The workers made these decisions in meetings which they held on a regular basis on company time. Within a short period, these meetings yielded new ways of performing the work and even resulted in the special tools for performing the work better. As a result, workers were soon able to finish their day's production in less than eight hours. This resulted in a new question for the workers to consider: ''What are we going to do with this extra time?'' (Already management had agreed not to increase production standards by reason of this quality of work life program.) First, they decided to go to the cafeteria where they could play cards or talk. But this, they later concluded, was a waste of time. So the workers decided that when they completed the assigned production for eight hours, even if it took only seven hours, they would go home. They called it ''earned idle time.'' This decision created difficulties for management and especially the union. Some workers could go home earlier because they had made their production, others could not. This difference could create all kinds of disruptions inside the plant which the union officers did not want. The union, therefore, made the counter-proposal that this earned idle time be used to expand the workers' horizons by setting up a school where they could take courses of their own choosing. This idea was finally accepted and the first course to be offered was a welding course. (Many of the workers were also small farmers whose equipment occasionally breaks down, and they would like to be able to weld it themselves.) Soon, little by little, the courses multiplied; some wanted sewing classes, and one was set up; others wanted a piano class, even a dancing class, and they were set up. It was also discovered that a number of workers had not completed their high school education. Arrangements were made to provide high school courses for these workers. Some workers wanted a black studies program, and one was initiated. Eventually, over 200 courses were offered.

All of this is really quite extraordinary, and it came about by workers making their own decisions about how to design their own work to reach reasonable production standards. They helped the company too because it recently won a major contract which might otherwise have been lost. Most importantly, these workers are learning how to use earned idle time to enrich their own capabilities as human beings. No one imposed upon them the kinds of courses to be offered; the workers made those decisions themselves. The union and management responded by finding the instructors, some of whom came right out of the work force. For instance, the instructor in welding is a worker who is now learning what it means to be a teacher.

We are, to be sure, only at the threshold of what can be done. We know how successful some of these experiments can be, and we recognize the risk of failure. We know that by experimenting and testing we can determine a measure of success. But yet, we do not know whether that success is transferable. Each plant has its own practices and traditions. What works in one plant may not work in another, or may have to be adapted to fit the special traditions, practices, and work habits of another plant. This is even true within a plant; there is no guarantee of transferability from one department to another. It is best, therefore, to let the workers on the shop floor find out what works best for them, which is the way it should be.

We Can Democratize the Work Place

I could go on writing about these experiences because I have great, and maybe unique, enthusiasm for this subject, I say "unique" because within the labor movement there is major resistance to implementing "quality of work life" programs. Many of my fellow unionists feel that it is a kind of gimmick that management will use solely to its advantage. They see it as a way to increase production, to have the workers work harder, or even as an excuse to lay off workers. Others worry about the worker's loyalty to the union as workers become more satisfied with their existence inside the plants. I argue strongly though that with appropriate safeguards very little of this will happen. I believe that the future of collective bargaining will grow out of the experiments I have recounted, and as we improve the quality of work life, we will strengthen not only the loyalty that the worker has toward his job and toward management, but also we will strengthen his loyalty toward the union as well.

But there is something deeper in all this. I started out talking about democracy—the choices and rights which are inherent in the kind of society we cherish in this country. The most glaring exception to these basic democratic precepts is the industrial plant; it lies at the workplace. I believe that this is the fundamental weakness in our American system.

Unless we can democratize the workplace as we have democratized other aspects of our society, our future looks dark. More importantly, we will be missing that level of potential which is possible for humans to reach. It is my belief that in the years ahead, as more and more of these experiments become standard practice in the shops, as workers are increasingly given responsibility to make their own decisions within the framework of what needs to be produced, this will strengthen our society, not weaken it. It will mean that the worker in our democratic society has come into his own *in the shop* as he has in the other aspects of his life.

NOTES

1. More specifically we agreed to carry out a number of joint activities: encouraging members of labor and management to develop experiments and projects, calling upon members of both sides to cooperate in these endeavors, providing for the joint funding of outside consultants, and reporting and evaluating these activities.

2. To provide a contrast between this experiment and what more typically occurs, the following testimony by a Lordstown worker and union officer will be helpful: "The job assignments within the plant in the same classification are solely the right of management, no say for the employee. The job content, and there is not much to that because when you have 36 seconds [to perform the operation] . . . all we are left with is the dead end jobs . . . jobs that offer little challenge to the more educated worker, little chance for advancement, and hardly any chance to participate as a worker. . . . [The worker] is brought into the plant and his orientation session ends and starts with his papers on insurance and his assignment to a foreman who immediately puts his warm body on the [assembly] line." (*Worker Alienation*, 1972, p. 10)

3. *Editors' Note:* The chief executive officer of this company, Sidney Harman, has a Ph.D. in organizational psychology. Dr. Harman is an extraordinary motivator who is willing to take risks in letting workers "problem solve" for themselves. Four principles were established for all the experiments: (1) workers must be secure in their jobs, (2) there must be fair treatment, (3) needs must be respected, and (4) workers must have a say in any decision making that affects them. A fifth principle evolved: all parties must respect each others' differing roles in a climate of trust.

REFERENCE

Worker Alienation, 1972. Hearings before the Subcommittee on Employment, Manpower, and Poverty of the Committee on Labor and Public Welfare, 92nd Congress, second session, July 25 and 26, 1972. Washington, D.C.: U.S. Government Printing Office, 1972.

It Doesn't Add Up: The Role of Human Resource Accounting in Effecting Work Humanization

by Ken Milani

CORPORATE MANAGERS RECEIVE ABUNDANT INFORMATION ABOUT THE FINAN-
cial and physical resources within their organizations from sophisticated data
processing equipment and information systems. They secure data in an almost
endless flow about financial (e.g., cash, receivables, investments) and physical (e.g., buildings, equipment, inventories) resources. However, there is one
resource about which very little concrete information is developed. This is the
human resource.

Rensis Likert (1967) has called for the development of an accounting or
information system which would provide managers with data about the value
of people in their organization. Likert's call for human resource accounting
(HRA) stems from his belief that traditional reporting practices (which tend to
emphasize short-run changes in sales volume or profits) lead to a long-run
deterioration of the human resources of an organization. Because the changing value of the human resource is ignored when organizational activities are
measured and reported using the traditional short-run emphases on sales or
profit, two effects are generated: (a) most managers are either unaware of or
unconcerned about work humanization activities and (b) work humanization
efforts are perceived by most managers as peripheral.

Likert believes that an HRA system would lead to greater humanization
of the work setting because managers would receive concrete information
about the changes in the value of human resources as these changes occur.
More importantly, this information would be generated from the firm's accounting system—an integral and important source of information used by

179

managers in daily decision-making activities. This paper will examine Likert's hypothesis that the explicit inclusion of human resource information in major corporate financial reports (i.e., the balance sheet and income statements) would have a positive effect on work humanization efforts.

A Short History of Human Resource Accounting

Although HRA procedures have never been accepted or adopted by a significant number of organizations, accountants recognized the value of people to an organization as early as the 1930s. Gilbert (1970) notes that the 1932 *Accountants' Handbook* "suggested the origin of goodwill was certain values arising from the personal qualities and technical skills of owners, managers and employees" (p. 295).

More recently, the Milwaukee Braves baseball team "capitalized the cost of player contracts acquired from the prior owner of the club and the subsequent farm club, scouting and recruitment operations of the new team" (Weiss 1972, p. 45). In 1967, Internal Revenue Service (IRS) Procedure 67-379 was developed. It required the capitalization and amortization (for tax purposes) of contract and rookie bonus costs for all terms.

At the present time, HRA efforts range from "proposals to account for the costs of recruiting, hiring, training, and developing employees as capital investment for management planning and control purposes, to proposals to account for the value of an organization's human resources as capital assets for financial reporting purposes" (McRae 1974, p. 32). No one denies that the asset or resource which is most valuable to an organization is its human resource. However, as Figler (1975) points out, "typical management actions in most businesses today show little understanding of this . . . let alone how to acknowledge . . . it" (p.23).

The Pros and Cons of Human Resource Accounting

HRA has both its proponents and opponents. In addition to citing the contribution of HRA to work humanization, HRA advocates frequently contend that "the information enables management to make hiring, training, development and replacement decisions on the basis of realistic cost-benefit analysis and provides investors with an improved basis to assess the value of an enterprise and to make better investment decisions" (McRae 1974, p. 32). Opponents of HRA have attacked it on several fronts including conceptual, methodological, and ethical perspectives.

Advocates of HRA feel that information about an organization's human resources is a necessary element of a well-managed and humanistic organization. On the other hand, HRA opponents contend *no* accounting information about the value of the human resource is better than *some* accounting information.

This section of the paper will focus on the pros and cons of the HRA movement before moving into a discussion of its applicability to work humanization efforts. The reason for this synopsis of the arguments for and against HRA lies in the writer's belief that acceptance of HRA has been somewhat hindered by the lack of agreement surrounding the development and use of an HRA system.

Definition of an employee as an asset or resource

The arguments in favor of formally including people as organizational assets are based on the following economic concept: an asset or resource is an organizational factor which can provide future benefits. Gilbert (1970) indicates that "economists equate assets, resources, expected future service, and factors of production which clearly justifies human resources being considered assets" (p. 25). Weiss (1976) considers an accounting concept—the going concern—and argues certain employee expenditures "are incurred on the assumption that these employees will continue, and that justifies . . . capitalization . . ." (p. 46). Earlier, Weiss (1972) confronted arguments which suggested the requirement of ownership for asset recognition by citing "capitalization of rental payments under long-term leases [as] an example of asset treatment where the item is not owned in the legal sense" (p. 47). Jaggi (1976) notes that "in order to be classified as an asset, a resource must have service potential for more than one period" (p. 41). Jaggi concludes that this criterion justifies the treatment of "employees service resources . . . as assets" (p. 41).

Jauch and Skigen (1974), however, are opposed to defining employees as assets because "the length of time the human asset is under the control of the firm is solely at the discretion of the asset" (p. 33). In other words, the future benefits to the organization are not assured. Generally accepted accounting principles (GAAP) do not allow the recognition of the human element of an organization as an asset. Accounting Principles Board Opinion 17 specifically states that intangibles generated internally (such as human resources) should be expensed. Under GAAP, ownership is a necessary criterion for asset recognition in all but a few situations. In a similar manner, McRae (1974) indicates that "an enterprise acquires only a contractual right to the services of its human resources" (p. 34). Newell (1972) summarizes the anti-asset position as follows: "The means used to disclose this information need not and should not take the form of an asset until we have established a theory which would allow us to report other similar costs as assets" (p. 16).

Thus, the battle over the definition of what constitutes an "asset" is still unresolved.

Measurement concepts/models

While some accountants, economists, and others have fought the definitional battle over what constitutes an asset, others have turned their attention to the problems of measurement of the value of human resources within an organization. Following the suggestion of Brummet et al. (1969) for "multiple measurement concepts" (p. 15), several concepts and models have been developed. Unfortunately, their advice to record these measures as "an interrelated and complementary set of concepts" (p. 15) has gone largely unheeded. Thus, another battleground has been created concerning the various measurement concepts and models which have evolved. In the sections which follow the more prevalent of these models will be discussed.

Historical cost.   Measurement of human asset value by means of historical cost or book value is the method suggested by Brummet et al. (1969) "until tools capable of measuring the appreciation or depreciation in the value of human resources can be fully developed" (p. 15). Since this technique (which involves the capitalization of acquisition, development, and other personnel-related costs) conforms with GAAP, it has received a great deal of attention and criticism. Perhaps the strongest criticism which has been raised is its failure to reflect the "current value" of a human resource. In most situations, certain costs are capitalized early in the employee's career and amortization starts almost immediately. Figure 1 depicts the typical patterns developed under the historical cost (book value) measurement model.

Pattern A reflects the capitalization of acquisition costs (e.g., recruiting, screening), in this case assumed to be $18,000, and its amortization (i.e., expensing) over the person's expected work career (assumed to be thirty years). Notice in this model that the employee's value begins to decrease as soon as the employee joins the organization. Pattern B illustrates the capitalization of the acquisition costs (assumed to be $18,000) plus early developmental costs (assumed to be $6,000) and the amortization of these costs over the anticipated career length of the employee (again assumed to be thirty years).

Capitalization of costs.   This approach is closely related to the historical cost method since it involves capitalizing certain costs including acquisition, start-up and developmental disbursements *as well as* the employee's salary. This approach has been critized on the same grounds as the historical

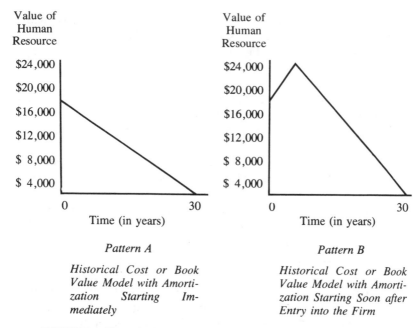

Pattern A

Historical Cost or Book Value Model with Amortization Starting Immediately

Pattern B

Historical Cost or Book Value Model with Amortization Starting Soon after Entry into the Firm

FIGURE 1. Historical cost or book value measurement model used in Human Resource Accounting

cost approach, but Jauch and Skigen (1974) feel that it has an additional drawback since in some instances there is "absolutely no correlation between the salary paid and the actual value of the employee to the organization" (p. 34).

Opportunity cost. This measurement model contends "the value of resources is determined by the amount that the human resources could earn if . . . used in an alternative function" (Jaggi 1976, p. 42). For example, if an administrative officer of a management consulting firm could generate $100,000 in fees for the firm if used as an operating consultant, his or her human resource value would be based on the $100,000 figure. While an attractive proposition in many ways, the opportunity cost model developed by Hekiman and Jones (1967) does not enjoy widespread support since it tends to focus only on those individuals in an organization with special skills or talents. Jaggi (1976) feels the most striking drawback of the technique is its failure to "provide necessary information for managerial decisions" (p. 42).

Triangle/Quadrangle/Pentagon model. This model recognizes that as an employee spends more time with an organization, he or she is likely to become more valuable to the organization. This growth in value may continue throughout the employee's career, or it may hit a high point, hold steady, and then start to decrease slowly. Figler (1975) described this pattern and noted that some individuals will increase in value until they retire while others will reach a peak and "thereafter remain static or begin to deteriorate" (p. 24). Jauch and Skigen (1974) alluded to the same pattern in arguing against acquisition cost as a measure of human resource value. Figure 2 illustrates the "triangle, quadrangle and/or pentagon" model in both of Figler's states.

Other models.   Several other models and concepts have been introduced or discussed. These include a replacement value model (Brummet, Flamholtz, and Pyle 1969), a salary surrogate economic value model (Lev and Schwartz 1971), a stochastic model (Flamholtz 1971), a group valuation model which stresses the Markov Chain technique (Jaggi and Lau 1974), a behavioral variables approach (Likert 1967), and a behavioral outcome costs model (Mirvis and Macy 1976).

None of the models discussed above has yet gained widespread acceptance. Indeed, the introduction of a new measurement concept or model creates another barrier to the acceptance and implementation of HRA since the development of a model is most often prefaced with criticism of existing models. Thus, the entire philosophic controversy is set in motion once again.

Use of human resource accounting information

Another area of controversy in HRA development is the question of whether HRA information should be provided for external and/or internal use. That is, should it be provided to stockholders, creditors, etc., or should its use be limited to internal operating personnel. At this stage, Jaggi (1976) and others conclude "the inclusion of human assets in external reporting has not yet received wide acceptance . . ." (p. 42). Nevertheless, one pioneering effort at external reporting occurred at the R. G. Barry Company in the late 1960s. The company developed two sets of financial statements, one with and one without human resource information. Weiss (1972) described the Barry system as one which "departs from original outlay cost . . . by using a replacement cost approach to establish an initial HRA balance, and then adding to this a combination of outlay costs and company development . . . costs" (p. 43). Shown below are examples of the statements prepared by the R. G. Barry Company under conventional practice, and using HRA information (Gilbert, p. 27).

Figler (1975) and others (e.g., Brummet et al. 1969; Weiss, 1976) feel that priority should "be given to developing the HRA techniques needed to

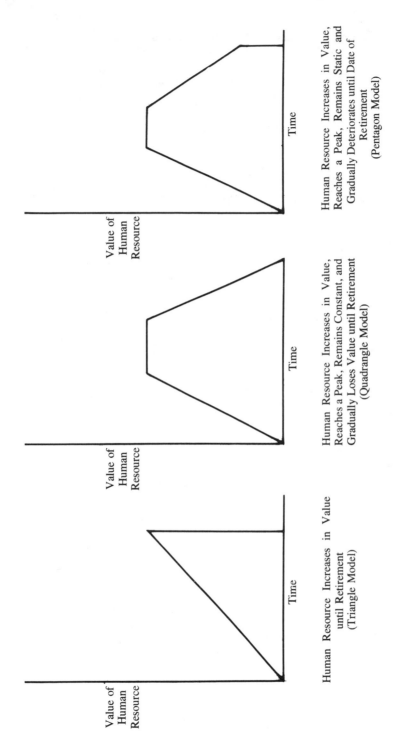

Human Resource Increases in Value until Retirement (Triangle Model)

Human Resource Increases in Value, Reaches a Peak, Remains Constant, and Gradually Loses Value until Retirement (Quadrangle Model)

Human Resource Increases in Value, Reaches a Peak, Remains Static and Gradually Deteriorates until Date of Retirement (Pentagon Model)

FIGURE 2. The "triangle, quadrangle and/or pentagon" model of human resource measurement

"THE TOTAL CONCEPT"
R. G. Barry Corporation and Subsidiaries
Pro Forma
(Financial and Human Resource Accounting)

	1970 Conventional and Human Resource	1970 Conventional Only	1969 Conventional and Human Resource	1969 Conventional Only
BALANCE SHEET				
Assets				
Total Current Assets	$10,944,693	$10,944,693	$10,003,628	$10,003,628
Net Property, Plant and Equipment	1,682,357	1,682,357	1,770,717	1,770,717
Excess of Purchase Price of Subsidiaries over Net Assets Acquired	1,188,704	1,188,704	1,188,704	1,188,704
Net Investments in Human Resources	942,194	—	986,094	—
Other Assets	166,417	166,417	106,783	106,783
	$14,924,365	$13,982,171	$14,055,926	$13,069,832
Liabilities and Stockholders' Equity				
Total Current Liabilities	$ 3,651,573	$ 3,651,573	$ 5,715,708	$ 5,715,708
Long Term Debt, Excluding Current Installments	2,179,000	2,179,000	1,935,500	1,935,500
Deferred Compensation	77,491	77,491	62,380	62,380
Deferred Federal Income Taxes as a Result of Appropriation for Human Resources	471,097	—	493,047	—
Stockholders' Equity:				
Capital Stock	1,087,211	1,087,211	879,116	879,116
Additional Capital in Excess of Par Value	3,951,843	3,951,843	1,736,253	1,736,253
Retained Earnings				
Financial	3,035,053	3,035,053	2,740,875	2,740,875
Appropriation for Human Resources	471,097	—	493,047	—
Total Stockholders' Equity	8,545,204	8,074,107	5,849,291	5,356,244
	$14,924,365	$13,982,171	$14,055,926	$13,069,832

"THE TOTAL CONCEPT"
R. G. Barry Corporation and Subsidiaries
Pro Forma
(Financial and Human Resource Accounting)

STATEMENT OF INCOME	1970 Conventional and Human Resource	1970 Conventional Only	1969 Conventional and Human Resource	1969 Conventional Only
Net sales	$28,164,181	$28,164,181	$25,310,588	$25,310,588
Cost of sales	18,252,181	18,252,181	16,275,876	16,275,876
Gross profit	9,912,000	9,912,000	9,034,712	9,034,712
Selling, general and administrative expenses	7,546,118	7,546,118	6,737,313	6,737,313
Operating income	2,365,882	2,365,882	2,297,399	2,297,399
Other deductions, net	250,412	250,412	953,177	953,177
Income before Federal income taxes	2,115,470	2,115,470	1,344,222	1,344,222
Human Resource expenses applicable to future periods	(43,900)	—	173,569	—
Adjusted income before Federal income taxes	2,071,570	2,115,470	1,517,791	1,344,222
Federal income taxes	1,008,050	1,030,000	730,785	644,000
Net income	$ 1,063,520	$ 1,085,470	$ 787,006	$ 700,222

provide information for daily management decision-making" (p. 23). Elias (1976), however, while viewing HRA information as being completely internal, is fearful the use of HRA may "encourage overspending or more investing in human resources than is economically justifiable" (p. 43). Additionally, he feels HRA could magnify and aggravate certain internal disputes, such as personnel transfers, "because an amortization expense will have to be transferred along with the employee" (p. 44).

Ethical considerations of human resource accounting

Mirvis and Macy (1976) directly address the ethical question of human resource valuation. Indicating a natural reaction by some to equate HRA with slavery, they feel the ethical issue is serious enough to "counterfeit the largely humanistic motives expressed by human asset accounting advocates" (p. 75). Jauch and Skigen's (1974) attack on HRA states "that humans simply do not qualify as assets under the usual definition of the term where assets are defined as something of value owned by a firm. [Their] primary objection . . . is that people are no longer owned" (p. 33).

On the other hand, Gilbert (1970) recognizes the ethical arguments against HRA but concludes that "one could argue that by having his value recognized, a person would be motivated to better himself and increase his worth" (p. 28). And Weiss (1972) feels "the notion that employees would resent treatment as 'assets' is probably the weakest argument against HRA, since the implementation of such a system would be accompanied by a general upgrading of management practices and employee morale" (p. 47).

As with the other HRA features cited previously, its ethical side has drawn out disagreements among writers. And for the first time, the humanistic foundations of HRA are viewed as a matter of concern.

Practitioner Acceptance of Human Resource Accounting

Prior sections have concentrated on the pros and cons of HRA from an academic or theoretical perspective. This portion of the paper examines the issues from the perspective of the practitioner.

Figler (1975), a member of an international firm of certified public accountants, feels that HRA can be applied practically in an organization "through full cooperation of the accounting and personnel department with management." Unfortunately, Figler states, only "a small percentage of all the managers in the country are aware that HRA exists . . ." [and] "the majority of practicing accountants have developed little enthusiasm for HRA"

(p. 25). Similarly, he notes personnel people could "view the challenge of measuring human assets as presenting so many difficulties that their attitudes toward it would be essentially negative" (p. 26).

A telephone survey by this writer of accounting executives (e.g., controllers, assistant controllers) in Midwest firms has substantiated Figler's comments.[1] Of thirty-two executives interviewed, eighteen (56 percent) were not aware of the HRA concept (see Table 1). The majority of those familiar with or aware of the concept were not convinced that the types of information generated by an HRA system would be beneficial to shareholders and/or management (see Table 2).

Arguments against HRA information incorporated many standard criticisms, including the notion of HRA data being too subjective and/or too costly

TABLE 1
**Accounting Executive Responses to Question Concerning Familiarity
With the Concept of Human Resource Accounting**

Are you familiar with the concept referred to as Human Resource or Human Asset Accounting?	*Number of Respondents*	*Percent*
Yes, I am very familiar with the concept	1	3
Yes, I have some familiarity with the concept	4	13
Yes, I am aware of the concept	9	28
No	18	56
	32	100%

TABLE 2
**Accounting Executive Responses to Question Concerning the
Usefulness of Human Resource Accounting Data**

Do you feel Human Resource or Human Asset Accounting information is potentially beneficial to shareholders and/or management?	*Number of Respondents*	*Percent*
Yes, very beneficial	3	21
Yes, beneficial	2	14
Yes, but of little benefit	4	29
No	5	36
	14	100%

to collect. Nonetheless, an understanding of the human condition was also reflected by a number of comments offered by respondents:

> The uniqueness of each person makes it hard, almost impossible to place a value on them. There's too much lost in the translation.

> To do an effective valuation, I would have to gather information about the personal lives of our people. I've been around long enough to know that problems at home carry an impact on the job.

Several executives cited high turnover as an argument against HRA. At least two felt they had more important issues to handle before getting involved in any HRA effort. One concluded his interview by stating, "I've got payrolls to meet and a business to run while you 'ivory tower' types sit around and talk theory."

Several controllers felt that the HRA system would involve a control-subsidiary account relationship. The control account would reflect the value of all personnel in a department, division, or organization while the subsidiary accounts would provide detailed information about the value of each individual in the unit being measured. The executives were particularly concerned about the "leaking" of this information to the personnel involved. One controller felt that HRA values would be "more sensitive than payroll information." An assistant controller expressed similar concern about employee reactions to their value relative to the values assigned other personnel within the firm.

About one-half of the controllers who were familiar with HRA indicated that their personnel departments were engaged in human resource measurement activities. However, the types of projects they cited (e.g., skills inventories, personnel development reviews and age/experience profiles) do not truly fall within the HRA framework. Nevertheless, they may be stepping stones to future HRA activity. Overall, the survey confirmed a general lack of information about and/or acceptance of HRA on the part of practicing accountants.

Human Resource Accounting's Role in Effecting Work Humanization

Likert, Bowers and others have frequently stated their belief that the development of an effective HRA system is a necessary component of any meaningful effort toward work humanization. Bowers, summarizing this line of thought elsewhere in this volume, asserts "there is a major flaw in the financial and economic thinking of organizational managers with regard to the human asset. Work in this field, . . . any attempt at applicational efforts in humanistic work design, . . . is still expensed, rather than treated as an investment. As a result [these] efforts are considered a luxury or frill, to be cut or canceled whenever there is a downturn in the business cycle.''

Human resource accounting as a positive force in work humanization efforts

Brummet et al. (1969) believe HRA can be a positive force in making managers more aware of the worth of people in the organization. They feel the lack of HRA information perpetuates short-run efforts which put people under a lot of pressure to ''temporarily increase productivity or reduce costs with the effects upon employee motivation, loyalty, willingness to cooperate, and labor relations going unmeasured'' (p. 15). Elias (1976) exhibits similar rationale, believing HRA would motivate a manager to initiate or increase human resource expenditures ''since the impact of more spending will not be reflected in the income measure immediately'' (p. 43). In effect, Elias sees HRA as having a direct, positive, and immediate impact on work humanization efforts.

Human resource accounting focus is not on work humanization

With few exceptions, the overwhelming majority of writers have argued for or against HRA while ignoring work humanization as either a major goal or even a minor objective of HRA efforts. Liao (1974), for example, argues that HRA would have a positive effect on productivity by ''measuring and reporting the changes in (behavioral) variables in the way management is accustomed to dealing with them'' (p. 20). Jaggi (1976) states similarly that HRA is ''not concerned with humans per se. Rather its primary concern is the performance of employees' services'' (p. 41). McRae (1974) reports that the HRA analysis being conducted at American Telephone & Telegraph (AT & T) is used entirely for management planning and control. The director of the AT & T project contends ''management can determine the payoff on a specific personnel program or evaluate alternative programs in terms of their impacts on the loss of employees and the related costs and, in turn, on future earnings. Also, local offices are . . . more cost-conscious because the information is available'' (p. 34).

It is possible to look beyond the statements presented above and see work humanization as an outcome. However, the HRA outputs stressed by these writers (e.g., performance, earnings, cost-consciousness) are not those normally associated with work humanization. Perhaps, this line of thought could be expected since accountants are not trained, nor are they utilized, in a manner that would generate or expand their awareness and/or sensitivity to work humanization. Several examples of this "tunnel-vision" syndrome so frequently displayed by accountants can be cited:

> *Managerial accounting efforts which stress the development of standards and ways of measuring and reporting deviations from these standards.* Work humanization may enter tangentially into the development and analysis of standards, but the emphasis is clearly on maximizing the output of each resource including the human resource.

> *The one-year time frame which accounting tends to impose on both internal, and especially, external reporting.* The life of the organization is cut up into twelve-month segments and the comparison of these segments can significantly influence, among other things, a manager's rewards as well as the price of the company's stock. The short-run "pressure cooker" practices described earlier can only be encouraged by this temporal slicing of the organization's life.

> *Tax laws encourage immediate expensing of HRA efforts.* Other than IRS Revenue Procedure 67-379 mentioned above (dealing with professional athletes), the law permits a company to immediately expense employee acquisition and development costs. The alternative of the capitalizing human resource costs (and usually increasing the firm's tax liability) is not very appealing.

Conclusion

The proponents of HRA feel that it would expose human resource mismanagement and/or make managers more aware of and concerned about the people resource within their organizations. However, one manager at R. G. Barry Company "recalls minimal impact of HRA on management decisions" (Mirvis and Macy 1976, p. 75). The survey of accounting executives conducted by this writer found that financial executives consider the "people" side of a decision to include the standard issues (e.g., costs of turnover, start-up costs, retraining costs related to layoffs, and production cost benefits derived from a stable work force). Their conception, however, did not include the development of HRA information about other policies and decisions.

At this stage in its development, HRA is a mechanism similar to the use of busing as a means to achieve and/or encourage integration. The mechanism is not as important as the attitudes which prevail. If meaningful integration is to occur, positive attitudes toward integration must be fostered or reinforced. Without this positive attitude busing is a cosmetic or "Band-Aid" approach. Similarly, HRA is viewed as a mechanism which will encourage more work humanization efforts. However, unless there is a positive attitude toward work humanization, HRA cannot be expected to play a key role in improving the quality of work life.

Brummet et al. (1969) feel that HRA "requires a different way of thinking about people and about the functions of managing human resources" (p. 15). The survey results presented in this paper indicate most accountants have not yet developed this new way of thinking. Figler (1975) offers a potential explanation for these results: "The accounting profession is oriented primarily toward measurement in discrete units and deals with events that . . . have some degree of predictability. As objects of study, people are far less predictable than are the subject matters with which accountants normally deal, and it would be highly advantageous if the accounting practitioner involved in HRA were knowledgeable about human behavior" (p. 26).

Elias (1976) feels that HRA will not have a significant impact upon business behavior "since long-term results will tend to be the same as with conventional accounting" (p. 43). Elias' focus is not typical, however, but his observations include several examples of corporate resource mismanagement resulting from HRA activity.

If HRA is to be effective in stimulating and/or reinforcing work humanization efforts, each firm will have to develop its own approach. The survey of accounting executives uncovered several human resource measurement efforts, both formal and informal. These systems should be developed and/or improved in a manner which will provide useful outcomes for that particular firm. Continued efforts to develop *the* definitive HRA model will result only in a continuation of the present "splintered" approach which has, in general, ignored the work humanization foundation of HRA. If positive change is to be effected, organization managers will have to be reminded constantly of the impetus behind HRA's development, that is, the desire to effect greater humanization of the work place.

The concept of human resource accounting as introduced by those stressing work humanization is based on a premise that "decisions will be made differently and human assets will be managed more effectively with the addition of information provided by a human resource accounting system" (Brummet et al. 1969, p. 15). However, after nearly a decade of research, debate, and other academic and practical applications, it appears unlikely that HRA will be a panacea for the work humanization field.

There are, however, several types of activity which indicate that the new generation of accountants will be more able and more willing to deal with the problems generated by an HRA system. The growth in importance of behavioral issues in accounting is one specific phenomenon which is likely to have direct impact upon the future of HRA since it focuses attention on the "people" side of accounting (e.g., psychological and sociological issues).

The survey of executives conducted by this writer also found some evidence of accountants being involved in efforts which stress the human resource. One firm, for example, has a human resources committee which is chaired by the firm's vice-president of finance. Another firm uses its internal auditing staff to develop a "skills inventory" of all technical personnel within the organization. A third company stresses "profit-reinvestment-in-people" while developing its annual budget. All these activities offer hopeful signs for future HRA activity.

NOTE

1. The telephone survey included four firms listed in *Fortune's* 500 and ranged downward to small service and/or manufacturing firms.

REFERENCES

Brummet, R. L., E. G. Flamholtz and W. C. Pyle. Human Resource Accounting: A Tool to Increase Managerial Effectiveness. *Management Accounting,* August 1969, pp. 12–15.

Cullather, J. L. The Missing Asset: Human Capital. *Mississippi Valley Journal of Business,* Spring 1967, pp. 70–73.

Elias, N. Behavioral Impact of Human Resource Accounting. *Management Accounting,* February 1976, pp. 43–45.

Flamholtz, E. A Model for Human Resource Valuation: A Stochastic Process with Service Rewards. *The Accounting Review,* April 1971, pp. 253–267.

———. Toward a Theory of Human Resource Value in Formal Organizations. *The Accounting Review,* October 1972, pp. 666–678.

Figler, H. R. Accounting for Human Assets. *Management Accounting,* November 1975, pp. 23–26.

Gilbert, M. H. The Asset Value of the Human Organization. *Management Accounting,* July 1970, pp. 25–28.

Hekiman, J. S., and C. H. Jones. Put People on Your Balance Sheet. *Harvard Business Review,* January-February 1967, pp. 105–113.

Jaggi, B. Human Resources Are Assets. *Management Accounting,* February 1976, pp. 41–42.

Jaggi, B., and H. Lau. Toward a Model for Human Resource Valuation. *The Accounting Review,* April 1974, pp. 321–329.

Jauch, R., and M. Skigen. Human Resource Accounting: A Critical Evaluation. *Management Accounting,* May 1974, pp. 33–36.

Lev, B., and A. Schwartz. On the Use of the Economic Concept of Human Capital in Financial Statements. *The Accounting Review,* January 1971, pp. 103–111.

Liao, S. S. Human Assets, Human Resources and Managerial Decisions. *Management Accounting,* November 1974, pp. 19–22.

Likert, R. *The Human Organization, Its Management and Value.* New York: McGraw-Hill Company, 1967.

McRae, T. W. Human Resource Accounting as a Management Tool. *The Journal of Accountancy,* August 1974, pp. 32–38.

Mirvis, P. H., and B. A. Macy. Human Resource Accounting: A Measurement Perspective. *Academy of Management Review,* April 1976, pp. 74–83.

Newell, G. E. Should Humans be Reported as Assets? *Management Accounting,* December 1972, pp. 13–16.

Weiss, M. Where "Human Resource Accounting" Stands Today. *Administrative Management,* November 1972, pp. 43–48.

———. Human Resource Accounting. *Management Accounting,* March 1976, pp. 45–46.

Postscript: Toward the Person-Centered Organization

by Gary R. Gemmill

THE FOUNDATION OF TODAY'S BUSINESS ORGANIZATION—ITS BUREAUCRATIC structure and processes—which was built upon the ground of the Industrial Revolution appears to be cracking under the weight of a multitude of contemporary economic and social pressures. Many people, and behavioral scientists in particular, are beginning to sense that organizations as we now know them are (from a human standpoint) unnecessarily repressive, unlivable, and in many respects, unmanageable. This is one of the basic themes that underlies the collection of essays presented in this book on the humanization of work. In my own work with executives, managers, and laborers in many different types of organizations, I have been struck by the deep sense of despair, the frustration, the loneliness, the sense of impersonality, and the sense of helplessness that people feel as they strive to carry out their lives in organizational forms they perceive as stifling, fearful, boring, game-playing, and dehumanizing.

One of the central and pressing issues of our time is how to design organizational forms that foster the process of self-realization and the development of authentic relationships, a sense of personal power, and a sense of self-worth based on a personal valuation of one's unique identity in the world and one's valuation that his work experience is deeply meaningful. What is sorely needed are organizational forms that are more responsive to the needs of the whole, organic person. It is tragic that the dominant, if not sole, criterion for designing organizational forms has been (and still is) the efficiency and effectiveness of the work process, regardless of its impact on the self-worth and self-realization of people caught up in that work process. The need for organizational effectiveness and efficiency in the accomplishment of work is not in question, only the false dichotomy that persists between task effectiveness and concern for human development. These are not mutually

197

exclusive alternatives. The tendency to dichotomize and to view human and organizational needs as a win-lose proposition has had an inhibiting effect on the search for alternative task environments which are more responsive to human needs. It is also of dubious moral and social value to defend prevailing organizational practices simply because they are efficient and effective when the evidence is clear that people are malaffected in the process, even though they are allegedly willing victims.

Rollo May (1969) seems to capture well the pathos of our times when he suggests that many people experience their lives as having no real significance and experience themselves as powerless to make it more significant. They feel apathetic, give up wanting, give up feeling, and resign themselves to adjusting to what they experience as a relatively meaningless world. May speculates that such apathy will eventually erupt into violence "... for no human being can stand the perpetually numbing experience of his own powerlessness."

While May's prognosis is open to question, the rampant sense of powerlessness and meaninglessness in our culture is not. Behavioral scientists have been extremely proficient in documenting and describing the human stresses and strains of contemporary organizational life; however, they have not been very proficient or imaginative in generating or developing alternative organization forms that would help to ameliorate these conditions. (To be sure, there are exceptions which I will mention at a later point.)

Dangers of empirical determinism in the documentation of contemporary conditions do exist. As Chris Argyris (1969) so clearly points out, the problem with conducting only "naturalistic" and "descriptive" research is that there is the danger of viewing what exists at the present time not only as inevitable, but as the way things *ought* to be. Truly, if we study only what currently prevails in organizations, we face the risk of developing a concept of a person whose "natural" behavior is concealing feelings, playing games, mistrusting, being bored with work, being passive, and not taking risks. A lack of awareness of alternative systems in which these symptoms are minimized or even eliminated forces us to resign ourselves to accepting as human nature the status quo we "see" evidenced in our data. By not experimenting with alternative work forms we doom ourselves to the continuation of meaninglessness and powerlessness in our lives within organizations.

There are significant numbers of people in all work roles (e.g. behavioral scientists, managers, teachers, etc.) who are extremely pessimistic about whether more person-centered organizational forms can be designed and implemented. Mainly, they feel hopeless and cynical, believing that one has to be nongenuine and "play the game" to survive. The only real alternative they perceive for themselves is dropping out; and yet, they are uneasy about doing that since they sense it is becoming more difficult to carry out. Not only have they lost faith in the "system," but in each other, and most importantly, in themselves. Occasionally, I have shared this pessimism, sensing on the one hand that something is very "sick" or "wrong" with the current organizational form in which we imprison ourselves; and yet, on the other hand, feeling incapable of changing or improving the situation. The task, at times, seems overwhelming and insurmountable.

Much of this pessimism is grounded in the primitive desire for a "magical solution" and, more importantly, in the lack of awareness of viable alternatives to our present way of organizing ourselves for work with each other. Several essays in this book (e.g., Sexton, Bowers, and Bluestone) deal specifically with one or both of these issues. Personally, I feel that the search for a magical solution to the myriad of human problems that press for attention in contemporary organizations arises largely from the desire to avoid the reality of change and growth. Growth often involves pain, frustration, discomfort, and uncertainty. Often it is our unwillingness to face such birth pains that predisposes us to cling to out-moded organizational forms and relationships. Whether we care to admit it or not, *significant* changes in the quality of life in organizations will come about only through the acceptance of ambiguity, much risk taking, experimentation, and frequently, even error. Courage to face such conditions, I suspect, only develops when people have a strong faith and trust in themselves and in each other. Personal resignation and pessimism, both born out of hopelessness, are obviously detrimental to the development of work environments that are more responsive to human needs. Resignation constitutes a decision to permit the dysfunctional conditions which exist to continue.

Lack of awareness of viable alternatives and limited experimentation have been, perhaps, the greatest impediments to the creation of more person-centered organizational forms (although Ken Milani's essay suggests that accounting procedures may at least be partially contributory). In some sense it is probably true that we are children of our times and are so caught up in the prevailing cultural fabric that it is problematic whether we can transcend it enough to invent new social and work forms. While the task of invention seems staggering and monumental, I am personally hopeful about the possibilities for creating more person-centered organizations. Indeed, much of what is necessary is already available—the work has begun. The basis for my optimism is the number of ongoing developments in our society which constitute pro-active forces lending to a greater humanization of the work process.

The essays in this book are an encouraging sign, since they indicate that many dedicated scholars and practitioners are seriously concerned with examining the dehumanizing aspects of work and are involved in searching for more person-centered options and alternatives. Although not sufficient in itself, such inquiry and awareness is a necessary step toward humanizing the work process. There are indications that other scholars and practitioners are also seriously enmeshed in inquiry and in the application of the behavioral sciences to improve the human quality of organization life. This is evidenced by the emergence of such journals as the *Journal of Applied Behavioral Science,* the *Journal of Humanistic Psychology, Small Group Behavior,* and *Group and Organizational Studies.* In such journals one can find systematic reporting of concerns and experimentation with more personally enriched work and organizational forms.

Another optimistic sign is that both industrial organizations *and* unions are experimenting with organizational alternatives—limited though they may be. Companies who have been active in this attempt include, to name a few, TRW Systems, Texas Instruments, Corning Glassworks, Union Carbide, and Saga. Departments of "organization development" are also finding their way into the corporate structure. To be sure, the trend is presently a ripple. And perhaps, as David Bowers suggests in his essay, some companies who have delved in it have become disillusioned because advocates have oversold the benefits as well as the speed and ease by which organizations can be made more person-centered. However, the realities are that any approach to re-vitalizing the human organization is not likely to be easy or painless. I am encouraged by the work described by Ted Mills and Irving Bluestone, who have called for and sponsored organizational development programs designed and implemented jointly by unions and management. Elsewhere, Bluestone (1973) has expressed an awareness that "magical" and quick solutions are unrealistic:

> Finding the precise means to achieve the goal of "humanizing" work . . . is not conducive to crisis negotiations. It is not the same as settling a wage dispute in the face of a twelve midnight strike deadline. Rather, it requires careful experimentation and analysis (p. 9).

That unions are concerned with the humanization of the work process is itself a hopeful sign. In most instances, unions have always functioned to protect and to serve the needs of their constituency and their movement toward creating more meaningful work seems a logical (although difficult) extension of their activity.

The continued growth of the laboratory method of education and expe-riential learning methodology are yet other helpful signs. The laboratory method, pioneered at the National Training Laboratories (NTL), has consis-tently focused on planned action for improving group and organizational effectiveness by integrating and incorporating the full humanity of the persons who are involved (Benne et al. 1975). Perhaps more than any other approach, it has led to greater experimentation and to greater inquiry into alternative work and social forms. The laboratory method has provided a basis for study-ing and experimenting with the effects of interpersonal openness, trust, and risk-taking on the work process and has encouraged the development of inter-ventions which promote such behavior. It encourages the creation and testing of alternative structures and humanly well-functioning groups that are rarely found in contemporary organizations. Coupled with the growth of the labora-tory method is the growth of the so-called "California" or "encounter group" movement. While the former is more group process oriented, the latter focuses on the barriers persons construct for themselves that diminish their vitality and humanity. Neither of these movements is to be taken lightly. Indeed, Carl Rogers (1970) suggests that the intensive group experience is perhaps the most significant social invention of our time. Of course, there is much controversy over the efficacy and implications of these methods for creating a more person-centered society. However, the controversy itself is an optimistic sign. To be sure there is a need for more experimentation, research, and theory construction. And efforts along these lines are increasing (Gibb 1975; Smith 1975).

There are three very important issues that are explicitly dealt with or alluded to in the essays assembled in this book: (1) cultural values and goals for guiding organizational development efforts, (2) the scope of work humani-zation, and (3) the appropriate targets and methodologies for effecting change in the design of work and work organizations of a more person-oriented form.

The issue of cultural values and goals is an extremely crucial one, but one which has largely been neglected in our thoughts about organizational restructuring. While amplified awareness of the factors and processes that facilitate and inhibit the development of organizational forms responsive to the human needs of its members constitutes an important first step in design-ing more person-centered work environments, by itself it is not sufficient. Unless one has a set of "operational values" to use in directing one's energies for change, amplified awareness becomes largely reactive and directionless. Unfortunately, the word "values" often evokes feeling of some abstract, philosophical concept that has no real bearing on the everyday world in which we live. Many of us have had people attempt to impose vague, superficial, or inconsistent values upon us with the result that we experience them as toxic, foreign bodies and resist having anything to do with them. What I mean by "operational values" is a person's conscious choice of a way of being or relating in his everyday world. The choices serve as guides to our behavior and in a sense constitute the "rules" by which we choose to live.

It is a myth to believe that one can be a value-free person—just as much a myth as the notion of a value-free scientist. Rejecting values which others have tried to instill in us still leaves us with the task of working out a set of values of our own. If we do not do this consciously, we do it outside our immediate awareness and the result is behavior lacking the force of intention-ality. Not being clear about what we value, we can become passive agents responding only to what we experience as capricious life forces. We lack a center from which to operate and experience ourselves as powerless and helpless. The more we avoid dealing with the question of our own values, the more directionless and fragmented we experience our organizational lives to be. For this reason I believe that attempts to humanize work must also provide a basis for clarifying values and for raising into awareness the value decisions that lie dormant (i.e., those which are not outcomes of conscious choice). We need to make explicit our values for work and for our treatment of each other in carrying out work processes. As Eric Fromm (1955) suggests, we must stop treating each other as things and stop allowing ourselves to be used as if we were things. When concern for persons becomes a scope value, persons are an end in themselves, not a means to an end. In his essay, John Julian Ryan clearly recognizes the importance of such a value decision when he states:

> the primal needs and rights of every person as a full human being [must] be respected as sacred, not the least of these being that of leading a meaningful, consciously creative, life as a worker serving others skillfully, personally and honorably.

We need not view such a value position as mere rhetoric or idealism. Rather, we need to find the means to make it operational in the development of our relationships with each other.

If we value work and authentic relationships, we must—each of us—act in such a way as to promote it, even though it may not be a popular view. As Francis Fiorenza suggests in his essay, work is not a curse brought about by humankind's fall from grace; it is a curse we have inflicted upon ourselves. Organizations were created by humans and can be changed by them. It is time for each of us to begin to reclaim responsibility and personal power and to nurture courage in ourselves and in each other to pursue uncertain paths. The alternative is to continue to lock ourselves in dehumanizing structures which have been around for a long time and which we have become "used to." Not to choose is a choice—a choice to settle for something less than what might be, should we experiment and grow with each other.

The issue of the scope of work humanization is an important one in the sense that it determines what aspects of the work culture we focus upon in making the organization more person-centered. Focusing upon making work itself more intrinsically meaningful is, in my opinion, too limited a scope of endeavor. Such efforts are laudatory and necessary, but so are efforts devoted to improving the quality of the interpersonal and social milieu within which work takes place. In my mind it is every bit as important for organizations to establish a work culture in which relationships are authentic, people have a constructive intent toward each other, people express concern and caring for each other, and people freely express both their emotional and cognitive sides. We must deal with the whole person in humanizing the work process. Research from psychotherapy attests to the importance of such a work culture in promoting self-worth and personal power. We must learn, I suspect, not to be so afraid to display our full range of humanness and emotions (which we so typically conceal from each other). We are free to relate to each other in any way we desire; we are limited only by our own imagination and fears. I am also in accord with what Kasl states in his essay on work and mental health: there is a need for clearer understanding and more studies of the relationship of the meaninglessness and powerlessness we experience in our work roles to performance and well-being in other life roles. This too is an important issue of scope.

The issue of the target of change is a perplexing one, dealing with the selection of the appropriate social unit for implementing changes intended to improve the quality of work life. Some scholars (Harman 1974; Nord 1974) suggest that the *economic system* is the appropriate target for reducing meaninglessness and powerlessness in the work process. However, as Houck indicates in his essay, Marx was somewhat naive in thinking that the demise of capitalism and the advent of socialism would eliminate the alienating conditions of work. Evidence that is available suggests that neither capitalism nor socialism has been particularly effective in solving the problem of worker alienation (Tannenbaum 1975).

A second suggested target for change is the *individual* (Tichy 1974; Leavitt 1965). However, approaching work humanization through altered individual awareness and changes in individual skills have not been particularly effective either. There are a number of reasons offered for this failure, including the lack of reinforcement of newly acquired behaviors by the work culture and the lack of supportive structural change. A third frequently cited change target is the *group;* and it too has been found deficient in and of itself (Gibb and Gibb 1971). As Bowers states in his essay, a changed group may become ''an indigestible element in the larger unit of which [it] is a part.''

Structural change has also been offered as a potential remedy for many present organizational difficulties. The codetermination face of industrial democracy described by Mills in his essay on European developments in work democratization is one such effort in that direction. So are the ''de-statused'' and matrix organizations described by Bowers and the autonomous work groups cited by Mills, Bowers, and Bluestone. A final potential change target is *technology*. Although considered by many since the beginning of the Industrial Revolution to be the principal focus for organizational design, as Heisler points out in his historical sketch of the concept of alienation, it too has been frequently found to be deficient as a mechanism for organizational improvement. While it is true that some advanced stages of technology (i.e., automated or continuous processes technologies) hold forth hope for the improvement of organizational functioning, both in the technical and human sense, certain stages (i.e., mechanization or mass production technologies) decrease human potential within the system and are themselves generators of dissatisfaction, alienation, and poor mental health.

The appropriate focus for change most clearly involves all of the targets cited, since the problem of organizational change is by definition a systemic one. If we are truly to achieve our objective in constructing organizational forms that are more person-centered or humanistic, a great deal more experimentation is needed employing various combinations of change targets on a planned, system-wide basis. The essays presented in this book provide an interdisciplinary and multifocused body of knowledge and experience that can be useful in increasing one's awareness of the scope of issues and concerns involved in such attempts.

REFERENCES

Argyris, C. The Incompleteness of Social Psychological Theory. *American Psychologist,* 1969, 24:893–908.

Benne, K., L. Bradford, J. Gibb, and R. Lippitt. *The Laboratory Method of Changing and Learning.* Palo Alto, Calif.: Science and Behavioral Books, 1975.

Bluestone, I. Worker Participation in Decision-Making. Paper delivered at the Conference on Strategy, Programs, and Problems of an Alternative Political Economy, Institute for Policy Studies. Washington, D.C., March 2-4, 1973.

Fromm, E. *The Sane Society.* New York: Rinehart, 1955.

Gibb, J. A Research Perspective on the Laboratory Method. In *The Laboratory Method of Changing and Learning,* K. Benne, et al., eds. Palo Alto, Calif.: Science and Behavioral Books, 1975, pp. 56–71.

Gibb, J., and L. M. Gibb. The Process of Group Actualization. In *Language Behavior,* J. Akin et al., eds. The Hague: Mouton and Co., 1971, pp. 171–187.

Harman, W. "Humanistic Capitalism: Another Alternative." *Journal of Humanistic Psychology,* 1974, 14 (1):5–32.

Leavitt, H. Applied Organizational Change in Industry: Structural, Technological, and Humanistic Approaches. In *Handbook of Organizations,* J. G. March, ed. Chicago: Rand McNally, 1965, pp. 1144–1170.

May, R. *Love and Will.* New York: W. W. Norton, 1969.

Nord, W. The Failure of Current Applied Behavioral Science—A Marxian Perspective. *Journal of Applied Behavioral Science,* 1974, 10(4):557–576.

Rogers, C. *Carl Rogers on Encounter Groups.* New York: Harper & Row, 1970.

Smith, P. Controlled Studies of the Outcomes of Sensitivity Training. *Psychological Bulletin,* 1975, 82(4):597–622.

Tannenbaum, A. S. Rank, Clout, and Worker Satisfaction: Pecking Order—Capitalist and Communist Style. *Psychology Today,* 1975, 9(4):40–43.

Tichy, N. An Interview with Max Pages. *Journal of Applied Behavioral Science,* 1974, 10(1):8–26.

Contributors

Mr. Irving Bluestone

Mr. Bluestone is vice-president of the United Auto Workers International and director of the UAW General Motors Department. Beginning his career as an employee of the Hyatt Bearing Division of GM, he soon became active in local union affairs. In 1970, after serving as assistant to president Walter Reuther, Bluestone was named director of the UAW General Motors Department; he became a vice-president in 1972. Bluestone received a B.A. degree from the City College of New York and pursued postgraduate work at the University of Bern (Switzerland). He is a member of the National Trade Union Council for Human Rights and a member of the advisory committee of the National Quality of Work Center.

Dr. David G. Bowers

Since 1971, Dr. Bowers has been a program director at the University of Michigan's Institute for Social Research. He has conducted or participated in major research reports on organizational practices and has published several books and articles, including *Management by Participation, System 4: The Ideas of Rensis Likert; The Survey of Organizations;* and *Systems of Organization: Management of the Human Resource*. Dr. Bowers earned his Ph.D. in industrial psychology from the University of Michigan in 1961.

Dr. Francis Schüssler Fiorenza

Dr. Fiorenza is assistant professor of theology at the University of Notre Dame. A former Kent Fellow of the Danforth Foundation, he received his doctorate from the University of Muenster (West Germany) in 1971. Dr. Fiorenza has taught at the University of Notre Dame since 1971 and has served as chairman of Notre Dame's Summer Program in Theology. Fiorenza is a member of the board of directors of the Catholic Theological Society and is an active member in several other professional theological organizations. He has also served as associate editor for the journal *Continuum* and the Councilium Series, the Seabury Press.

Dr. Gary R. Gemmill

Dr. Gemmill is an associate professor of organizational behavior at Syracuse University and has been a staff member and trainer for numerous programs in human relations, team building, and personal growth, in both the U.S. and Canada. He received his formal business education at Michigan State University (M.B.A., Ph.D. in organizational behavior). In 1976, he received a postgraduate diploma in Gestalt training from the Gestalt Training Center at San Diego. The author of articles on power, conflict management, communications, and group processes, Dr. Gemmill has also developed and published several structured experiential exercises for facilitating personal and interpersonal growth.

Dr. William J. Heisler

Dr. Heisler, as an assistant professor of management and organizational behavior at the University of Notre Dame, was a co-director of the S&H Lecture Series. He earned his M.B.A. and Ph.D. in organizational behavior from Syracuse University. Joining the University of Notre Dame in 1972, he has developed a variety of interests in fields related to the quality of work-life, human resource management, and organization development. A 1974 AACSB–Federal Faculty Fellow, Dr. Heisler is presently an associate professor of management at the Babcock Graduate School of Management, Wake Forest University, and an active member of the Academy of Management and the American Psychological Association.

Dr. John W. Houck

Dr. Houck is a professor of management and organization at the University of Notre Dame and a codirector of the S&H Lecture Series. A former Danforth teaching fellow, Houck earned a J.D. degree from Notre Dame, an

M.B.A. from the University of North Carolina, and a master of laws degree from the Harvard Law School. He is a former president of the Notre Dame Chapter of the American Association of University Professors, and director of the South Bend Urban League. In addition to authoring a variety of articles and reviews, Dr. Houck is editor of *Outdoor Advertising: History and Regulation* and coeditor of *Academic Freedom and the Catholic University.*

Dr. Stanislav V. Kasl

A former Woodrow Wilson Fellow, Dr. Kasl earned his Ph.D. in psychology at the University of Michigan in 1962. Having taught psychology at the University of Michigan from 1962 to 1968, he is now professor of epidemiology at the Yale University School of Medicine. Dr. Kasl has served as a consultant to the American Heart Association, Social Security Administration, Department of Housing and Urban Development, Bureau of Community and Environmental Management, the National Institute on Drug Abuse, and other agencies. He has authored numerous articles and technical reports dealing with work and mental health.

Dr. Ken Milani

Dr. Milani is an associate professor of accounting at the University of Notre Dame. He formerly worked as a cost accountant with Johnson & Johnson (Chicago, Illinois). He has been the recipient of both the Haskins and Sells Foundation Fellowship and the American Accounting Association Fellowship. Professor Milani has written several articles dealing with taxation and the behavioral implications of accounting. He is the coauthor of *Programmed Learning Aid for Federal Income Tax* and a certified public accountant (C.P.A.) holding memberships in the American Accounting Association, American Taxation Association, American Institute of Certified Public Accountants, and the National Association of Accountants.

Mr. Ted Mills

Mr. Mills is director of the National Quality of Work Center in Washington, D.C. Having served as special assistant for productivity to the chairman of the Price Commission in 1972, Mills created and developed the Quality of Work Program and later, in 1974, formed the National Quality of Work Center. From 1962 through 1971, he was president of his own consulting firm specializing in quality of life and communications research and programming for such organizations as AT&T, Kodak, Hoffman LaRoche, and many others. From 1948 through 1960, he was an executive broadcaster and producer of NBC–TV shows and films, working predominantly in the public affairs area. The professional recognitions of his achievements include two "Emmy" nominations.

Dr. John Julian Ryan

Dr. Ryan is a professor of English at St. Anselm's College in Manchester, New Hampshire. Previous to his present appointment, Ryan taught at Harvard, Holy Cross, and Catholic University. His most noted works include *The Idea of a Catholic College, Beyond Humanism,* and *The Humanization of Man*. Ryan has written often for such publications as *Cross Currents,* and *Commonweal*.

Dr. William P. Sexton

Dr. Sexton is associate professor of management at the University of Notre Dame. Having received undergraduate and M.B.A. degrees from Ohio State University, Sexton also earned his Ph.D. in administrative management from that institution in 1966. Possessing industrial experience in the areas of personnel, labor relations, and manufacturing supervision, he has engaged in extensive consulting work and has conducted seminars for various firms in areas such as leadership, group dynamics, personnel, and organizational development. He has published numerous articles in organizational behavior, and a book entitled *Organization Theories*. A second book, *People, Leadership, and Organizations,* is presently being developed.

Index

211